BETWEEN ACTS
An Irreverent Look
at Opera
and Other Madness

BETWEEN ACTS

An Irreverent Look
at Opera
and Other Madness

by
Robert Merrill with Robert Saffron

McGraw-Hill Book Company
NEW YORK   ST. LOUIS   SAN FRANCISCO   DÜSSELDORF
MEXICO   TORONTO

Book design by Sallie Baldwin.

123456789 DODO 79876

Library of Congress Cataloging in Publication Data

Merrill, Robert, 1919-
Between acts: An irreverent look at opera and other
madness.

1. Merrill, Robert, 1919-   2.   Musicians—
Correspondence, reminiscences, etc. I. Saffron, Robert,
joint author. II. Title.
ML420.M42A3   784'.092'4 [B]   76-20467
ISBN 0-07-041501-3

To my friends and colleagues:
those who are gone, I miss;
those who are still active in this wild
and wonderful business, I treasure.

Contents

Introduction

You will find no burning issues of the day here—nothing on rescuing the Republic, feminism, self-analysis, or singing to your plants. This book is an irreverent mosaic of tales from the performing arts that I have reveled in for over 40 years: smokers, burlesque, vaudeville, radio, film, television, Las Vegas clubs, musical comedy, and, for three decades, the Metropolitan Opera.

If there is very little of redeeming social value in these stories, they may reveal some offbeat insights and a smattering of gloriously mad laughter.

Mad?

Yes. For opera, as Samuel Johnson so accurately described it, is an "exotic and irrational entertainment." All entertainment thrives on the exotic and irrational, and uses it to lift the audience out of the mundane world around it. But in grand opera, we spend so much of our lives pretending we are kings, witches, princesses, Don Juans, irresistible courtesans, gods, and demons that some of our humanity clings to these characters, while their melodramatic gestures, grandeur, and sheer nonsense seep into our souls.

After we wipe off our makeup, the fantasy lingers on. The irrational becomes normal. A casual smile becomes an invitation to a grand passion; a single misstep turns into a grand catastrophe.

On November 16, 1906, Enrico Caruso took a stroll in Central Park. Everyone knew the warm round face, nestled in the mink collar of the alpaca overcoat, the cane, the derby, the cigarette at a cocky forty-five-degree angle. He loved to stand at the monkey house, mimicking the animals' cries and facial quivers.

A woman with a well-rounded posterior stood next to him, smiling. Now Caruso had for ten years been living with a soprano who could not obtain a divorce in Italy, and she had borne his sons. He was entirely faithful to her, yet he evidently could not resist displaying approval of the stranger's *derrière* in the Latin fashion.

A policeman promptly arrested him for "molesting" this Mrs. Hanna Graham, who charged the tenor with pinching her bottom. He claimed he had merely smiled, but he was clapped into jail for a while, until $500 bond was provided. He went to his hotel, locked himself into his room, and moaned in despair.

At the hearing, the irrational took control. Reporters found that Mrs. Graham, who had given a fake address, had previously filed the same complaint against another man, and he had been arrested by the same officer. Mrs. Graham never testified because, the police said, she feared reprisals by Caruso's friends of the Black Hand. This arresting officer testified he had observed the tenor also following a girl of twelve and a "large black woman." The next day a heavily veiled woman charged that Caruso had been in the audience at the Met the night she was there, and as she left he "fondled" her.

The Police Commissioner labeled Caruso a pervert, who had to be removed from society. The magistrate agreed and fined him $10. Several newspapers called for his deportation. Demonstrations appeared outside the Met, and Caruso feared his career was finished in America.

Standards for fondling have been elevated in the years since then. Ezio Pinza, the greatest Don Giovanni of the Met for two decades, arranged a rendezvous with one of the ballet girls on a Met tour train—then forgot which berth she was in. As he and I walked back to our Pullman after dinner, we passed through the chorus car. Lights were out, so Pinza reached into each upper and lower berth on both sides of the aisle, squeezing every girl to find his inamorata. Since Don Giovanni, as his valet enumerates onstage, had possessed 640 women in Italy, 231 in Germany, 100 in France, only 91 in Turkey but 1,003 in Spain, Pinza was only carrying on the grand tradition.

Mario Lanza set a new standard for public display. He was a young man in a hurry, endowed with a tremendous natural tenor voice but unwilling to take lessons or direction; he demanded instant fame. He came into a restaurant with a baritone and a soprano, with whom he was on tour presenting operatic excerpts. Service was slow that night, and Mario began to feel that the waiter was ignoring him. He stood up, opened his trousers and whacked the table with his other tremendous natural endowment. He was recognized instantly.

Why then would I, a shy, fat kid from Brooklyn, so afraid of singing for relatives that I would lock myself into the bathroom and throw up, become part of this exotic, mad world? For a perfectly irrational reason:

My mother wanted to be a singer.

1

The Girl Who Stripped for Animal Husbandry

Well, very few people in this world set their hearts and minds on a goal and reach it. I first ran into Richard Burton about two decades ago, aboard the *Queen Mary*; he was on his way to Hollywood to make his first movie after a moderate success with the Old Vic. A shapeless tweed jacket hung open over his wine-cask chest, and his head seemed too large for his body.

"You're not as big as I am," he said, in a slightly sardonic but wonderfully resonant rumble. "How did you acquire such a God-bless voice?"

"Practice."

"Good God, I'd give up *Hamlet* to sing in just one

opera!" (Fortunately he didn't. His singing in the musical *Camelot* hardly brought Rudolf Bing to his knees, but his *Hamlet* at the Old Vic, which Winston Churchill called the most virile he'd ever seen, had the longest run in the play's history.)

And Laurence Olivier, after an evening of singing operatic arias with Danny Kaye and me in Danny's home, sighed, "It's all gift and skill. I wish I'd had the gift to sing *Otello* or *Falstaff*—I might have abandoned the theater." A startling admission from probably the greatest actor of the Western world.

I've known only one person in the entertainment profession who chose her destiny and achieved it, even though for a woman the path to success is usually more tempestuous and thorny. She was Zonia Duval. Sometime in 1943, I was booked as a headliner with comedian Pinky Lee into a theater in Philadelphia, presenting *Hats Off to MacArthur*, a tribute to our hero in the Pacific. When I arrived at the theater, there was a cardboard blowup of me, "The Star-Spangled Baritone," and one of Pinky Lee, but obviously the real headliner was Zonia ("Strip for Action") Duval, whose body, spectacularly ennobled in cardboard, made clear what this public would pay tribute to.

It was my dumb luck to follow her act, an exotic dance that was loudly acclaimed for its grace and vision of a better world. She had flaming red hair that stretched down below her knees, and she used it to whip and caress her entire body. Waiting in the wings to go on, I noticed that many of her devotees in the first rows carried newspapers—a rather strange place for serious readers, I thought.

As Zonia ran off, nude, she bumped into me and I was propelled onstage as if I'd touched a thousand-watt cable. Well, no man could compete with that act. The audience screamed for more of Zonia all through my "Donkey Serenade," and I got their message. I dropped "Figaro" and closed with two fast choruses of a special number, "Hats Off to MacArthur," which at the time was equivalent to our national anthem, and that quieted them down.

Pinky Lee followed me with his comedy routines. In

one he did eccentric foreign dances, responding to requests from the audience. I made the requests, running to various corners at the rear of the house and calling out, in the appropriate accent, "Russian kazatska! . . . the polka . . . Viennese waltz." Pinky was—and is—a very funny man, but I'm afraid that week the audience's eyes were glazed with the afterimage of Zonia Duval.

She was something of a mystery. She locked herself into her dressing room and had meals sent in. None of the usual callers appeared at the stage door. After the performance, Pinky and I and the chorus girls went out for coffee and gossip; Zonia slipped into a cab, to reappear in time for her performance the next day. She never spoke to anyone. We all believed that someone in the crime syndicate was keeping her—and watching her.

The mystery of her fans' newspapers was cleared up by one of the girls. In burlesque they were called "newspapermen," because the papers covered any private gratification the stripper might arouse.

After the last show, I hopped the milk train to bring me into New York early in the morning. As I walked down the dreary aisle I recognized the blazing red hair of Miss Duval. I reintroduced myself, and we had a pleasant, rather surprising, dialogue all the way to Penn Station.

Duval was actually her name, and she was a shy, sensitive, remarkably beautiful woman from an upper-middle-class family—French-Russian as I recall—who had given her vocal and dance lessons and a taste for operatic and symphonic music. She had gone into burlesque stripping to make money—she averaged $1,500 a week—to buy a farm in eastern Pennsylvania, where she planned to retire soon with her husband and child. She wasn't being watched by any mobster—she had spent her time in the dressing room studying agriculture and animal husbandry.

Fifteen years later: When I sang on the *Tonight* show, I mentioned my star-spangled days in Philadelphia. Soon after that, a letter arrived from Zonia. She had quit burlesque a short time after our meeting and now lived happily on the farm with her husband and children. She had grasped exactly what she wanted from life.

My mother was a woman of ferocious determination to make herself into an opera singer. But, as Olivier said, it's the gift and the skill that make for success, and she never had the opportunity to develop the skill. She was the daughter of a Warsaw tailor, the only man in the family not a cantor. "So you see, your gift came from me," she told me, "and my gift came from God." A wealthy Pole had heard her soprano voice and offered to subsidize her training for opera. Since relations between Jewish tailors and Polish aristocrats were not at the time well integrated, her family rejected the offer. She never forgave her parents or my father, also a tailor, for not having the money to make her an opera star. And she never let me forget it, either.

I made my unpromising debut in this world, yowling and kicking, on the kitchen table of a sixth-floor cold-water flat on South Second Street, Williamsburg. It could only have been a very conventional scream, but somehow it persuaded my mother that I was a singer, and from that moment my life was laid out for me. I would be her replacement.

OUR CAST

In America, my mother, Lotza Balaban, became Lillian. My father, Abe Millstein, became Abe Miller through the confusion of a clerk at Ellis Island. I was named Morris, but on our block that turned into Fatso.

What I wanted to do was play baseball. And she persistently blocked the baselines. As soon as I learned to walk, she decided I had a weak heart, a "leaky valve," and I would have to walk slowly, breathe deeply, and not "run around in the sun like a crazy dog." When I wanted to sell newspapers to make money for a ball and gloves, she said, "No, that's how gangsters start." I did not realize she was preserving my hands for piano lessons. I had to wear heavy gloves in fall and winter, and the slightest scratch on my fingers brought out an armor-plate of gauze wrapping, Vaseline, and bandages torn from tattered sheets.

I managed to see the Dodgers play, but that was my father's secret. Boy Scouts were admitted free to Ebbets

Field once a week. Though my father now operated a sewing machine in a factory, his tailor's fingers had not lost their skill. He found a fabric that matched the Scouts' uniforms, and my brother Gil and I became instant Boy Scouts, all the way down to the long green stockings. The Dodgers were giants in those days—Dazzy Vance, Babe Herman, Hack Wilson—and I even saw Babe Ruth clout two homers at Yankee Stadium by courtesy of the Scouts.

I was in demand on our block when the sides were chosen—and an empty lot was available. I had a knuckleball and a floater that went up like a balloon and looked so easy that they wrenched their backs reaching for it.

The block was my whole world. It demanded, and I gave, complete loyalty. Entire wards and square miles of Brooklyn, the Lower East Side, the Bronx were transplanted European settlements, filled with families from the same town or province in Lithuania, Latvia, Poland, Russia. Other neighborhoods, I heard, were transplanted from Sicily and Naples and entire counties of Ireland.

Our block stank in summer and froze in winter, and many of my friends died of the flu or pneumonia. We were always short of money, but we never thought of ourselves as underprivileged or hopeless. Since I never ventured far from our block, I assumed this was the way everybody lived. All of us had to pal around with each other. If you strayed into one of those Irish or Italian blocks, who was going to help you?

But my security here was undermined by Momma's goddamn Caruso records. Bing Crosby and Russ Columbo were what we listened to on the radio and whistled on the street: "Let's Fall in Love," "It's Only a Paper Moon." Caruso was "long-hair stuff" and suspiciously sissy. Merely listening to opera music could brand you a fruit. And then whom would you have to hang around with? Your sister.

My mother worshipped Caruso's voice. This was one of her few pleasures; she scrimped dimes and quarters to take occasional voice and piano lessons. The throb of Caruso, so like the cantor's, reached out to her soul. And—who knew?—filling the air with the tenor's voice might somehow make me sing like him.

These records in the early thirties cost $2 each. Since my father earned about $25 a week, laboring on piecework ten hours a day, each record meant half a day's efforts thrown away "just to hear an Eyetalyan scream!" Momma kept these jewels in a closet, wrapped in old towels and quilts.

The Goddamn Carusos revolved relentlessly on a hand-wound machine with a large brass horn. Momma bought it secondhand, using money borrowed from her cousin Abe Bernstein, who had become rich by owning a garment factory, not by working in one. He thought she was crazy. To me, the most insane folly was that she played Caruso so *loud*. And the windows were wide open in baseball weather.

I had nightmares of my pals turning their backs on me, with dirty winks, when they chose up sides. My life turned into a clear-cut fight: the block versus Momma—the Dempsey-Tunney battles.

I'd shut the windows of the room facing the street, and my father would yell, "I'm dying—open the windows!"

"Oh, no." I said. "So much racket in the streets I can't hear this great music."

And he'd raise the windows again.

The records and Momma's drive for my future were intermingled with food—"eat, eat, my genius"—so that by the time I was twelve I was a child prodigy: I wore size forty pants. And I never could steal any bases. I also developed the hay fever syndrome, although little ragweed could possibly grow in those fields of asphalt and cement. And somewhere along the way I managed to fall into stuttering in moments of tension. Momma's reaction was characteristically accurate. "You're cutting off your throat to spite my face. It's all right. To be a mother is to suffer." I was the one who suffered: I was the stu-tu-tu-tering F-f-f-atso who t-t-took the nee-needling on the b-b-block.

(SCENE: On the sidewalk. We're waiting for some guys to arrive with a bat and ball.)

JOEY: *What's all that longhair stuff comin outta your window, Fatso?*

ME: *Where? It's n-n-not my fuf-fuf-floor. It's the guy n-n-next door. A op-op-opra nut.*

SAMMY: *Where? Where?*

ME: (Waving to another floor) *Over the-the-there! I keep ye-ye-yellin' turn the god-goddamn Ca-Ca-rusos off, it's dr-dr-drivin' me cu-cu-crazy.*

SAMMY: *Must be some kinda fairy.*

(The new kid on the block, big as the iceman and hairy, appears on the stoop next door.)

ME: *Tha-that's him! Tha-that's the g-g-guy!*

JOEY: (Astonished) *You just can't tell, can ya?*

Desperate times require desperate measures. How was I to know that the wretched insecurities of my childhood were basic training for the even wilder insecurities of show business?

After a while, the golden voice did get to me—but not when Momma was around. "O paradiso" and "Vesti la giubba" gave me goose bumps. I would listen to them alone; after closing the windows and drawing the shades, I sat in darkness, wondering how the hell did he do it? But I would never admit this to her.

> *In my later teens, I managed to play a lot of sandlot ball on Sundays without her knowledge. Teams were sponsored by churches and bars, and I pitched for $10 a game, which made me a semi-pro. Tommy Holmes, who compiled a lifetime batting average of .320 in the major leagues, played on our team.*

Momma began to study English at night school. I thought this was a very progressive step: She might become interested in the outside world and stop bothering me. Until the Day the Piano Came.

The old dark-oak upright arrived in a truck from the Henry Street Settlement House, which had given it to her for only $10. Nobody on the block had a piano, so a crowd gathered to debate how it would get up to the sixth floor. Carry it up the stairway? Impossible.

Another truck pulled up, boldly proclaiming THE ORIGINAL AARON ABRAMOWITZ HAULING CO. A pulley was hauled up to the roof while the window panels were removed from our front room. The piano, cradled in a rope sling, floated up to yells of "They'll never make it!"

They did. The next day, a little bent-over German came to tune it. Momma next brought in a voice coach to employ her newly developed English in building up a repertoire: "Because," "Kashmiri Love Song," Victor Herbert melodies. She performed at weddings and on Station WEVD for carfare and a few dollars.

Her coach, a Russian perfectionist, was persuaded to give me piano lessons on the assurance that I would then become his voice student. I immediately developed a debilitating backache, I was detained in school, my fingers stiffened into arthritis. After two lessons he gave up. Still, rumors spread on the block: " . . . the piano's not just for the old lady . . . " A secret piano player was just as fruity as a Caruso player. I sabotaged half a dozen teachers before my mother abandoned that campaign.

The battle with the boy soprano never ended. When I sang, I discovered, I lost my stutter. And after Momma discovered me singing along with her coach while I was in the next room, her bombardment intensified.

Every time our relatives visited, Momma cajoled and threatened, they all applauded, and I absolutely refused to sing. I lived in terror of that one awful moment that would force me to run away from home and the block: Suppose a pal raps on the door to tell me the game is starting, and he catches me in the middle of " . . . pale hands I loved, beside the Shalimar . . . "? So I would escape from the relatives into the bathroom, the only room with a lock, and throw up.

We moved to Brownsville, into an area boasting the chic name of Crown Heights and a newly built apartment with heat and hot water. I started the eighth grade at New Utrecht High School, which was an entirely different ball game. I didn't have the comforting embrace of the old block, the school was so crowded the boys sat on the

radiators, and the English teacher mocked my stutter. My
stomach churned in his class, and I hated the written

homework. I was all alone, fat, at war with the world.

Coney Island: That's where the action was. Starting in
spring, we wore bathing trunks instead of underwear to
school so that, after classes, we could take the subway and
go in for a swim. As twilight approached, we gathered
under the boardwalk and sang, accompanied by a ukulele,
love's old sweet songs that we'd picked up on the radio. We
chose a position where the boards overhead were separated,
so we could watch the girls parade by. Our lookout would
signal the approach of the good-lookers, our voices swelled
up louder—and we were surrounded by them. The Young
Communist League girls were not the best-looking but they
did follow the party line: from each according to her
abilities, to each according to his needs. And as the sun
slowly sank over Coney Island, the sands under the boardwalk became a make-out resort.

For everyone but Fatso. I consoled myself at a boardwalk stand with hot dogs and soda.

One day I took a positive step—I acquired a ukulele. I
mentioned to my mother that my friends were making
music, and next day, there was the ukulele on my bed.
Since only three chords were needed for accompaniment I
quickly became the boardwalk troubadour, my soprano
ringing out cleanly with the Crosby and Russ Columbo
favorites. I remember the afternoon, the song, and moment
on which my voice changed: "Everything I Have Is Yours."
I took the melody down a half-tone, then another . . . and
another. What a delicious feeling—I was a baritone, a *man*
at fourteen and a half. I was singing "Everything" with
Crosby's own whistle and hum when I saw, through the
boardwalk slats above, a girl peering down at me in
disbelief.

"Say, you fellas got a *radio* down there?"

Her question gave me the answer to changing my
whole world. Crosby was a millionaire now, making movies too, but he'd started in radio; so had Russ Columbo, and
Dick Powell had begun as a crooner. A pulsating stream of

images flowed over me: a network studio in New York, a Pierce-Arrow with uniformed chauffeur . . . apartment on Park Avenue, then Hollywood, spotlights lighting up the sky for a premiere at Grauman's Chinese . . . I'd have to swat the girls away. Of course, I'd have to lose twenty-five or thirty pounds. I came home fired up to follow Crosby on the Road to Riches.

(SCENE: At the dinner table.)

ME: *I want to take lessons. There's a guy at the Fox Theater building, used to work with Crosby.*

MOMMA: *I know one that worked with Caruso.*

ME: *Well, first I have to learn how to read music.*

MOMMA: (Nodding carefully) *How much could it hurt . . . ?*

The man in the Fox Theater building, sitting behind the door labeled MUSICAL INTERPRETATIONS—ACTS BOOKED, was no teacher, and he had never been closer to Crosby than an orchestra pit. Cigarette dangling from his lips, he worked over my every inflection of "How Deep Is the Ocean" with a Crosby record on his phonograph. Occasionally he hammered at a piano, faking any song in any key, but he didn't bother me. I had at last removed my mother from my back.

I was lucky he was not a teacher, improving my tone and stretching my voice. He could have destroyed it. I was not yet fifteen; a male voice can mature at about eighteen and a female's around fifteen. The proper age of consent is as difficult to establish in singing as it is in marriage.

When I was twenty-four, doubling at Radio City Music Hall and the NBC network, I was waiting in a voice teacher's studio to meet a girl for lunch. A woman introduced herself to me as Mrs. Silverman, and urged me to listen to her daughter, Bubbles, also a student here. She was fourteen and had already made a singing radio commercial. Well, prodigies come and go every year and I was hardly an expert on sopranos, so I agreed vaguely, hoping that the mother would forget it.

She met me at an NBC studio with an accompanist and her cute daughter, who sang the mad scene from Lucia *and several other* prima donna *showpieces in perfect Italian and bowled me over. It was a glorious, mature, incredible voice. Still, I suggested, "She ought to wait two or three years. If she sings too early she's likely to hurt herself. In the meantime, keep studying and see what happens."*

Mrs. Silverman thanked me fervently. I don't know whether she took my advice, but Bubbles became Beverly Sills.

My voice deepened and developed timbre. Station WFOX was in the same building as my teacher, sending me a clear signal from heaven. I walked into the studio and landed an agreement to sing three times a week without pay. Some of the other performers were the rankest of amateurs, but I was broadcasting. Although I could not lose weight, the unseen and unseeing audience made me a different person. I moaned my romantic imitations of the crooners without mercy or humility, and received a few letters from girls who could not spell.

One day I looked through the glass of the studio door and there was Momma, singing her reliable medley from Victor Herbert. We lasted eighteen months on WFOX, but I refused to sing duets with my own mother. And to distance myself further, I changed my radio name to Merrill Miller. By now I had cut so many classes at New Utrecht that the principal recommended a trade school. After two aptitude tests, he assured me the career for which I was best fitted was carpentry.

The trade school, with dirty red-brick turrets and screened windows, had an uncanny resemblance to Sing Sing, and the primary function of the teachers was to keep the students from clobbering each other with the lumber. I did my best. I sawed, planed, and sandpapered trays and shoeshine boxes, and when I brought them home, they looked as if they'd been whittled freehand with a dull knife.

That June, my father mercifully took me out of school

to wrap shoes in a store managed by Uncle Max. In August, my mother prevailed on her cousin, whom we called Uncle Abe in honor of his riches, to take me into his dress business. The floors of his apartment, including the kitchen, were covered with Oriental rugs, which had slipcovers. We relatives were never permitted to walk on them, though. He would lift the edge of the cover to show the design, and that was it. He paid me $8 a week to sweep the floors and push a handcart loaded with his frocks to and from his suppliers in the garment center. And every day I passed by the old Metropolitan Opera House at 39th Street.

The yellow brick building looked more like a garment loft or a warehouse, particularly on the Seventh Avenue side, where the scenery was stacked under tarpaulins until it could be brought inside. I read over the casts posted on the walls and occasionally recognized the name of the opera from the Caruso records. It was the twilight of the Met's Golden Age, but it all had a wonderful glow in the afternoon sun.

Stagehands were dragging the flats through the huge iron roll-up door when I passed by, glumly pushing my cart in the rain. I slowed down. From the dark void, I dimly heard a piano and singing above the street roar and honking cars. A rehearsal—*live* voices. I had never heard live opera singers. The impulse grabbed me: Why not? At least it would be dry inside. I waited until the last flats were shifted, then followed behind with my cart, mumbling "costumes" to the man in a cap at the entrance. I continued pushing the cart until I reached the darkest corner of the backstage brick wall and hid behind the clothes.

My hand separated them and I could see, as if framed in a movie shot, a man in a velour shirt and a woman at a piano. He was tall, with a barrel chest and the strong face of an athlete. I did not know who they were. Then I remembered the listing outside: "Next week, *Don Giovanni* with Ezio Pinza and Rosa Ponselle." They sang a duet I had never heard. The glorious sound filled the stage and soared up to a vast, dim roof, as high as the Ebbets field bleachers. I sat there and let it sink in. Our home records were an echo, a scratchy groan, compared to this. This was the real thing, and it gave me the real goose bumps. Goddamn! What if Momma was right? Was this for me? . . .

And then somebody with a clipboard under his elbow threw me out.

At dinner I told my mother I'd heard Ezio Pinza in person. She was not impressed. In her mind, only a tenor could be a Caruso or a Cantor Rosenblatt; baritones or basses were merely for supporting roles.

Casually I asked, "Do we have money for a real voice teacher?"

Her eyebrows implored heaven. "Money I can always find—a son who listens to me is another story."

I promised to listen.

Her energies, pent up for years, were unleashed. In two days she'd found a friend who knew a cantor who also sang with the Salmaggi Opera Company at the Brooklyn Academy of Music. His wife sang for Salmaggi, too. "A good sign," Momma said.

The maestro was a pudgy tenor whose eyes darted from side to side, as if watching for a curtain that might close any second. He started me singing high Cs, to show a baritone had a wide range, and I hit those high Cs until I was hoarse. After the third lesson ($2.50 each) I refused to return. Momma, convinced I was malingering, invited her own coach to dinner for an appraisal of my voice. Obviously surprised, he urged her to take me to a teacher who actually had a studio in the Metropolitan Opera building. A Mr. Samuel Margolis.

(SCENE: The Margolis studio. Autographed photos of men and women in opera costumes cover the walls. Mr. Margolis, a man of quiet dignity, is finishing a phone call as Momma and I wait.)

ME: (Whispering) *He d-d-doesn't l-look like a si-si-singer.*

MOMMA: *So? You look like a singer? Don't talk—you'll make a mess. I'll talk.*

MR. MARGOLIS: *Mr. Siganari has told me about you.*
First I want you to vocalize.

(I sing scales. He makes small suggestions in technique.)

Now sing any aria you know.

(Aria? I don't know any. I give him "One Night of Love" from the Grace Moore movie.)

MR. MARGOLIS: *He can become a baritone or a tenor.*
We'll see—

MOMMA: (Instantly) *You'll* take *him? Oh, God bless*
you!

MR. MARGOLIS: *He must work, of course.*

MOMMA: (Sadly) *... Still, to pay you ...* (Hopeless shrug) *My husband is not a strong man and, God forbid*
... (Her voice trails off) *... these are hard times for us.*

MR. MARGOLIS: *He could be a big star. Then he can pay*
me.

(Momma is speechless. I pump his hand anxiously.)

ME: *I-I will, I-I will! I pro-pro-promise, Mi-mi-ster*
Mar-mar-golis.

(Margolis blinks, a little puzzled by my stutter.)

I was on my way now—I was not sure where. A trained voice could bring me to opera, but that was like going to heaven while you were still alive enough to enjoy it. In the meantime, radio was broadcasting more and more classical music, and dozens of musical comedies were being produced each season to cheer up Depression audiences. I was still a Crosby fan, and best of all, I enjoyed singing now, for my audience of one. Four times a week, after work, I walked to the Margolis studio in the Met building. The routine continued for years without variation; only my jobs changed.

Uncle Abe harangued me daily—"singing is philanthropy, not feasibility"—so when Uncle Max found a partner and opened the Paradise Bootery in Times Square, I picked up my option: wrapper and delivery boy. These shoes, at $10 to $14 a pair, were designed for showgirls and other glittering types.

Deliveries allowed me to explore the Upper East Side and Park Avenue. I carried a dozen pairs to one apartment on East 55th Street, where a pleasant little housekeeper accepted them and handed me a $20 tip.

"You're an artistic-looking young man," she said. "Why are you delivering shoes?"

I explained I was studying opera. She sat down with me on the upholstered bench in the hallway and gave me a lecture on working hard to achieve my dreams, being nice to people and never giving up. "If you do what you like most to do, you'll be successful and rich."

When I told Uncle Max about this, he laughed. "Get a towel, mop behind your ears. That's Polly Adler." He suggested I use the $20 to treat myself to one of the girls. I nodded nonchalantly and kept the money for cigars and cigarettes—a passion I'd acquired in the cellar of his shop.

I don't smoke cigarettes any more. During the summer, when I'm not singing, I indulge in several cigars a week after meals. As soon as I sniff the fall air, which announces the arrival of opera and concerts, I lose all desire for the aroma of tobacco. I stop smoking. Cold turkey.

Momma moved us to Bensonhurst, where I discovered that most of the guys my age were out of work and joining the Civilian Conservation Corps, to live in the mountains out West, chopping trees and building muscles. When I told my father that a couple of years with the CCC would turn me into a Charles Atlas and take me away from the city's bad air, I noticed a rare tear trickle under his glasses. "My boy," he muttered, "what do you know of hard work? Are you crazy?"

Hoping he could somehow introduce me to a solid job—"a singer is not like a Singer machine"—he brought me into his own shop that summer. To stamp buttonholes in women's garments. The sewing machines stretched for half a block in an Eighth Avenue loft; since the operators were paid by the piece, they seldom stopped. Poppa's body became an extension of his sewing machine. His head and shoulders rocked to its whirring flywheel; arms and fingers jabbed the fabric under the needle. He did not leave the table to eat, but pushed the homemade sandwich into his mouth, as if his hand was a plunger, while the other guided the fabric, and all the while the sweat poured from his forehead like lubricating oil, over his glasses, down his cheeks, and onto the sandwich. It was degrading, heart-wrenching. I understood why he was miserly, why he screamed against Momma's records and my "loafing." His work was real—it hurt. My singing was play, dreaming, ultimately crazy because no sane man could think of making the rent that way.

> *The Star Burlesque in Brooklyn: When I played hooky from school, I would save the bus fare and lunch money so that I could attend on Saturday afternoons to observe the tassel twisters, the bumps and grinds—and there, several rows in front of me, sat Poppa. I instantly retreated to a dark corner at the rear. God knows what surcease from work and Momma he found there, but it must have been important for him to pay $1.25. For a moment I thought of walking over to him, to show we were both men of the world. But I didn't have the courage. I never went back.*

We left for work before the sun rose and returned to Brooklyn after it set. Since the loft was on 36th Street, I was actually creeping closer to the Met.

Momma now hinted to Mr. Margolis that I should see a real, live opera. He obliged with three tickets to the Met's Family Circle for *Trovatore* with Giovanni Martinelli, Richard Bonelli, and Elisabeth Rethberg. We climbed the stairs up, up, to our seats on the right side, close to the proscenium and at about the same level as the immense chandeliers. The hazy view backstage had given me little preparation for the red plush and gilt magic of the house. Mr. Margolis thoughtfully brought opera glasses, which revealed the audience below in tuxedos, long gowns, furs.

In these depressed days, people still dressed for the Met.

At last, absolute stillness, and the curtain rose on the heavy marble rooms of the Aliaferia Palace. I had never seen singers acting. The bigness of everything over-whelmed me: The volume of the voices, the facial move-ments, the glow and richness of the costumes. Bonelli, the Count di Luna, sang effortlessly, enjoying it, reaching out to me with all the fervor that had thrilled me in Caruso. He seemed to sing directly *to me*, and I was hypnotized. "You see how easy it is?" he sang. You can do it, too.

(SCENE: The express train to Brooklyn. Momma and I are rereading and savoring the *Trovatore* programs.)

ME (Without the stutter): *Count di Luna. That's what I want to sing.*

MOMMA: *You would look nicer, too . . .*

ME: *He's marvelous . . . but I know I can do it.*

MOMMA: *What makes you so sure, all of a sudden?*

ME: *I can sing louder than Bonelli.*

2

Merrill Miller:
The Japanese
God of War

It was unmitigated, vulgar gall. But after my paralyzing self-doubts, I really believed it. I was eighteen, growing older by the hour, and I wanted to hear that audience shout "Bravo!" to me.

I borrowed books from the Brooklyn library, which I had avoided in my school days, to study the lives of the great singers, and I listened closely to my mother's records, searching for the secret ingredient that raised their voices above all others. The wherewithal came from my first aria, coached by Mrs. Margolis: "Largo al factotum," the show-stopper from *The Barber of Seville*. It's the tale of Figaro, the resourceful, brash barber who is beloved by all for his many useful talents—an early Sergeant Bilko. Bonelli had propelled me toward opera—Figaro paid my bills until I got there.

It began with a friend named Cal, who used to hang out at the candy store on my block. I ran into him in Times Square. After I intimated I was on the verge of making it big at the Met, he asked if I could sing anything like "Donkey Serenade." I auditioned it right there on the sidewalk, and he recommended me to his father, who was arranging a dinner for a Masonic Lodge in Brooklyn. For $10 I sang "Chloe" and "At the Balalaika," closing with a smash "Figaro." It would have been suicidal to announce it as "Largo al factotum."

The word-of-mouth about the Figaro Kid spread slowly through Brooklyn. With "Donkey Serenade" I now had a surefire repertoire of four numbers for weddings, anniversaries, farewell dinners, neighborhood clubs, smokers, bar mitzvahs and engagement parties. These jobs had a built-in bonus—I could take home the excess turkey, chicken, smoked meats, pastries. And I always became hungry seeing people eat while I worked. Since I never knew when I'd have a pianist who could play "Figaro," I worked out a special arrangement: The musicians faked the melody by vamping under my singing and then we finished—frequently at the same time—on a smash C-major chord.

One afternoon, on Sixth Avenue, I noticed a sign:

MAJOR BOWES AUDITIONS
ONE FLIGHT UP→

Well, I could win this one. Bowes had started the show on WHN in 1935; it was now network but the talent I'd heard was mostly kazoo players and bird imitators. I walked upstairs into a room packed with young people, mandolin and banjo cases, managers, and mothers. This was evidently a second hearing for performers who had passed a screening, so when a man asked me for my "form," I said I forgot it. He glared but gave me one to fill out. After an hour, I was called into the next room, where several judges sat around a piano. The staff accompanist was one of those ebullient Russian musicians whom I was later to encounter in orchestras all around America; next to tailors, the chief export of Russia in the 1900s was violinists and pianists. This one had white hair that wreathed his bald head, huge horn-rim glasses and the inevitable name of Mischa.

"Verr's your music?" he asked.

"I lost it in the subway."

He cursed softly in Russian. "Hokay, vee fake it. Vot can you sink?"

"You know 'Largo al factotum' from—?"

"I know *from*—just giff me *key*."

"The original."

He sighed, "Ah, thank Gott," and played the entire aria perfectly. I was as impressed by his feat as he was by mine. The previous entry had played "Waitin' for the Robert E. Lee" on tissue paper wrapped around a comb.

Three weeks later I was called for a rehearsal conducted by the Major himself, with an audience, in what is now the Ed Sullivan theater, 53rd and Broadway. There were ten of us: a child who sang like Baby Snooks, tambourine and ukulele virtuosos, a fellow who tapped out "America the Beautiful" on glasses of water. My "Figaro" won a $10 check and a chance to repeat for the network's national audience. The audience vote came in next week and Merrill Miller won. The bottle tapper was a weak runner-up.

With my victory came a three-week tour in a Major Bowes unit. He had seven units out, and I was paid $75 a week, including transportation but not housing.

I was instructed to meet my unit in Fort Worth, Texas, which unsettled me and drove Momma to tears. She knew what a fort was—it protected Texas from the Indians—and I couldn't argue the point because, in the back streets of Bensonhurst, everything west of the Hudson River was Indian territory.

I took the train wearing my only blue serge suit, and sat up three days and three nights, peering out the windows for men on horseback. I arrived at the theater just in time for a rehearsal of the first show at 10:30 A.M. Now I met the rest of the company, all certified amateurs: ventriloquist Paul Winchell, Jack Carter, Ted Mack (who played clarinet and emceed), the comedy team of Mickey Ross and Bernie West, who much later became chief writers for the *All in the Family* TV series. I sang the first show utterly exhausted, in what had become my blue serge sweatsuit.

We then had two hours, until the next performance, to find hotel rooms. Jack Carter and I paired up in a rooming house at $1 a night. I felt quite safe in the room after I discovered several peepholes in the door, to look out for strangers. Carter, who was a lot more worldly, explained later this was a free-lance brothel that rented rooms to couples off the street, and the peepholes were for looking *in.*

"Figaro" received a rousing welcome in Oklahoma City, St. Louis, Indianapolis, and points east. I'll always have a soft spot in my memory for Buffalo, where Jack insisted he would not room with me unless I bought another suit. A tailor near the theater advertised "Suits made to order in 3 days—$30—Satisfaction guaranteed." He delivered, as promised, a midnight blue worsted and it fit perfectly.

We returned to New York for our final week—at the Roxy. The Roxy was big-time, the new Palace of vaudeville; Frank Sinatra was out with another unit, but ours was the hottest unit of all.

Some years later, Frank was making the bobby-soxers swoon in the aisles at the Paramount theater, while a few blocks south at the Met, I was singing an Errol Flynn variation of Escamillo in Carmen. *For the first time I heard, to my astonishment, the matinee teenagers scream- ing and sighing at me from the balcony. Frank kidded me on his radio show: "Who asked that longhair to muscle in on my territory?"*

After reaching the summit of his career as the most acclaimed entertainer in the country, Frank decided to retire a few years ago. But after a while he decided he wanted to sing again. He played several engagements and found that his voice was tiring after a half hour. Frank is a serious artist; he delivers his best, and if he doesn't, he knows it.

The vocal cords are like any other muscles. If you lie in a hospital bed for four weeks, you must learn to walk again. Frank canceled several appearances and called me in New York. "I've got a string of one-nighters coming up—I start with a big one out on Long Island—can you recommend someone to work with me on my voice?"

Since I have faced similar problems with a tired throat, I volunteered to do what I could. We went to work in his suite at the Waldorf, vocalizing and relaxing his cords so that he would not have to force the sound. After several one-hour sessions, which he taped, he was ready to go on with his first show at the Nassau Coliseum.

I sat there, more nervous than Frank, because I was listening for each note. He started off tentatively, but at the finish his voice was stronger than when he started. He mesmerized 17,000 people; I have seldom seen such love and excitement in any audience. A few more vocalizing sessions, and he went on to complete the tour that ended in several concerts in New York with Ella Fitzgerald and Count Basie. Ol' Blue Eyes was back, all right.

I came home from the Bowes tour with $90, primed with tales of my safari out West and the importance of my coming debut at the Roxy. What interested my father most was my $30 suit.

Nobody in our family had ever owned a custom-made suit, not even rich Uncle Abe. Poppa telephoned his brother, a tailor; Uncle Looey, now a retired tailor; and Uncle Abe. Tea and sponge cake were laid out, and they meticulously analyzed the incredible workmanship: "The shoulders . . . hand-pressed!" "See the inset here?" "Hand-stitch on the lapels." "Three buttons on the sleeve, and they open up, so you can roll it back like a shirt." Uncle Abe poohpoohed the work, but my father nodded his head serenely; he had seen the future and it was wonderful. "Ah,

America, America! They can make a beauty like this for thirty dollars, not by Three Gs on 14th Street, but out in the woods, God knows where it is, *in Buffalo!*"

Inspired by that suit, I called on a man named Lew who produced and booked and hired all the Bowes units. I demanded $200 a week for the Roxy, or I would quit.

"You nuts?" he roared. "We got ninety for you. That's top price."

"I quit." I walked out, under a hailstorm of shouts and curses and "you'll never work in New York again, you hear?"

He called back next day: He would give me $175 if I didn't tell the other acts. I accepted graciously.

The Roxy engagement set me on the track for vaudeville just in time for its bankruptcy. One locomotive was Sammy Rausch, who also sent me to a newsreel company to sing "The Star-Spangled Banner" as the introduction to all their films. America had entered the conflagration in Europe and the Far East, and movie houses wanted to assist in the war effort. My voice appeared on screens all over the country for several years while I was classified as 4-F because of my allergies.

Another agent, with the name of Mike Hammer, booked me all over the five boroughs on Fridays and Saturdays for engagements that added up to a considerable income in those days—$50 a weekend. I moved fast, chauffeured by my younger brother Gil in his thirdhand Ford, from wedding to banquet to synagogue to dance hall. The car enabled us to carry home enough cold cuts and Danish to last all year.

I had cards printed:

MERRILL MILLER
Bensonhurst 0640
Baritone available
for any occasion

I sang solos with a choir on the High Holy Days. Oscar Julius, who conducted the choir, also secured bookings for us in nearby towns. He once arranged a night's accommodations in a Turkish bath, where we were directed to sleep on the wooden benches. It was as damp as a tomb, and just as eerie. I dressed after midnight and walked around until I found a $2 rooming house. Without peepholes.

Oscar Julius taught me the invaluable art of sight reading; Mr. Margolis worked on my voice, and Mrs. Margolis coached me in the leading baritone roles. And every Monday I'd pay Mike Hammer his 10 percent in cash, on the sidewalk in front of the Palace theater, surrounded by dancers, comics, unicycle virtuosos, dog trainers, the true believers who kept telling each other that radio and movies were bound to resurrect vaudeville. Soon.

Vaudeville was still strong in the Second Avenue Yiddish theaters, although it was often called musical comedy, featuring stars such as Moishe Oysher, Menasha Skulnik, and Molly Picon. Some of the most renowned comedians in America had been incubated here: Eddie Cantor, George Burns, Fanny Brice, the Marx Brothers.

I worked only on Saturday and Sunday, singing operatic arias translated into Yiddish by a friend of Momma's for $2 each. The "Toreador Song" became "Song of the Bull-Killer." "Figaro" was switched to "The Fixer."

The musical comedies were a series of sketches, separated by songs and dances tailored for the talents of their stars. These shows appealed to the audience's old-world morality and free-flowing tears with certain motifs that recurred as relentlessly as any in Wagner:

The daughter seduced by a gentile.

The father who abandons his wife and runs off to America.

The son who abandons his faith seeking American riches.

The mother's constant sacrifices.

The father who works himself to death in a sweatshop.

The rise to the top and fall to despair, forbidden romance, divorce, and a happy ending—all enveloped in warm laughter. The essential message was: Stick together—the family knows best.

When I saw my first show here, I was appalled at how closely it resembled my own family's problems, which may explain why the tales were so popular. They had a foundation of reality, and if some families did not live that way, they felt they should; they expiated their guilt by coming down to Second Avenue on weekends to pay $2.20 and $3.60 to see this life at a safe distance. The shows had a slapdash, homemade quality that was hard to resist.

To sub for a sick star, I rehearsed his specialty with the pianist. When I went on that night, the orchestra used the star's own tenor arrangement. I became a tenor.

We had a Yiddish "Tribute to General MacArthur." This was utter fantasy, involving imitators of Fanny Brice, Supreme Court Justice Louis Brandeis, Al Jolson, Judas Maccabeus (the Jewish hero of 160 B.C.). Merrill Miller was the Japanese God of War.

In another show, I secured a free box seat from the impresario for a fellow voice student, Paul Richards. After I'd finished an aria, I stepped forward and announced, "Ladies and gentlemen, we have with us tonight one of the greatest singers of the Metropolitan Opera! I want you to meet my good friend, Ezio Pinza!" The spotlight picked him out and Paul, surprised but obviously pleased, stood up to bow. Tremendous cheers. I was able to find box seats for all of Margolis's pupils by introducing them as Lily Pons, Martinelli, Lawrence Tibbett. I never attempted Caruso.

Second Avenue also had its own brands of ham: Great Actors, Actor-Directors, Actor-Director-Impresarios. Some excellent actors emerged here, to appear on the English-speaking stage and in films—Paul Muni, Luther Adler (the Adlers were the downtown Barrymores), Ricardo Cortez, who picked his name from a cigar band. The prototype of the Actor-Director-Impresario was Maurice Schwartz, a virtuoso performer in the tradition of nineteenth-century opera. His great moments were prose arias; sound and emotion were more important than meaning.

Actor-Directors dressed in pince-nez, canes, snap-brim fedoras and, in winter, greatcoats with wraparound fur collars. Their Players Club was the Café Royale (later celebrated in a Broadway play as Café Crown), where they could sip tea through lumps of sugar, read newspapers, and receive their courtiers.

The caste system was strictly enforced. Actors sat in the large front section, to which the public also had access. Actor-Directors presided over smaller rooms at the rear, where the headwaiter rejected tourists and autograph hounds. I was admitted to the Actor-Director orbit because one of them claimed me as his protégé "from the opera."

I usually worked four shows a day, leaving little time for the Café Royale, so I lived off huge platters of knishes brought in from Yonah Schimmel, our own Fauchon. They cost 10 cents each, which you paid to the guard at the stage door. One was a meal; if you ate two or three, it was hard to squeeze out of the dressing room.

My parents attended every Saturday night. The eight performances netted me $50—that is, $6.25 a show.

One evening in May, as I left Mr. Margolis's studio, now on 57th Street, a friend ran into me. "Hurry up, they're auditioning for Scaroon Manor."

"What's that?"

"Hotel in the Adirondacks."

I ran across the street to Steinway Hall, where I found the hotel's entertainment director, Dave Bines. He listened to my "Chloe" and "Balalaika," nodding with little enthusiasm until I admitted I also sang "Figaro." After he heard that, he hired me for a summer in the country at $250.

Another kind of vaudeville was emerging here. In the forties, the mountain resorts had no indoor-outdoor pools, ski lifts, giant theaters that paid headliners $10,000 a week. A hotel had "class" if it had an outdoor *filtered* pool. They were mainly small, family-operated establishments that had begun as boardinghouses for the summer. Instead of sitting on your sidewalk or fire escape, sweltering in the New York heat as you played cards, snacked, and gossiped, you could come to the mountains, sit in the fresh cool air, and do the same thing.

Scaroon Manor was as idyllic as I'd imagined the CCC

would be. Mountains, fresh air, lovely greenery, a lake. I shared a small cabin with a tenor from Texas; the others on the professional entertaining staff were a girl singer, six chorus girls who danced in production numbers, and a five-piece band that sounded like fifty. We performed on weekends with headliners such as the Three Stooges and Red Skelton.

It was an outdoor stage, which drew audiences of 600 guests and several hundred visitors. An outdoor audience, I learned, was the most difficult to hold, because of the competition of birds, wind, threats of rain, and mosquitoes. During the week the staff entertained with nightclub-style numbers, and "Figaro" became the hero of the Borscht Belt. Whenever I appeared, someone would offer me $10 to sing it for him and his wife or family.

I worked as a patsy for the Three Stooges, who tore up my only tuxedo jacket, and I stooged for Red Skelton. He did his classic doughnut-dunking routine, in which he played six different people (a fastidious little lady, a truck driver, and others) characterized by the way they dunked at a lunch counter. I was the man behind the counter, handing him the doughnuts.

Red was on the way up from vaudeville. He had recently developed this routine after a theater manager in Montreal told him the audience was a little tired of his pratfalls. "Can you imagine that?" he said, raising his cinnamon-colored eyebrows. "I dunked those damn dozen doughnuts three shows a day for three years and put on thirty-eight pounds."

His eating problem now was getting his favorite break- fast food, pork chops, in hotels that advertised "kosher only." He carried a cast-iron skillet and an electric hot plate as props, and delegated me to pick up the chops in town. He'd plug into his dressing room outlet, close the stage curtain, and lock his door to hide the aroma. The owners came sniffing around but Red would explain, through the locked door, "I'm warming up my nose putty."

Red had some peculiar obsessions. He was so afraid of the dark he kept a light on in his room, and he was always on the alert for some unknown "they," who, he was convinced, were out to destroy him. He carried money in his shoes to fool "them." Offstage, he called himself Red. Onstage, in rehearsal, he referred to himself as Victor Van Bernard. "My real name is Richard Bernard Skelton," he confided to me, "but I'm not sure." He solved the smoking problem by chewing—not smoking—twenty cigars a day. "I know I'm nuts, but if I keep 'em laughing, they'll never put me away." He kept them roaring.

I came in late for a show one night, so hungry I gobbled up four of his doughnuts. When he reached the truck driver, I had none to hand him.

He screamed, "Where's my doughnuts?"

I pretended the prop man had forgotten them.

"I want my doughnuts," he yelled, and fell off the stool onto the floor, where he gave a wonderful impression of a child kicking and bawling. The audience assumed this was part of the act and roared along.

Then he leaped up to grab me by the throat. "If you don't get those doughnuts, I'll strangle you," he mumbled. I shook loose and run off into the kitchen. He ad-libbed a desperately hungry man, slipping off the stool and wrapping his six-foot skinniness around the lunch counter. If the laughs stopped for a second, he did a backward dive to the floor. When I returned with the doughnuts, he licked my cheeks like a happy hound.

Before he returned to New York, he left me with this parting thought: "Like my mother used to say, kid—don't take life too seriously. You'll never get out of it alive."

Several years ago, rehearsing with Red for one of his TV shows, I admitted my doughnut theft. He screamed, "*You* were the sonofabitch!" He took that part of his life seriously.

The chorus girls were closely chaperoned by Dave Bines's wife, Cookie, the choreographer. Still there were lovely moonlit nights on the lake, and canoes. I was a failure under the Coney Island boardwalk, but under that moon I discovered I could maneuver in a canoe.

Through Dave Bines I received a position on the S.S. Rotterdam *cruising to the Bahamas. A hundred dollars and all I could eat. It was an elegant ship, from the accommodations to the dining room to the black tie and gowns for dinner. My accompanist was a Dutch pianist trained in the classics.*

The first night out, it was so balmy we were asked to perform on deck. Directly in front of me sat the imposing William Mackenzie King, Prime Minister of Canada, and his retinue. Having never worked in front of anyone this eminent, I was a little shaky. "Donkey Serenade" was well received, and when I announced "Largo al factotum" in honor of the PM, he applauded vigorously. At that moment, the wind came up and blew my music sheet over the rail. Silence. I whispered to the pianist, "Okay, fake it. Vamp in C." He shook his head dolefully. He couldn't do it. I smiled helplessly as the Prime Minister said, "Well, get on with it."

"I don't have my accompaniment," I said.

The Prime Minister rose from his chair and sat down at the piano. "What key do you wish, sir?"

"C . . . Can you vamp in C, your honor?"

The Prime Minister vamped better than my ex-teacher in the Fox building, who'd been faking for thirty years. Ovation.

I came home feeling very pleased with myself; I'd leaped out of my cocoon. Hoping to surprise Mr. Margolis and my mother, I breezed over to the sixth floor of NBC to enter the Metropolitan Opera Auditions of the Air. Wilfred Pelletier presided over the preliminary weeding-out, which I passed with—of course—"Largo al factotum." At that time I was under the influence of a recording by Titta Ruffo, whose magnificent comedic joy, reveling in his control of the world around him, surpassed, I thought, even Bonelli's. Now that I had worked with several masters of comedy, I knew I was ready.

I never reached the semifinals. Just as in my early years I'd achieved a bit of success as a Crosby mimic, now I assumed I could ride into the Met on the shoulders of Ruffo. Imitation may be the sincerest flattery, but it is also, for artists, the shortest path to oblivion. I sank back into the routine of my voice lessons, depressed and shaken. But not for long.

3

In and Out the Window

Soon I was at the very top of the Met—eighty feet above the stage. Charlie Siegal, the electrician at Scaroon Manor, had been hired by the opera; he escorted me in through the stage door as his out-of-town nephew, and up to the fly gallery, where I sat on a narrow iron balcony. I saw only the tops of heads and torsos—they grew legs and feet when they moved—but the voices floated up to me beautifully. With the Met programs in my hand, outlining the plots, I learned to recognize the stars by the density of their hairdos and the prominence of their chests.

And next summer I sallied out again into the Catskills,

booked by Charlie Rapp, the indefatigable Machiavelli of the mountains. He set me for Young's Gap Hotel for six weeks and proposed to double my salary by doubling me. The strategy was simple, requiring only speed and a flexible mind.

I had signed for three shows a week—Tuesday, Saturday, and Sunday. Charlie tried me out for speed by booking me into other hotels on my nights off, without the knowledge of the Young's Gap owners. "Your contract does not require exclusivity," he pointed out. And my accompanist, Sasha, a huge amiable bear of a Russian who played the accordion, raced his Plymouth over slippery hills and corkscrew roads.

Satisfied with my velocity, Charlie next proposed to book me in another hotel on the same nights I had to appear at Young's Gap. "You'll open the show here," Charlie explained, "applause—thank you—walk out for some fresh air—Sasha is waiting in the Plymouth—over the mountain to the other hotel, where you come on in the middle of the show—three numbers—applause—thank you—out for the fresh air—into the Plymouth—and back for the finale at Young's Gap!"

"What if I can't get out for fresh air?"

"They have to give you time to wash your hands—it's in the contract. Then—out the window—into the Plymouth—"

"What if the window doesn't open?"

Charlie threw up his hands. "I'll *break* it open!"

I came home breathless and twice as rich.

Next summer: same place, same scheme. Except that I was caught at the President Hotel by Mr. Leschnick, co-owner with Mr. Podolnick. Podolnick was the overseer of the kitchen who, it was rumored, slept in the walk-in refrigerator and allotted twelve potato chips to a plate. Leschnick was the impresario, a short, bald, volatile man. When he hired me, he asked if I could do some numbers from that opera—he didn't recall the name, but it had a famous detective.

"I don't remember any detective."

"You know . . . Pinkerton!"

Leschnick grabbed my legs as I hung out the window of his "Music Hall." He cried out triumphantly, "Ha! I'm going to trow you and your mudder off the show!"

That was a double embarrassment. My mother, in a fit of prosperity, had rented a summer cottage near the hotel. It was a *kuchelen* (cook-it-yourself) that provided communal cooking facilities and little else. The *kucheleners* brought their own bedding and utensils; it was much less expensive than the President and they could appraise the hotel shows at night. Guiding their way with flashlights over dirt paths and around trees, these patrons of the arts moved silently onto the hotel grounds like a column of fireflies. The hotels retaliated with a security system, marking their registered guests' wrists with an invisible ink that could only be revealed by a special light. Often members of the audience with bulging pockets were searched by hotel guards for the incriminating flashlight, and interlopers would be ejected.

My mother had prevailed on Leschnick to include her repertoire of Polish songs on the week-night shows. The audience loved her, and now Poppa, Gil, and even their friends were welcomed as legitimate guests to the shows.

"Mr. Leschnick," I said, dropping from the window to the grass, "I'll sing two extra numbers on every show."

"And no running to udder hotels."

I assured him his people came first.

"Remember—actors I can buy by the gross—people it's not so easy."

The chief *toomler* at Camp Tamiment in the Pocono mountains, just a little west of the Catskills, was a skinny guy six feet tall, with watery blue eyes, a mop of red hair, a Pinocchio nose and a Dick Tracy chin. Since the function of a *toomler* was to raise a tumult, to keep the guests off-balance so they wouldn't check out of the hotel in bad weather, that chin was in constant motion. He was frantic, he was insulting, he was hilarious, even if you couldn't understand a word of his doubletalk. You had to stay at Tamiment.

Danny Kaye was six years older than I. He came from

Bradford Street, in the East New York area of Brooklyn; he had dropped out of high school, was a Dodger fan and the son of a garment worker. He used to spend a lot of time sleeping, he told me, because he didn't know what to do with himself. "My father slipped me a few bucks under my pillow once in a while, and when my mother caught him, he said, 'It's like sending the boy to college. When he wakes up and finds out what he wants to be, he'll be a happy man.'"

The piano player was a petite, rather serious brunette who, Danny discovered, had also lived on Bradford Street and attended PS 149 (where Danny made his stage debut playing a watermelon seed); Danny had even watched the office during lunch hour for her father, a dentist. Sylvia Fine also wrote hilarious lyrics that Danny delivered like the sputter of an outboard motor. They eloped to Florida, and a few years later I heard that Danny Kaye, playing a swish photographer in the Broadway musical, *Lady in the Dark*, was rattling off a catalog aria of fifty Russian composers in forty seconds. And, just as quickly, he became a multimedia star.

Some time in the fifties, after I sang the national anthem at a benefit show, Kaye grabbed me backstage: "You—so *you're* Robert Merrill! I was driving out in California and almost ran off the freeway. I heard this voice on NBC coming out of somebody named Robert Merrill, but I knew it had to be from Tamiment. You never looked like a Merrill Miller to me."

It was as much a tribute to his memory as it was to my voice. He had remembered my *sound* for over ten years. Toscanini was the only man I knew who had a memory like that. And this may help explain why, when Danny Kaye woke up, as his father predicted, he found out he wanted to do—everything. He is the truly fulfilled Walter Mitty. The not-so-secret life of Danny Kaye reveals this versatile performer is also an accomplished operatic singer, a surgeon, an orchestra conductor, a low-score golfer, a jet pilot, a great chef . . .

"I've never really had to work hard for anything in my

life. I just concentrate totally on anything that strikes my interest." And nearly everything does.

I introduced Danny to Rudolf Bing (he immediately called the general manager Rudy), and Rudy asked Danny to play the non-singing jailer Frosch in a new production of *Fledermaus*. This is the only moment I've ever known Danny to fail: He couldn't arrange his schedule to fit the opera.

Danny never bothered to learn to read music because all he has to do is hear a melody sung or recorded and he can repeat it perfectly—years later. He has stunned me with arias I had sung twenty years before on records. Danny's two-octave range mimics anything from a dramatic baritone to an Irish tenor to a coloratura soprano and even her high C. He improvises harmony to any melody, which few trained singers can duplicate.

In a taxi to the theater, I sang a melody from *Traviata*. Danny instantly harmonized on the tenor notes. When we finished, the cabby remarked, "Hey, you guys are pretty good. [To Kaye] Tell me, mister, aren't you a professional singer?"

He loves to introduce children to opera, and on the *Met Opera Look-in* on television not long ago, he sang the "Largo al factotum" with me and a duet with Beverly Sills. He was kidding it, but his voice was too close for comfort to that of an opera singer.

His uncanny musicianship extends to his conducting of symphony orchestras for benefit concerts. He listens to the music on a record or at rehearsal and he is ready to conduct. He is not faking—he does lead the orchestra. This astonished Dmitri Mitropoulos, who sat next to me at a benefit in Carnegie Hall for the New York Philharmonic. He turned to me: "Is it true your friend has never studied music?"

"I'm afraid so."

"Incredible. What a stick technique! He might perhaps have been a first-rate conductor."

For a long time, Danny was interested in surgery. With the permission of friendly surgeons in New York and Los

Angeles hospitals, he spent hours observing the cutting and sewing. And, sure enough, a surgeon told me later that Kaye could, in an emergency, perform minor surgery. The American College of Surgeons made him an honorary member.

When Danny was a youngster one of his friends was Al Weller, a surgeon who also played the guitar. As Danny tells it, Weller and he sat in on a jam session where the doctor started to explain an operation. Danny took over, pantomiming the incisions and forgetting the sponges, explaining it all in nonsense doubletalk. That may have been where Danny first realized he could manage the staccato tongue-twisting that brought him to Broadway and seventeen movies.

I played almost all the large hotels in the Catskills. Their entertainment facilities varied, but one show remained constant: the parents' acts trying to marry me to their daughter. The fact that I was a budding operatic singer added a cachet of culture that raised me, in their minds, above the budding pharmacist or accountant. My calculated determination to remain single at that time was only a minor complication in their scenarios.

> (SCENE: The hotel lounge, after the show. I have been invited to tea and cake with Mr. and Mrs. A. He is an effervescent man who plays guitar and, incidentally, owns a chain of supermarkets.)
>
> MR. A: *I like your voice, my boy. A great gift.*
>
> ME: *Thank you very much.*
>
> MR. A: *Still, talent has to be nursed along, correct? . . . You know my daughter, Anna? What a personality!*
>
> MRS. A: *And a beautiful cook and a college girl. She studies piano with a teacher that comes to the house.*
>
> MR. A: *Well, I just got word from my partner, he's retiring soon and I'll need help in the business . . .*
>
> MRS. A: (Brightly) *You'll always have groceries on the table.*

ME: *I make enough for my teachers . . .*

MR. A: *Fifteen thousand a year brings the best teacher.*

ME: *I don't want the complications of a wife—I need to be free to travel—*

MR. A: *Who's talking about marrying? So she'll wait. My Anna likes to travel. Already she's been to Miami.*

MRS. A: *Come over to the house. She plays so pretty—you'll sing, I'll make a spongecake . . .*

MR. A: *Look. I can raise the job to $20,000.*

ME: *I'm going out to California . . .*

MR. A: *Keep in touch. Here's my card.*
(He winks at me broadly)
What a smart negotiator you are, young fella!

Negotiator? As soon as I returned to New York, I was a notorious patsy for agents. They rented my voice out for cash, deducted 10 percent, and since I seldom knew what actual fee they received, often kept an additional $20. Sometimes I was booked into the Catskills on off-season weekends, with Phil Foster or Phil Silvers, and the agent would try to pay us off separately, so we wouldn't know the total fee. One of the Phils usually discovered what that fee was, and the agent would reluctantly pay us at the same time—under a bright light so we could count the bills.

> *Singers of the nineteenth century insisted that managers pay in cash before the show started. Adelina Patti, who demanded $5,000 a performance on her American tour in the 1880s (the equivalent of $50,000 in today's pauper dollars), delayed a matinee because her impresario, Col. J. H. Mapleson, had only $4,000 in the box office.*
>
> *Very well, said the amiable Adelina through her agent, she would be costumed and ready to go on as Violetta, except for her shoes. As soon as the remaining $1,000 was paid, she would put them on. By curtain time, Mapleson turned over $800. Her agent announced that she now had one shoe on, waiting for the other $200. Mapleson started the* Traviata *without her, and somehow raised the $200.*

Mme. Patti went on, fully shod, in the middle of the first scene and gave a superb performance.

Maria Callas continued that pay-in-advance tradition. To discourage this, Rudolf Bing paid her manager, Battista Meneghini (who was also her husband at the time), in $5 bills. Bing kept trying.

When I sang my "Figaro" at Grossinger's on a Thanksgiving Day, an amiable guest assured me I was an artist who deserved a national radio audience. I thanked him carefully.

"Please see me at my office in New York," he said. "My name is Moe Gale."

Some agents I knew had their offices in the Automat, but Moe Gale was different. He had a large suite, a secretary and, it seemed, a direct line to NBC and H. Leopold Spitalny, who had a stranglehold on conducting and hiring of musicians there. As musical contractor, he hired and fired all instrumentalists in consultation with the union; as conductor, he chose the music, rehearsed, and led several network shows. His brother Phil conducted an all-girl orchestra.

I auditioned for NBC the day after I walked into Gale's office. The NBC vice president in charge of something or other wanted a crooner; Spitalny and Samuel Chotzinoff, the network's music consultant, insisted on me. I was signed at $90 a week for the fifteen-minute *Serenade to America*. I would sing four songs on three shows a week, and I calculated that each show paid as little as a banquet in Brooklyn. But this was network radio, and in 1943 it was soaring to the zenith of its influence in America's affection. An audience of millions, I was assured, awaited me.

Leo Spitalny was a small man, a very live ringer for Woody Woodpecker of the movie cartoons with a heavy Russian accent. His ferocious energy and irascible temper and kindness to me were all, I suppose, tied up with being Russian. Most of his index finger was missing; the rumor was that he had cut it off himself, for without a trigger finger, men escaped service in the Czar's army. He did not consider this any bar to his conducting. In radio, a conductor held up four fingers to signal a four rhythm; two fingers indicated a half (two) rhythm. When Leo held up his first two fingers, the musicians complained they could not play a one and a half rhythm—but not in front of Leo.

His arrangements for orchestra were not handicapped by the fact that he wrote them in committee. NBC had several of the best arrangers in the business, and Leo called them into conference around a large table. I attended because I had to find out what key I was singing.

"Awright, gentleman," Leo began, "vith zee 'Home un zee Range' I vant zee first zthree barrs should be like horzes, vith zee cowboys . . . zee second hate barrs I vant zee smell from zee barrn, zen gallop! gallop! For zee finale, zomezing like zee heavenly choir, but more earthly, clomp, clomp. You undersztand?" The arrangers would chorus, "Yes, maestro," and write out the wonderful arrangements for which H. Leopold Spitalny was famous.

Ours was a superb orchestra of forty men, most of whom also played in the NBC Symphony, but we had only a half hour to rehearse *Serenade*'s four numbers. Near the end of the third piece, "Bolero," we would suddenly hear a disembodied voice, "Okay, you're on the air," and we'd go into the theme. Then Leo would start conducting "Bolero" instead of turning back to the first number, my "Road to Mandalay." Fortunately, our first violinist, Mischa Mischakoff, another Russian but more methodical, took over after the first few notes, conducting with his bow until Leo could shuffle his score into order.

He conducted the first international hookup of music from both London and New York. I was to sing in the NBC studio with Leo conducting the orchestra, and an English soprano was to sing in the London studio—accompanied by our orchestra in New York. The usefulness of this stunt escaped me. Leo had earphones and microphone connected to London, and he assumed therefore that the soprano could somehow see him, too. Leo yelled, "Dummy! vy dontcha votch me? I'm holding upp too fingerrs, no? Vy you zing eet een four?"

The English voice came over the studio speaker. "Mr. Spitalny, would you be good enough to clarify that?"

"Fur gudssakes, speak Heenglish!" Leo yelled again. "Vatch my hands. Be a moosishan, canchya? Guddamn raddio! . . ."

In a short while I was doubling again, from NBC to Radio City Music Hall; it was much more remunerative than the Catskill hotels and I did not have to climb out of windows. Erno Rapée, general music director of the Music Hall, heard my voice on a newsreel and hired me for four shows a day. The stage door opened on 49th Street. After my second stage show, I'd hurry to the NBC entrance on 50th Street, between Fifth and Sixth Avenues, take the elevator up to the studio, run out after fifteen minutes and arrive, breathless, at the Music Hall for the last show.

I had to keep my makeup on, and since the tremendous size of the Music Hall (it seats 6,000) required heavy eye shadow, rouge, and lip brightener, I drew unbelieving stares from tourists and invitations to lunch with strange men. Leonard Warren and Jan Peerce were alumni of the Hall; they had the same awesome experience, singing out into a vast space whose boundaries could not be seen in the darkness. All I could see were the spotlights, somewhere out there in the rear, like the headlights of trains in the night.

The population backstage was the equivalent of a small town, ruled—in the dictatorial tradition of Mayor Hague of Jersey City—by Rapée.

A short, sardonic Hungarian with a thin mustache that looked penciled-in, Rapée had led symphonies in Europe and written the theme music, "Diane," for the 1927 silent film *Seventh Heaven*. Now he waged a continual war of attrition with the stage show producer, Leon Leonidoff, an effervescent Russian. They'd shout obscenities at each other, in front of Music Hall corporate executives who came to see the final run-throughs; as soon as the money men left, Erno and Leon threw their arms around each other. It was a recurring routine the two played, to prove they were geniuses and earning their pay as a team, but I noticed they never exposed their backs to each other.

Rapée bullied and fired talent with calculated ruthlessness. He had been a top conductor at NBC until he was fired, as I heard it, for taking kickbacks from the musicians. A call to his office in the Music Hall meant a tongue-lashing or a dismissal. He sent for me after I'd had a small crisis onstage.

The night before, I'd eaten dinner in one of those inexpensive, sidestreet Greek restaurants with the table d'hôte afterburn. On the last show, as I sang "Home on the Range" in my sequined cowboy suit, a great bubble slowly worked its way up my chest. Waiting for the end of a phrase, I gaily waved my ten-gallon hat over my face, and belched into it.

Rapée, dour as ever, stood up behind his mammoth desk as I came in and, before I said a word, he farted. I didn't know whether this was an instrument of terror or simply a warning, and since nothing registered in his face, I pretended not to have heard.

"What was that business with the hat?" he said.

I explained the origins of the great bubble and, in view of his own problem, expected to find him sympathetic. Not at all. "I can't have people see this on my stage," he snorted. "Don't you dare do that again."

I promised I wouldn't.

"I heard you on that lousy radio show," he said.

(I was now on a weekly program conducted by Dr. Frank Black, musical director of the NBC Symphony.)

"Black is a faker. Why do you sing with him when you can have Rapée?"

I shrugged helplessly.

"You tell them at NBC you want Erno Rapée to conduct your shows, and nobody else."

I promised I would.

Working for the NBC network gave me a muted illusion of power. Their well-dressed, smiling page boys (Gordon MacRae was one) brought us coffee at rehearsals and always answered, "Yes, sir." Years later, Schuyler Chapin revealed that he had been one of those "gofers" to whom I'd called, "Say, boy, can you get me a cup of coffee?" On his opening night as general manager of the Metropolitan

My sense of having arrived—well, not at the Met but somewhere up high—was made almost believable by the penthouse of Sigmund Romberg. Good old Leo Spitalny arranged the audition for a summer replacement show, *An Evening with Romberg*. The cigarette sponsor paid me a happy $700 a week, but most exhilarating, Romberg became Rommy and a good friend.

He'd been born in a Hungarian town near the Austrian border, so he always thought of himself as Viennese. "Let me tell you the difference between the Viennese and the Hungarian. Both of them will sell their own mother. But the Hungarian, Merrill—the Hungarian will deliver." Certainly his greatest successes, *Maytime, Blossom Time, The Student Prince, New Moon*, no matter what their setting, were his rose-gold memories of the Vienna he knew as a music student at the turn of the century: the city of cafés, the wines of the *heuriger*, the Strauss and Lehar melodies.

Romberg had immigrated to New York in 1911, and played piano in restaurants; after two years he went to work for the Shubert brothers' musical factory, turning out four shows a year. He wrote forty musicals and revues for them, none of any great distinction. After his first personal success, *Maytime*, the money rolled in. In the 1920s, the Shuberts had nine road companies simultaneously playing *The Student Prince*. After Friml had two flops in the thirties and retired to Hollywood, Rommy was the last master of the Viennese operetta, and he was conscious of time passing by. "I'm two wars behind," he told me. "And now I'm fifty-seven. I must write a show genuinely set in America."

An incessant smoker, dapper in vested suits that barely hid his comfortable belly, he indulged his taste for the good life in a twenty-fifth-floor penthouse with a flowered terrace that rivaled Rockefeller Center's gardens. He assured me he expected to attend my debut at the Met, and took me under his well-tailored wing. We had dinner on his terrace, evenings at the theater, and he talked wittily about new trends in music, painting, theater—but never politics. He introduced me to hand-embroidered napkins and baroque Italian table silver. It was a champagne summer, a taste of what success in the arts could bring. My wide-eyed eagerness to drink it all in, I suppose, appealed to his detached, quizzical view of life. Possibly I was a substitute son. No matter, he had style and he loved to share it.

He engaged me to sing under his baton with the Philadelphia Symphony at Robin Hood Dell in that city. His chauffeur drove us down the night before the performance. Next morning, we rehearsed, it rained, and the performance was postponed to the next night. "It's so dreary in Philadelphia, even without rain," he said, and we were driven back to New York for dinner at home with his wife. In the morning, back to Philadelphia.

I had never had a birthday party. Rommy remedied that deficiency when I turned twenty-five. Grace Moore was there on the terrace, one of those lavishly beautiful creatures who exuded womanliness, a star of the Met, movies, radio, musical comedy—she had it all. She lifted a glass of champagne to me: "Happy birthday. See you at the Met."

I lived on that toast for weeks. I asked Mr. Margolis "When?" and he assured me I was not ready yet.

In January of 1945, Rommy came up with the genuine American musical of which he was enormously proud, *Up in Central Park*. It was a charming story, set in New York during the days of the Tweed ring and lavishly produced by Mike Todd; it ran for fourteen months. A hit, but the critics carped that Romberg was still echoing Strauss and even parodying his own earlier work.

I had an appointment with Jeanette MacDonald to rehearse for an album of Up in Central Park, *and after half an hour, it looked as though she had forgotten me. She did appear, out of breath and apologetic: Autograph hunters had besieged her. I was glad I'd waited because she was one of those film beauties who looked even better offscreen: She actually flashed emerald eyes. At recording time, we faced each other across the mike, but she faced*

*the conductor, Robert Russell Bennett. I was, as usual, ill
at ease. Hell, I thought, why do they always maneuver me
like this? . . . She must have read my eyes, for she asked
me to change places with her, so that I could face the
conductor.*

In January, two years later, Rommy asked me to
accompany him to the opening of *Finian's Rainbow*. He
was entranced with the music, keeping time with his head
and humming the melody. In his car, returning to the
penthouse, he sighed softly and said, "Why can't I write a
show like that?"

Rommy's last musical, *The Girl in Pink Tights*, was
produced in 1951, some months after his death. It was a
quick failure and the end of a wonderful era: Romberg had
written seventy shows.

The name Merrill Miller came to an end in 1944. I was
rehearsing a benefit for the Red Cross with Mark Warnow,
who conducted the *Hit Parade*. "You know something?—
you don't look like a Merrill to me. You're a Bob. Let me
introduce you as—Robert Merrill. That has star quality."

My mother handed me a scrap torn from the corner of
her newspaper. There was a number scribbled on it.

"Somebody called for you to sing. He wants you to call
him back."

"Didn't he leave his name?"

"Who can say such a name? Some kind of foreigner."

4

Always Pencil
the Mustache
under the Mustache

The next morning I phoned, and an affirmative voice
identified itself as Michael de Pace, operatic manager, who
rattled off an impressive string of Metropolitan Opera
singers for whom he handled outside engagements. He had
a possible one-night stand for me in Newark, New Jersey, at
$250. It all sounded like a gag by one of the sidemen in the
Radio City orchestra, especially when de Pace announced
his address: RCA Building.

I checked with Moe Gale, who knew him, and dropped
in on Mr. de Pace. He was a swarthy six-foot sea of calm
and consideration. "I'm casting *Aïda*, and you have an

interesting dark quality in your voice. Do you know Amonasro?"

"Of course," I said. "I've been working on it with Bellini."

> *Bellini was a volatile, finger-waving coach who specialized in Italian operas. He admitted to direct descent from the great composer Vincenzo Bellini and found the English language an incurable affliction. I spent a third of my hours with him diagnosing his English. "Sing it chipper, chipper!" he'd cry. "You know, more potato chip." After much pantomime of popping chips and crunching, I realized he meant sing it* crisp.

"What's more, you'll have the opportunity to sing with one of the world's greatest tenors—Giovanni Martinelli!" De Pace waited for that to sink in. "He's been at the Met since 1913."

Nineteen thirteen? That was six years before I was born. "L-l-look, I've go-got to-to tell you," I stuttered, caught between fear and disbelief, "it's my first opera . . . I m-m-mean, he m-m-must be sixty—how c-c-can he love Aï-Aï-Aïda, my da-da-daughter? I'm twenty-five!"

"We have a great makeup man."

I hustled over to the Margolises, who were as surprised as I was, and delighted. Mrs. Margolis immediately picked up the score—she was primarily a pianist—and we worked through the role. I had a week to learn it before rehearsing with Martinelli, so I studied into the night and occasionally slept over on a couch in their studio.

My mother brought out a Victor record of "Celeste Aïda" that Martinelli had made in 1918. I was gratified to be working on the same stage with him, but I now realized that his act would be impossible to follow.

Momma was immediately convinced the next step was the Met. "A man like Martinelli, a voice from heaven, you don't think he sings with any *nebbish* they pick up in front of a candy store? Oh, no. But don't be afraid of him. Remember, he stands on two legs, the same like you."

My father was much cooler. "A Caruso he ain't—but Caruso's dead."

Martinelli lived in the Buckingham, down the block from the Margolis studio. He was my height, with a mop of white hair as fluffy as Ben-Gurion's and the powerful chest of a longshoreman; his quizzical glance as I entered was softened by the world-weariness in his eyes. He put me at ease immediately, helping me over my crudities, with a genuine desire to help. It was a rare opportunity for me. Martinelli was still a stalwart of the Met's Italian team, even though his voice was not in its prime, and his acting was formidably convincing.

Our Aïda was a handsome girl with a voice of exquisite sweetness. I had heard on the 57th Street rumor line that she would soon be signed by Edward Johnson for the Met, but I couldn't relate to her. I felt an aloofness, almost iciness; she literally looked down her nose at the shaky Brooklyn boy. She was also distant from Martinelli, as if she felt he was fortunate, in his declining years, to find her singing opposite him.

For the Newark *Aïda* the scenery, props and costumes came from Stivanello's, a huge loft on lower Fifth Avenue. They bought up costumes from musical shows and opera companies that had closed, and could outfit a hundred productions. Tony Stivanello often mounted several operas simultaneously in different cities. I searched through the double- and triple-tiered racks for my costume: a loincloth of fake leopard with necklaces of bright brass rings and what seemed to be large brown teeth.

I confessed to Tony this was my first opera and I didn't know where to stand. It was easy in radio or the Music Hall—I merely stood in front of a mike. But on the stage, I would have to walk around—*act*. I had no concept of how Amonasro, King of Ethiopia, would walk.

"Okay," Tony said. "I'll give you lessons. I charge five dollars."

"I'll take two," I said quickly.

We worked in the Margolis studio. Tony coached me line for line on character, movement, and motivation of an Ethiopian king. He even threw in a pair of sandals so I wouldn't pick up splinters.

None of our family had ever ventured to Newark. Since

I had to report at three o'clock for the rehearsal, the family set out at noon on the safari. My mother packed sandwiches and fruit, and we took the subway to the Hudson Tubes. She knew we were traveling under water—"very bad air for the voice"—and urged my father to close the windows in the train.

During the rehearsal, I had to leave the family standing in the lobby. Our conductor was also from the Met, a harried veteran who could not face the terrors of a dark theater while sober. I rejoined the family at a lunchroom, where they had ordered tea and coffee for our sandwiches; all of this made me more jittery because the counterman was glaring at us. I dashed backstage for makeup.

The gray-faced old-timer slapped the blacking over my entire pale white body like a mud pack and topped it with a wig which today might be classified as Afro, then added a frizzy, square-cut beard and low-hanging mustache with spirit gum. The mustache immediately began to itch.

The first act rolled smoothly—Amonasro does not appear in it. Martinelli took command of the stage and held it like an old warrior. His singing was now a triumph of technique and experience, conveying the illusion of his once-glorious sound. I stood in the wings, caught up in the music, sweating and scratching my mustache.

At last I lined up for my entrance at the tail end of the Triumphal March. Behind one trumpeter frolicked a dozen dancing girls from a local academy in a well-bred bacchanale, and then Radames was carried in on a litter by four slouching supernumeraries of various heights. Martinelli cursed vividly in English and Italian, promising eternal damnation if they dropped him. I was shocked. I never dreamt that opera people talked to each other *sotto voce* while they worked; in radio there was absolute silence.

I staggered on stage as a captive in chains, scratching that damned mustache and followed by my defeated Ethiopian army: eight barefoot white boys in minimum makeup, recruited from a local high school for 75 cents each. They clustered together timidly and, when they heard the giggles that greeted them, smiled ingratiatingly at the audience.

Aïda, after a moment, recognized me as her father, and I embraced her fervently.

As I stepped back to sing my noble aria, "Ma tu," I heard a sprinkle of laughter. The mustache, loosened by my scratching, had somehow stuck to the side of Aïda's neck. She couldn't see it. I gestured toward her neck as I sang, but I was rewarded with steely disdain for what she must have construed as my abominable acting. Finally, Martinelli brushed off the clinging hair, and I finished in an outburst of applause.

After the curtain calls, Martinelli walked back to the dressing room with me. "Not so bad, my boy, for the debut. You have the quality." In my mirror I noticed that my face, as a result of my scratching, had acquired a peculiar zebra-stripe aspect. But what the hell, Martinelli, the living legend, liked me.

Mr. Margolis said, "Tomorrow we'll talk about the mistakes."

My father came backstage, shaking his head, glancing dubiously at the singers and chorus. "I hope for you the best," and he sighed, "but this looks to me like a business for Eyetalyans."

The ride back to Brooklyn on the subway was joyous, bubbling with "I-told-you-sos." Momma and Poppa took turns putting their arms around me, and Aunt Lesser pulled out an apple she'd saved for the occasion. It hadn't occurred to me that we could celebrate my triumph by taking a taxi.

My reviews were good: "Young baritone of promise . . . Surprising sonority . . . His future will no doubt be more secure than his mustache."

I never made that blunder again. If I had to wear a mustache, I always asked the makeup man to pencil another one underneath it. And in over thirty years, the top mustache has never fallen off.

Our soprano never forgave me. Years later, she did make her debut at the Met, and again she sang Aida to my Amonasro. At the rehearsal she asked why the mustache had stuck to her and not to me. And the complaints flowed on: *"So this is the wonderful Met! Why, the dressing room is* filthy!*"*

Her debut was a failure. She had not grown, she had not developed, beyond that night in 1943. Whatever fears she had masked with her assumptions of superiority had undermined her career.

De Pace called me a week later. Martinelli wanted me for Tonio in *Pagliacci*. In Worcester, Massachusetts.

Martinelli coached me in his studio, meticulously and with great consideration for my insecurities. Tony Stivanello gave me the concept of playing Tonio as a hunchback, the deformity forcing me to feel the character's bitterness. Our Nedda was the first truly professional actress I had ever worked with: Ethel Barrymore Colt, daughter of the great Ethel, a lovely girl with a brightly colored voice and a performer in the proud tradition of her family. Merely keeping up with her and Martinelli forced me into a deeper understanding of stage action and reaction.

I knew that the climactic scene, in which Canio hunted for Nedda's lover, was the tenor's big moment, so I kept out of Martinelli's way and concentrated on my own cues. I hadn't expected the overwhelming rage he created in performance. He overturned furniture and threw chairs, one of which grazed my leg. I reacted with genuine fear. His was a demonstration of emotion that overwhelms intellectual analysis: the ferocious face, the twitching body, the torment flowing out of him as if he was flagellating himself. And with all this, singing "Pagliaccio, non son," a formidable aria that tenors at the peak of their form can fumble. Martinelli's B-flats and top notes were not in his throat that night; he sang *on* the notes and somehow created an impression of his old sonority and luscious tone. What a marvel he was!

I am deeply indebted to Martinelli: He also taught me how to eat.

In my early twenties I weighed about 175 pounds. My mother was still stuffing me with starches and fats, out of love and fears and memories of privation in Europe. ("Eat,

eat, my son. Meat is worth more than money.") Our meat was usually roasted to a putty grey, and we never had raw fresh vegetables in the house—my father considered them food for animals.

As I rushed around to radio studios, singing lessons and odd jobs, I grabbed anything at hand: egg creams, pastrami sandwiches, potato chips, peanut butter, hot dogs, pretzels, Hershey bars, Goobers, Cokes and celery tonics, chopped liver, *derma*, pickles—oh, I loved pickles with anything! All washed down with coffee.

When I arrived at Martinelli's apartment at ten o'clock, he would be finishing breakfast: coffee and a piece of fruit that he chose, after much deliberation over the skin and texture, from a large cut-glass bowl holding bananas, apples, pears, grapes. He ate again, he told me, only when he was hungry—he had no fixed mealtime hours—and then it was usually a raw salad.

I started to have fruit for breakfast: in summer, with yogurt; in winter with hot cereal. In the middle of the day, I'd have a half cantaloupe with cottage cheese or a large vegetable salad. If I was at home, I'd splurge on a banana, lathered with peanut butter that was ground to order in a shop on Sixth Avenue. Or topped with wheat germ. And about five o'clock, on the day of a performance, I'd stoke up on a small steak and salad. After a while, I dropped coffee—it kept me awake at night. Most of my diet now is vegetable: If it can keep those immense elephants thrashing around, it's good enough for me.

I've weighed 145 pounds for the last twenty-five years. Bless you, Giovanni Martinelli.

Another de Pace call: Escamillo in *Carmen* in Hartford, Connecticut. I accepted with a blasé "Why not?"

And then he added, "Carmen will be Gladys Swarthout." Well, Grace Moore had assured me I would be welcomed at the Met. I now looked forward to charming Miss Swarthout. It seemed only inevitable at twenty-five.

Another visit to Stivanello's emporium of hope and memories revealed that the popularity of *Carmen* left little choice in toreador costumes. I rummaged around the loft to come up with knee pants, silver-embroidered jacket and vest, black hose, hat, and cape. They had been made for a performer approximately the size of a bull; all the adjustments for me were marked, to be delivered the night of the show.

I shared the dressing room with the Don José, Armand Tokatyan, an esteemed tenor in the twilight of his career; he had the vital, classic Spanish features, although he happened to be Armenian. And a relentless womanizer. His wife had discovered him with their housemaid on her kitchen's linoleum floor. When he saw my costume, he broke up. The knee pants wrinkled down to my ankle, the stockings were a network of holes, the embroidered jacket seemed to sparkle with rhinestones and sloped down off my shoulders. The hat lay over my eyes and ears like a dead cat. And where were the shoes?

At that moment, a visitor stopped in to say hello to Tokatyan, a young lady with the smile of a madonna and a kit of safety pins, needles, and thread in her pocketbook. The pants were pinned up, my skin under the stocking holes was painted black—"It'll look like black lace," she said. Nothing could be done about the grotesque zoot-suit jacket, and I would have to wear my own crepe-sole brown loafers.

Tokatyan assured me it would all blend together under the dim "mood" lighting onstage, and urged me to go meet Miss Swarthout. I stared at the Katzenjammer Kid in my mirror and decided I couldn't face her.

"It's better she sees you now," the tenor said. "If you come onstage cold, she might choke."

I rapped lightly on her door and heard a jovial "Come in." She was a vision of whipped cream, sparkling in a gown out of a Technicolor spectacular, layer on layer of multicolored lace.

"The chorus dressing room is down to the left," she said politely.

I introduced myself as her Escamillo for the evening. She only shook her head, her mouth half open, in shock.

"Escamillo? *You?* Good heavens, those stockings are positively *diseased!*" she exploded in a hysterical tremolo, then stopped suddenly. "I can't sing against those rhinestones—the glitter will blind me!"

I promised to keep my distance, and avoid the bright lights.

"Oh God, help us all!" She was overcome again by that tremolo, and waved me out of her sight.

Totally demoralized, I shuffled back to my dressing room, and opened the door to find Don José heavily engaged with the madonna of the safety pins on the floor—on my toreador cape. I shut the door instantly and sat on the steps outside, wondering where I had gone wrong.

The performances that evening meshed like a Swiss watch. Tokatyan was fifteen years younger, on key and on cue; I shook the dust off the balcony rail with my "Toreador Song," and Miss Swarthout displayed the acting skill that had won international acclaim: She embraced me in the pinned-up pants and cat hat as if I were her true heart's desire.

Faust was my fourth pickup opera, a complex work, with many scenes, crowds, magic and props. The promoter in Trenton, New Jersey, assumed we all knew our roles, so we did not have even a walk-through with the orchestra. There was no director, either; stalwart Tony Stivanello was out of town.

I wandered around the stage, trying not to step in front of any principal singer and looking up for the filament in the overhead lights. (A tip from my friend Charlie Siegal, the electrician: If you could see the filament in the bulb, you were standing in the brightest area. And since it was every man for himself, I wanted at least to be seen. I almost went blind.)

I have forgotten the name of our Marguerite. The Faust was Mario Bereni, a young tenor with a brilliant voice, who had married David O. Selznick's niece. He was the male counterpart of my unhappy Aïda, but the chip on his shoulder was solid gold.

It was my introduction to the singer who travels with

his own emergency ward. His wife was his nurse, and from under his dressing room door seeped odors of menthol or iodoform—or was it Chinese incense? His nurse stood in the wings with two colors of spray: one for the throat and one for the nose.

Hypochondria is one of those neuroses that serves as an insurance policy. If a singer has drunk too much champagne or had a disagreement with his wife, he can ask the management to announce, "Mr. Caruso is suffering from a severe cold today, but he has consented to sing nevertheless." No matter how he flats, he is applauded for his courage.

My guardian angel, Moe Gale, introduced me to Marks Levine, head of National Concerts and Artists Corporation, who arranged a series of concerts in small towns in the South. It was the beginning of the development of community concerts, for which committees in several towns banded together to hire the hall and spread the costs, reaching audiences from a wider area than any one town could manage. For my first tour, I had fifteen engagements at $200 each, out of which I paid transportation for my accompanist and myself.

It was barnstorming in wartime, long train rides, delays, layovers. I didn't worry whether the train would be on time—I was happy if it was on the track. My made-in-Buffalo suit took the tour in stride, but for me the Deep South was an eye-opener: new accents, new food, new music for my repertoire—French ballads, German lieder, Negro spirituals. It was also my introduction to the out-of-town artist phenomenon. Girls waved at me as I sang and left notes at the boxoffice. It took me some time to realize this was simply a way of relieving the small-town tedium, which in earlier days had been expressed by walking down to the railway station to wave at people in the trains.

The usual mishaps pursued me. My partner was Freddie Maranz, twenty-two, a first-rate pianist, an awkward accompanist and, despite years of study in Paris, painfully unsuited for this world. On the train to Alabama, he sniffled and groaned all night in the berth above me.

"What's the matter, Freddie?"

"Gee, Mister Merrill, I wish I had some pistachio ice cream."

"You don't have to call me mister. I'm Bob. Now please go to sleep."

"I can't. I always have ice cream before I go to sleep."

"Ah, for godssakes, there's a war on."

He was hooked on ice cream, for breakfast, lunch, dinner. This was not dessert—it was his entire meal. And if he didn't have a fix of vanilla at night, he had withdrawal symptoms, moaning and tossing all night. He also had a hernia and a truss.

I was slipping into my new Howard tuxedo jacket, awaiting the committee that would escort us to the Consolidated High School auditorium, when I heard his scream through the wall: "Mister Merrill! Help!"

Freddie was in his shorts, and holding a metal belt with a knob on the end. "There's a screw loose," he said.

I knew that. The only question was, where? "It fell out. I can't go on without my truss, Mister Merrill."

"Goddammit, stop calling me mister." I crawled under his bed, raking the rug for the screw. I heard a rap on the door, and in came the escort committee. Freddie hid in the bathroom. I dusted off my knees, and asked the group to please wait downstairs. The men stared at me dubiously, as they closed the door.

Ten frantic minutes later, I found the screw on his night table.

I tried to watch my diet, but when the local sponsors set up a buffet or a steak dinner, I couldn't ask for cottage cheese, and yogurt sounded very un-American.

Somewhere, deep in the heart of Texas, a gentleman in boots and a string tie insisted we accompany him to the local chili parlor ("*Best in the West*"). He slapped me on the back: "Why, boy, it's better'n a warm woman on a cold night!" Freddie stuck to ice cream. I swallowed one spoonful of the fiery lava and lost my voice overnight.

At the end of the tour, an elaborate dinner was laid out in a hotel dining room, enlivened by a five-piece dance band. My stomach was by now inflated, after weeks of receptions, so as I sat down to dinner, I loosened my trousers, just as I did at home. In those days, I wore suspenders. After dinner, I asked the young lady heading the sponsors' committee for a dance. When I stood up, my trousers fell below my hip.

How could I explain that I'd packed only one set of suspenders, and they were now holding up my tux trousers in my room? I murmured, "I lose so much weight after each concert . . ."

The young lady nodded graciously. "I sure wish you could tell me your secret." I was invited back next year.

Moe Gale now announced that I was ready for another try at the Metropolitan Opera auditions. I was not so sure. At times I dreamt I had that audience screaming "Bravo!"—and yet . . . what if my suspenders broke? What if I forgot the words? I had done it before and I was not too good to do it again. I recalled the wasted soprano in *Aïda*—if you don't grow, you atrophy. I had to try again.

Three national auditions on radio were the hurdles on the road to Olympus, each narrowing the contestants until only two were left. NBC's Studio 8-H was comfortable to me now: I was singing from there three times a week, and the audition announcer, Milton Cross, was a former tenor who had studied with Mr. Margolis.

Momma pulled my ears for good luck, and Poppa reassured me "More and more you look like an Eyetalyan."

I qualified easily enough. I sang "Figaro," and this time I knew I was Robert Merrill and not Titta Ruffo. It was precise and merry. The tender loveliness of "Nemico della patria" from *Andrea Chenier* brought me into the finals.

My choice was Iago's "Credo" from *Otello*. And from the opening bars, I was propelled by a powerful current of exhilaration. *I knew!* I knew I had it. After I finished, the first thought that popped into my head was: I'll throw away all the furniture in our apartment and move the family into a penthouse near the Met, so I can walk to work.

For the awards, Edward Johnson introduced me and Thomas Hayward, the winning tenor, on the broadcast from the stage of the opera house. My parents sat up front in the red plush seats, in clothes bought for the occasion. Momma was crying and applauding, and my father, recovering from a diabetes attack, was wagging his finger to tell me, "You see? I told you so!" Newlywed Gil was clapping Poppa on the back, and his bride was applauding for both of them. I had a thousand-dollar check from the sponsors and a contract to sing on Mt. Olympus.

Hayward and I sang our winning arias, and then we joined in "Del tempio al limitar," from *The Pearl Fishers*. Our voices coalesced like Siamese twins, and then I realized we were both muscling each other away from the microphone. We were already old campaigners.

A champagne reception followed in Sherry's, the opera-house restaurant. A swirl of congratulations, handshakes, raised wine glasses: Risë Stevens, Lawrence Tibbett, Lauritz Melchior.

Martinelli: "Roberto! So we work together again! eh?" I hugged him.

Gladys Swarthout: "I trust you burned Escamillo's costume?"

Wilfred Pelletier, who had conducted my disastrous first audition: "You have a great career ahead of you. Don't be a fool this time—work! I'll be watching you."

I turned to meet Richard Bonelli. "You don't know how much I owe you—" and then I had to stop.

"What? what?" he insisted.

Could I thank him for singing to me up in that balcony? For stimulating a cocky kid to think he could outsing the great Bonelli? I murmured something inconsequential, and shook his hand. (Some years ago, we met again, when he came backstage in Los Angeles after my performance of *Fiddler on the Roof*. He had been teaching, and his voice still boomed at 78.)

In June 1945, I signed my contract with the Met: $125 a week for as many performances per week as the management chose. And I could continue in radio and concert work. My roles for the season, as I discovered in a mimeographed sheet, would be bits: A herald in *Lohengrin*, Marullo in *Rigoletto*, and others I have since blocked out of my memory. I refused to study them. I was still featured singer every week on the *Voice of Firestone* show with an audience of about 10 million, and I just couldn't be interested in walk-ons. I was, after all, twenty-six years old.

Every week I asked an assistant conductor for the date of my debut, and he had no clues at all. Frank St. Ledger, the casting director, called me into his office and inquired if I was prepared to go on as A Herald. The *Voice of Firestone* overwhelmed any voice of reason within me. "I don't really care for that part," I said bluntly.

St. Ledger merely raised one eyebrow. "Indeed? And what does interest you?"

I recalled my mother's admonition for my debut with Martinelli: "He's got two legs the same like you." I answered St. Ledger: "Something challenging, like *Barber*."

I heard no more from St. Ledger. The season opened in November with *Lohengrin*, and my herald's role was easily filled. The war in Europe and the East had just ended, and with it austerity and mourning clothes. Tons of jewels and ermine and white ties came out of their vaults to glitter and be seen at the Met; the opulence was baroque, rivaling the legendary glamour nights of the twenties. And the cast of *La Gioconda* a few weeks later equaled any ensemble in opera's Golden Age: Risë Stevens, Zinka Milanov, Ezio Pinza, Richard Tucker, Leonard Warren.

And Robert Merrill was singing the *Voice of Firestone* theme, written by Mrs. Harvey Firestone:

". . . and now each flower is sweeter, dear,
I know it's just because at last you're here.
We sit alone in all the world apart
*And love is blooming full within my heart."**

*Copyright 1942, G. Schirmer, Inc. Used by permission.

Like hell it was! My heart was full of blooming paranoia: I had been blackballed by Met management for my arrogance and the plot was obviously to give me nothing until I quit in disgust.

It was a very cold December. I was looking over some thick-soled boots in the shoe store window at the Met's 39th Street corner when Edward Johnson walked by. He asked me to come up to his office. Well, I was not going to resign. Never.

> (Inside the office: Mr. Johnson, behind the desk, indicates a chair. I stand stubbornly.)
>
> MR. JOHNSON (Ever the gentleman): *I've been doing a lot of thinking about you.*
>
> ME (Stiff-lipped, unrelenting): *Really?*
>
> MR. JOHNSON: *Singing an aria on radio is far different from creating a character onstage, and developing it for several acts.*
>
> ME: *I know.*
>
> MR. JOHNSON: *We're doing* Traviata, *and I would like you to sing Germont.*
>
> (I sit down slowly. Germont is a major role, a man of the world in his fifties.)
>
> ME: *I'll do it! I know I can do it.*
>
> MR. JOHNSON: *We've never had anyone as young as you in that part.*
>
> ME (Quickly): *You have great makeup men. I've studied it. I'm ready for it.*
>
> MR. JOHNSON: *Good.* Traviata *is set for December 15th—a week from today.*
>
> ME: *Oh, my God!*

Here was one of those grand-operatic coincidences: Richard Bonelli had retired earlier that year, and his last performance was Germont in *Traviata;* I was to begin my career at the Met as Germont, only eight years after I saw Bonelli in my first opera.

We had company for supper that night—little Aunt Esther and Uncle Sam, who had thought I would make a good carpenter. I would wait for the appropriate moment before I revealed the dazzling news.

My mother was in the kitchen, tending a pot roast. Aunt Esther told me I looked too thin now. "You need a big stomach to make a big noise." Uncle Sam weighed in with: "Look at Sinatra—millions of fans, millions of dollars, girls fainting for him." My father, sunk down in his chair, murmured, "Better they shouldn't faint at the opera—better they should holler brave-o."

My mother brought out the pot roast, and I said, "Hello, Momma." She glanced at my eyes and asked, "Well, my genius, you have something to tell?"

The great news flowed out of me in one burst, to applause and heavy chords from Uncle Sam on the piano. Momma clasped both my wrists tightly. "No more fooling. *Now* you work!"

My father nodded encouragingly, "That's a good boy," and slumped over, falling out of his chair to the floor. Spittle oozed out of his mouth as he lay unconscious. The rest was uproar: screams, advice, pleas to God. I forced brandy into his mouth. Uncle Sam opened Poppa's shirt and diagnosed a heart attack or a stroke. Momma called our doctor. Aunt Esther collapsed in sympathy. I forced brandy down her throat. Our doctor, obviously irritated by being disturbed at this hour, diagnosed a heart attack. He gave Poppa an injection, but he remained unconscious. Uncle Sam drew me aside to whisper, "This doctor is jerk. I know a specialist, best in the world, thirty bucks a visit." I was by now paralyzed with grief; all I could do was nod. When the specialist came—a gentleman with a Trotsky goatee—my father was still unconscious. More stethoscope, careful listening, pursed lips. He could survive this heart attack in the hospital, said the specialist, if . . .

The ambulance orderlies came in time for my father's convulsion. They had to force the gentle little man into a straitjacket to carry him into the ambulance. I rode with him, wiping the glaze of sweat off his face. In the hospital, the spasms subsided. He suddenly opened his eyes and recognized me. "Don't worry . . . the opera . . . I'll be there."

After a night and day of anguish, I learned that the eminent specialist, our own doctor, even Uncle Sam had all been wrong. It was diabetic shock. Poppa would be there, all right.

I was to play opposite two of the ranking stars of the Met: Licia Albanese as Violetta and Jan Peerce as my son Alfredo. Our director would be Désiré Défrère.

Défrère was a cosmopolitan European, close to the age of Germont; he had sung the role many times, and knew every nuance of my part far better than I did. Germont for me was a dangerous stretch. He was a sophisticated man of the nineteenth-century world, bound by a complex code of class traditions in which women were either courtesans or virgins on a pedestal. I was a provincial twenty-six-year-old, still living with my family in Brooklyn, who had to learn Germont's language by rote. To complicate matters, it is a static role: I stand and listen to Violetta and my son most of the time. Germont does not appear until the second act; he enters without any musical warm-up into a dramatic duet with Violetta that lasts twenty minutes, and it is just a prelude to the emotional aria "Di provenza." This half hour of continual singing makes or breaks the baritone. For him, the remainder of the opera is all downhill.

Défrère was a taskmaster with a cutting edge. When I made my entrance, hand in pocket, to give a semblance of elegant relaxation, he growled, "Have you ever *seen* a gentleman?"

When I moved my arms to relieve my stiffness in "Di provenza," he muttered, "Don't make an omelette."

At the dress rehearsal, in front of Johnson and St. Ledger, I missed a cue in the duet with Violetta. I lost control and the scene began to disintegrate. Défrère leaped on the stage to my rescue: "Hold it! I want to change this . . ." He created some minor adjustments in our position, consuming several minutes to give me time to put

myself together. I breathed deeply and then, without looking at me, he signaled the conductor to resume. It was a
magnificent gesture of compassion. And Licia Albanese,
the most gracious prima donna, played to me as if I were
her equal and assured me, "You have nothing to worry
about. If you forget anything, I will cue you."

On the day of the performance, Jan Peerce became ill
and bowed out. I had welcomed the security of a veteran,
fifteen years older than I, playing my son. When Richard
Tucker volunteered to sub, my anxieties were scarcely
soothed; he had made his own debut some months
before—and he was only five years older.

He was Reuben Ticker when we were growing up in
Brooklyn. He played punchball in the streets, attended
New Utrecht High School, where he played tackle, and
both of us even had dreams of starring in sandlot ball. But
we had never met until we were introduced backstage at the
opera house. And now we had time for only one walk-
through for the performance in which I had invested so
much of my life.

My father was there in his first tuxedo; for insurance he
had insulin in his veins and, in his breast pocket hanky,
some sugar cubes. Momma was in her long black gown, her
chin up, surveying the audience with a trace of *hauteur* and
living up to a Met publicity puff that labeled her "a retired
concert soprano." Our entire family was out front, as well
as the Margolises, the Gales, and the Spitalnys.

My Catskill strategist, Charlie Rapp, cheered me with a
telegram: SO NOW YOU'RE DOWN TO ONLY ONE JOB
A NIGHT!

Edward Johnson, who had been a Met tenor and knew
the agonies of opening night, came into my room to buck
me up. "John Charles Thomas used to say, 'You're not
going to the electric chair—you're just going to sing.'"

Just before the overture, Tucker found me in the wings
and whacked me on the back. "Whattahell, Bob—let's do it
for the block!"

And I was home safe. To bravos and curtain calls . . .
Licia squeezing my hand—"You see? They love you!" . . .

and Tucker whispering, "They can't all be from Brooklyn—maybe they mean it." The audience was standing and cheering, and as the joy washed over me, I felt like the Count of Monte Cristo after he escaped from the dungeon and swam up to the surface of the sea—the world was mine!

Except for the small area called acting, of which— some critics noted—I did not have complete control. However, I retained my own show on NBC radio, and signed on for five years as featured singer and master of ceremonies of *Music America Loves Best,* an RCA-Victor sponsored show that presented guests such as Heifetz and Marian Anderson. Mine became the best of two worlds.

5

"I'd Rather Make a Movie with a Dead Genius"

Dinner at Danny Kaye's house, 1949: With a minimum of urging, I sang for the Pooh-Bah of MGM, Louis B. Mayer. He pursed his lips, vaguely bemused, while Danny nudged him to sign me for a movie. Mayer was not easily moved. Mario Lanza had recently completed *That Midnight Kiss,* and Mayer was awaiting the critical judgment of the boxoffice. "To tell you the truth," Mayer said, "I'd rather make a movie with a dead genius."

Despite Mayer's funereal disinterest, I was intrigued by the idea of branching out into film. Caruso had made two silent flops, but Grace Moore had been a great success in *One Night of Love*, and so had Lily Pons in *Paris in the Spring* and Lawrence Tibbett in *The Rogue Song;* even Kirsten Flagstad had had her fling in *Big Broadcast of 1938.*

Paramount came through with a quickie screen test: Makeup, sit down on a sofa, answer questions from off-camera—"You remember the Dodgers? . . . Talk about those early days in Brooklyn. . . . What impressed you most about Hollywood?" It ended with the inevitable "Figaro," and "We'll call you soon." I felt let down by the whole charade and flew back to New York to prepare for Rudolf Bing's first season at the Met.

But the executives at Paramount liked the test. George Seaton, one of their most successful director-producers, had a "property" for me, and would I take another test on it? Moe Gale and I agreed I would.

The project was *Anything Can Happen,* an amusing best-seller by George and Helen Papashvily recounting the mishaps of a Georgian (Russian) couple in adjusting to the strange customs of American life. I spent an afternoon with mustachioed, bubbling George at the Russian Tea Room, soaking up his accent. Seaton gave me a two-page scene to learn for this test: explaining to a judge why I, the immigrant, should not have been arrested for picking lovely flowers in Central Park.

Paramount liked that one, too, and offered me $65,000 for ten weeks of work in the summer, between opera seasons. I signed the one-picture contract. Then came one of those tricky switches for which Hollywood is noted. José Ferrer was hired to appear in *Anything Can Happen* and Robert Merrill discovered, from a paragraph in the *New York Times,* that he would make his film debut in April 1951, in *Aaron Slick from Punkin Crick.*

The problem here was not *Aaron Slick,* a title which made me go out and buy a spittoon, but the month of April. That was when the Met's spring tour started, and Bing had already advertised me for eight appearances. He had a valid contract with me and I had one, just as valid, with Paramount; the bleak fact was, I had signed with the Met first.

Somehow I thought that if he allowed me to make the movie, I would come back with an enhanced reputation which would in turn augment my boxoffice appeal for his opera. There was a great back-and-forthing of letters and ultimatums, and I was fired by Bing. Well, I would make a few movie hits and then, at a mutually appropriate moment, he could take me back.

I felt I was in the best possible hands in Hollywood. William Perlberg and George Seaton, the producers, had created a long list of hits; the writer and director was Claude Binyon, another experienced craftsman, who assured me, "It's going to be a great movie with a great cast." The movie was based on a play which was also great, I was told, because it had been performed 40,000 times, the all-time, all-American record. What I was not informed of, till much later, was the reason *Aaron Slick* had chalked up this awesome total: It had been played by every summer camp, backyard, high school and church social group in the country since it was written, in 1919.

It was, in short, as hayseed as its title. Dinah Shore, my co-star, would be the farm girl (Josie Berry) whose boy friend, Aaron Slick, is a sod-kicking, shy yokel, played by Alan Young, a "hot" young comic. In the end he outwits me, Bill Merredew, a con man on the lam from Chicago who wants to steal Josie's farm because he thinks there's oil under it. My blonde sidekick, Gladys, would be Adele Jurgens. A dozen songs had been written by a team of pop hit writers, and it all might have been fun if it had been done with some wit or satire, in the style of *The Music Man.* But no, the president of Paramount loved the play, and it was not to be tampered with. I was pleased, however, by the dressing room I shared with Alan—it had been used by my idol, Bing Crosby, and I finally met him in a Paramount office.

After a few days on the set, I realized that Dinah had eleven songs and I had one. I tried to beef up my role with that all-time hit "Figaro," but Perlberg patiently explained they already had a great team of songwriters and, besides, "Everybody knows you can sing, Bob. We're playing you *against* type—that's the entire psychology of it." In the quarter of a century that I've been thinking over that line, I've often wondered why our producer was never made Secretary of State.

My acting was a problem for the movies. On film, a threatening gesture was a raised eyebrow, with a slight tilt of the head; in opera, which has to project about half a mile, I stepped forward and drew my sword. In ten weeks, I could not become accustomed to letting the camera merely read my mind.

The big comedy scene was my being chased up a tree by a bull. It required four days and paid me an overtime fee of $13,000. A city boy to the end, I just could not climb that tree, so the director hired a double to shinny up, and my distinctive legs were seen hanging in closeup. The only scene that excited me was a song-and-dance sequence choreographed by Charlie O'Curran and titled "The Spider and the Fly." I was the spider, enticing Dinah into my web. Charlie worked us gamely into time steps and slap-shuffle-slap for about a week, although Dinah and I seemed to have three more feet than Astaire and Ginger Rogers. Charlie thought the rushes were "cute—it works." The producers cut it all out, of course.

Charlie was a close friend of Betty Hutton, who was shooting *The Greatest Show on Earth* at the same time, and he insisted I had to meet her.

(SCENE: Betty Hutton's dressing room)

CHARLIE: (At the door) *She's just the way she is on film—full of sock and a little crazy. Wild! Love that girl!*

(Inside the suite: it's all in zebra strips. Betty, stretched out on a sofa, is dressed in coordinating zebra-stripe leotard. A very impressive woman.)

CHARLIE: *Betty, this is Bob.*

BETTY: *Hey, is it true what they say about opera singers in the hay?*

(How do I know what they're saying about opera singers in Hollywood?)

ME: *Of course! It's all in the tessitura!*

BETTY: (Leaping up) *Oh, wow! Will you show me where that is?*

Charlie cooled off on me. I didn't know that he planned to marry her.

I adored Dinah: We had so much in common. After five movies, including *Up in Arms,* in which she had been overshadowed by Danny Kaye, she was still shy and lived with a scarcely hidden complex of insecurities almost as big as mine. She had been stricken with polio as a baby, and her mother had pushed her into sports, just as forcefully as mine had pushed me into singing. Dinah became a hard-hitting tennis player, but picked up the singing on her own, against the wishes of her parents.

She admitted "I never learned how to read music easily, it still scares me. I get my feelings across by breathing the lyrics as if my lips were an inch from a man's ear." And she felt she looked horrible in Technicolor—"I'm just not really photogenic."

Her childhood affliction made her ambitious. "I had to run farther and leap higher than anybody." She came to New York from Nashville in 1938, and got her first break on WNEW at about the same time I was crooning on WFOX; she had her own network show when she went into films. Dinah was now far from the public image of the girl next door in the plaid blouse; she was a sophisticated, intelligent woman, a proficient painter in oils—and as bored with making films as I was. Movies were a long series of waits, then ". . . walk over here, turn, hit this mark, and lift your chin about half an inch . . .Cut! and try it again." So we reminisced about the forties in New York—she had sung with Leo Reisman's band at the Strand Theater, right across the street from Uncle Max's Paradise Bootery.

I spent as much time as I could with her and George Montgomery in their Encino home. She loved to cook, and one of her great dishes was her mother's chili con carne. Where her Tennessee mother got it is beyond me; it was loaded with garlic, pepper pods, and jalapenos, a Mexican chili pepper, and we never ate it before a duet. Dinah laid out an Aaron Slick dinner in the backyard, on long tables, where the required dress was overalls, boots or barefoot, straw hats and hay behind the ears. (This was in the fifties, remember, before all stars went barefoot in jeans.) The dinner menu consisted of Dr. Krohn's mother's chicken (he was Dinah's obstetrician), mashed potatoes, soda biscuits, watermelon. I wish we could have communicated some of that night's joy to the movie.

The James Masons would arrive for Dinah's delightful dinners about two hours late, with their infant in their arms. Not because they couldn't find a baby-sitter, but to fulfill Mason's philosophy of child education. "We take the child with us everywhere," he'd explain. "It's time the little one learned the realities of life." The baby sat at the dinner table, on people's laps, rolled on the floor and fell asleep in a corner at about 2 A.M.

The Paramount press agents exploited my estrangement from the opera to promote their picture. They sent out a photo of me and Crosby, arm in arm, based on the dubious notion that whatever the Met's Bing might think, Paramount's Bing liked Merrill. Bachelor operatic baritones were something of a novelty here, so the publicity men turned me into the town's escort service. The faces of the girls blended into a whirl of deep tans, sunglasses, and glistening blonde hair. I danced with Sheila Graham, Cobina Wright, Jr., Lana Turner. I ate at Chasen's with a brunette whose name I never caught—I just called her Honey. And the next morning, Luella Parsons identified her as "Clark Gable's best girl."

Men who were in a position to give jobs to women held them in the same esteem as the runny-nose kids under the Coney Island boardwalk. At lunch in one of the studio dining rooms, I noticed a striking blonde girl in tight slacks and loose silk blouse wiggle by. A West Coast agent said, "You want that? I'm trying to help a friend get her contract renewed. She's the studio service station—calls herself Marilyn Monroe."

The same agent installed me in a six-room, $500-a-month apartment at the Chateau Marmont, at my expense.

"Why do I need all this?" I asked.

"You have to look successful out here, otherwise you're a bum. You have to entertain. Get a couple cases of liquor;

here's the home number of my assistant, he'll send a broad over anytime, night or day."

On a few occasions I did not have a full day at the studio, I came home to find rumpled beds. My open-hearted ten-percenter was entertaining his friends at my expense.

Somehow, in the midst of all this, I had several congenial chats with Gregor Piatigorsky, the giant of a cellist who resembled a gaunt Chaliapin. He commiserated on the fickleness of the music business, and urged me not to lose sleep. "When I was great in a concert, they invited me back in five years. If I was lousy, they called me back in seven. So what are you worried about?"

Without my singing teacher, I was worried. I practiced regularly, but having no opera to work toward, I felt cut off from music. I began to have a few extra drinks every night. One morning, about six-thirty, bleary and depressed, I sat in the Paramount makeup room. An older woman took the chair next to mine and nodded warmly. I couldn't think of one clue to who she was. When her makeup was completed, a fascinatingly soignée actress arose and floated out. I had dined with her the week before—Marlene Dietrich.

Yvonne de Carlo, as petite as Lily Pons and vibrating sensuality, came on our set to wish me well. She had studied seriously for opera, and I thought we might have something to talk about. We made a date for dinner at seven. I drove to pick her up at her home in the hills above Hollywood; the roads were narrow and twisting and in the rain I couldn't see the numbers of the houses set back among the trees. I pulled around to turn into her driveway, to discover this was not her house and my left front wheel was over the edge of the cliff. I took a few deep breaths and exploded into a wild laugh: My first picture was not completed and I was already over the hill.

I drove back along the cliff-hanging road, rang the bell, and this time I was in the correct house. Miss De Carlo's hair was in a wrapper; She handed a drink to me and apologized. "I'm awfully sorry we can't have dinner—I have a five-thirty call tomorrow on location."

A night at Cobina Wright's: Judy Garland, carefree and bursting with energy, belted out several duets with me. She had that yearning, passionate quality I've heard in very few other singers. I swallowed too many drinks and refused to drive home; I had been psyched out by those cursed mountains. Cobina called a cab. Judy and I and two others piled in, and as we lurched off down the winding road, she sank to the floor and clamped her hands over her eyes. She had a painful fear of heights and could not talk until she reached her home.

I attracted one of the town's leading homosexuals, a shock which Danny Kaye found mysteriously hilarious. "Oh, migod! what a loveable, naive boy you are!" It was at Danny's party in the Beverly Hills Hotel. Clifton Webb chatted with me as I walked into the men's room and out again. He invited me to dinner at his house, and as we shook hands, I realized he was holding on too long, and perspiring heavily. I excused myself with a five-thirty call on location.

That incident wrapped up—in one big ball of celluloid—all the feelings of embarrassment and exasperation I had felt since the first day of shooting. I left Hollywood next morning, two days ahead of my schedule, to sing with the San Francisco Symphony.

After *Aaron Slick* was released, in April 1952, it had the peculiar distinction of filling boxoffices from coast to coast with patrons demanding refunds. The brains at Paramount discovered, to their astonishment, that *Variety*'s classic sociological commentary still applied: "STIX NIX HIX PIX." The big cities gave it the same KIX.

Dinah went on to new heights in television, my dreams of movie musicals were effectively squelched, and Alan Young's promising career fell apart. He played Mr. Ed in a talking horse series for television, and later left show business to become a lay preacher.

The film continues to bedevil me on late, late television. Half the Met chorus and many of the soloists blame me for keeping them up late, but they swear they enjoy it. People come backstage or write notes from all over the

country, telling me how much fun they find in *Aaron Slick*.
And when I toured ten cities in *Fiddler on the Roof*, every
one of the local stations instantly scheduled the movie.

Dinah Shore has been afflicted with similar dubious
praise. She merely shrugs and says, "Anybody who stays up
that late to see that picture deserves it."

Las Vegas in the early fifties was still a small desert
town, where the dust was relieved by the oases in a few
good hotels. In the late afternoon, performers who had been
up all night gambling away their salaries would convene
around the bars and pools—Lindy's with wet feet—and
reminisce about the gray, cold days in New York. The
showgirls came out about this time, to relax with nude
swims, adding to the *gemutlich* ambiance.

Louis Armstrong and I teamed up in an act at The
Sands: opera vs. jazz. In white tie and tails, he'd growl
"Vesti la giubba" and I socked out "Honeysuckle Rose."
We were, as I learned in Hollywood, playing against type;
but this time the chemistry was right and we created a
laughing gas that kept the audiences high for four weeks.

You could not help smiling back at Louie. He had been
born on the Fourth of July, and for the rest of his life sent
up verbal and musical firecrackers. He dubbed me his
"wailer," his "living aspirin." His inventiveness overwhelmed me. He came back from a tour of the continent
and phoned to tell me, in that voice like a buzzsaw calling
to its mate, that he'd sat in "with those opera cats at the
cafés in Milano. You know, Puccini was there, and Verdi. I
told them I worked with you and, man, if they'd just get
their heads together on a new piece, we could really lay it
on audiences all over the world."

Between shows, he sat in his dressing room, writing in
longhand a book to demonstrate the evils of alcohol as
opposed to the benign effects of reefers. He was almost
always happy on marijuana, but "Booze—oh daddy, that
makes a man mean and uglies up the world." Beer was his
only alcohol; his contract specified a case of cool bottles in

his dressing room every day. "It makes you sweat, cleans out the pores, and mollifies the throat lining."

His mother had convinced him that the road to happiness and health lay through his stomach; if he kept it swept out nice and clean, he would never be sick. Louie's magic broom was Swiss Kriss, an herbal compound, of which he swallowed a heaping tablespoon in a glass of water every day of his adult life. "I don't want to take everything with me—you gotta leave some things behind." And he did live to seventy-one, despite more than a half century of one-night stands and food grabbed on the run.

He persuaded me to try his Swiss sweeper to "clear all them frogs out of your throat." I missed the midnight show and the next early show. "You gotta get customed to it," he said, "and you'll still be wailin' at the Pearly Gates."

In those days, blacks were not permitted to live in the hotels where they worked. The Sands offered to make an exception for Armstrong, but he refused. He and his wife Lucille stayed in a rented house on the edge of town, and this is where he introduced me to soul food—beans and rice and collard greens, very healthful natural foods. I've never been able to find those Louisiana red beans and rice done with the savor Lucille blended into them.

Louie suffered from a kidney ailment and a callus on his lips caused by lifelong pressure of the horn mouthpiece, yet he was—even in private—forever cheerful; I never heard him say one derogatory word about anyone. He exploded only once—at some musicians in the band who were goofing off. Louie simply walked away from trouble.

We and our wives went to hear his friend Billie Holliday at a Vegas hotel a few years before she died. The maitre d' stopped him: "I'm sorry, no black people."

He replied quietly, "Well, tell Billie that Louie Armstrong sends his best regards," and walked away. I telephoned a friend who knew the owner, but Louie said, "Just drop it, Pops." He did contribute money to black rights organizations and during the height of the violence in the sixties, he informed the State Department he would not perform on any goodwill jazz tours abroad "while they're beating up on my people over here."

He called progressive jazz "jujitsu music," yet even the avant-garde critics had to admit he brought jazz out of the back streets with his trumpet style and solo improvisations. His last engagement was, appropriately, the Waldorf-Astoria.

"I never tried to prove anything," he said in our Vegas dressing room. "I just tried to give a good show, you know? Music's my entire life—if I can't play, my life's not worth a bottle of beer, and if I don't have an audience, I'm nowhere."

"Daaahling! What in blazing hell are you doing *here?"* Tallulah wrapped her arms around me, smothering my reply with a wet kiss and squeezing me against the bar.

"I'm following your act."

"You poor misguided bastard! The only act that can follow Tallu is King Kong with an erection!"

I had come back to The Sands for a solo appearance, and for the next hour I remained just that—there was never a duet with her. She filibustered about our encounter on her radio show—the sun and dry air were sickening—" . . . and I've had the most blessed event in my young life—silicone injections—and my bazooms are absolutely *virginal*—oh, lawdy! I'm born again!"

She shifted her shoulders to separate her cleavage, and out came a beautifully formed bosom, fuller than a Bali maiden's but obviously virginal. "They fill it with this glop, but you can't tell the difference. Have a bite."

"Delicious," I said.

I first saw Tallulah Bankhead in 1939, from a second balcony seat, in her American triumph, *The Little Foxes.* Another hit, *The Skin of Our Teeth;* then a disaster, and the stage abandoned her. She stormed into network radio, drawing the biggest audiences in the country, and here she was at The Sands, caricaturing the grotesque gossip-column image of herself—booze, boys, girls, men, all in a swirl of ferocious energy. A force of nature, like Mount

Vesuvius, that could not be denied. Only the blue eyes and voluptuous mouth remained of the honey-hair beauty of *The Little Foxes.* She was utterly honest with herself, and the separation from the legitimate stage must have hurt— but, "Whattahell, honey, I've got it where it counts."

When I came onto her radio show, I had never spoken lines—the announcer merely introduced me and I sang. Tallulah would announce, "For the next hour and thirty minutes, this program will present, in person, such bright stars as—" and the guest would state his name. It was radio's most important variety show, with at least six top-name performers, and I was afraid I'd tense up, relapse into my old stutter. She saw me blinking nervously and tossed away the script. "I heard this beautiful boy sing today. He has a great voice and I love him!"

Relaxed, I stepped forward and spoke my line perfectly: "Robert Merrill."

For the next show I was given a few lines and invited to the script conference. She had the best team, headed by Goodman Ace, but she lashed them like sled dogs. Her long legs in floppy slacks propped on a desk, puffing a cigarette—she screamed and groaned and exploded in raucous sarcasm. "If I can't get any writers with balls, I'll have to write it myself!"

She took a phone call from Ethel Barrymore: "Ethel, I want you for a simply lovely sketch. About the old days in the theatah. And here's the blackout line. I say, 'I just loved your brother's performances,' and your line is, 'What did you see John in?' and I say, *'Bed!'* . . . But, *daahling!* he really *was* the best I ever had. . . . Well, let's have lunch. . . ."

Since she dreaded to be alone, she invited me often to parties in her house off Sutton Place. I suppose I was the straight man, relief for all the comedy of the exotic flora that surrounded her. I'd sing a few numbers and go home by midnight; Tallulah was on till five or six. I never saw her in daylight.

Even a volcano subsides eventually, and in 1968 her sister Eugenie asked me to sing, for Tallulah's funeral services, the theme of her radio show, "May the Good Lord Bless and Keep You." I was startled by the choice of that pallid tune, but she assured me it was what Tallulah would want to be remembered by.

(SCENE: The lounge at The Sands Hotel. Jack Entratter, who books the acts, takes me by the elbow.)

JACK: *I want you to meet a fascinating person.*

(We walk to a table in the corner; it's Susan Hayward and the fascinating person. At the next table, two heavies who look like bodyguards.)

JACK: *Bob Merrill, this is Howard Hughes and Susan Hayward.*

(Hughes is wearing his formal clothes: sneakers, jeans, and open white shirt.)

ME: (Extending my hand) *It's a pleasure to meet you.*

(Hughes continues eating; he doesn't meet my hand or look up.)

SUSAN: *I really loved your show. We don't hear a big voice like yours very often.*

HUGHES: (Mumbling) *The mike was too loud.*

SUSAN: *That Pagliacci aria, it almost made me cry.*

HUGHES: *Opera leaves me cold.*

(The air is very cold; I get the feeling Hughes resents me.)

SUSAN: *We Brooklyn people stick together.*

HUGHES: (To her) *You want anything for dessert?*

ME: *Well, I have to get set for the next show.*

(I extend my hand; he refuses it again. Baffled, I walk away with Jack.)

ME: *Why wouldn't he shake my hand?*

JACK: (Shrugging) *He's got some psycho thing about catching germs.*

(SCENE: My room at the hotel.
TIME: 3 A.M. that morning. The phone rings.)

VOICE: *Merrill?*

ME: (Half asleep) *Who is this?*

VOICE: *This is Johnny. Mr. Hughes asked me to call. He wants to know if you're interested in making movies.*

ME: *Look, I don't know who you are—*

VOICE: *Mr. Hughes has a large interest in RKO, and he feels you could be a popular star. He's willing to sign you to a personal contract, let's say a hundred thousand, with yearly options.*

ME: (Going along with it) *Does he have a property in mind?*

VOICE: *He'll build you up. Hell, he made a star out of Jane Russell just by engineering a bra for her. You'll have to concentrate on movies. No opera.*

ME: *That's out of the question.*

VOICE: *I think I can get you one-fifty.*

ME: *I'll have my agent call you.*

VOICE: *I'm in and out. I'll call you.*

(TIME: Noon. I call Moe Gale in New York repeating details of our meeting and the call.)

MOE: *Craziest thing I ever heard. I'll call you back.*

(An hour later.) *He can keep you dangling on options for years, while RKO pays for you. He could kill your opera career.*

ME: *Why would he do that?*

MOE: *He's a strange guy. I hear he can't stand to have his girl say something sweet to another guy.*

ME: *But I see his scouts bringing other girls up to his floor.*

MOE: *Sure, he's had a lot of girls around—Gardner, Turner, Jane Russell. Even if he only sees 'em once a week, he wants to feel he possesses 'em. They're all* his.

ME: (Astonished) *He's* jealous?

(TIME: 3 A.M. again. The phone rings.)

VOICE: *Mr. Hughes' offer is still good. What do you say?*

ME: *I'm not jealous.* (I hang up.)

6

Destiny Rides Again

Most romantic operas are elaborations of the boy-meets-girl theme, but the boy is always a tenor. The baritone hardly ever gets the girl because composers believe that love duets are more thrilling in the soprano-tenor range.

When I was thirty, I determined to challenge the eternal verities of art—I would get the soprano. She was the petite, blue-eyed Roberta Peters, who had made a sensational debut in *Don Giovanni* by taking over from an ailing star, five hours before curtain time, in the lead role of Zerlina. Roberta was only twenty; she knew the part but had never sung on a professional stage before, and she didn't even have a run-through with the orchestra. She became the darling of the Met with her *sopra acutissima*, a rare, very high coloratura voice.

I found her irresistible. We saw more and more of each other, to the great joy of gossip columnists and press agents, who labeled us the Met's "Love Duo." After a while, Roberta and I began to believe their fantasies.

The complications preventing our marriage were minor, I thought. She had signed a personal contract with Sol Hurok, the egocentric impresario, who once autographed a photo to his own daughter: "Your father, S. Hurok." Roberta's parents, who had invested a great deal of money in her musical education since she was thirteen, insisted, with Hurok, that her career would be hampered by marriage, especially to another singer.

At about the same time, I was also courting Rudolf Bing to resume my career at the Met. After he banished me for breaking my contract, he insisted, "As long as I am manager, Merrill will never sing here." No pleading by mutual friends or intermediaries would make him relent.

When I sang in Salzburg for American troops, I discovered he was staying in the same hotel. I managed to meet him for coffee, admitted my error, and apologized. "Never," he insisted. "Never." His voice, though polite, carried the chilling doom of Poe's raven, reiterating "Nevermore."

The 1951 season opened; George London replaced me very nicely in *Aïda*. I attended the opera three nights a week at intermission, sitting in Sherry's as close as possible to Bing. I stared at him until he looked up, and our eyes met. I lifted my eyebrow: "Yes?" With the legendary Viennese tact, he tilted his head slightly and reluctantly, almost sadly, turned away.

One night I accosted him. "Mr. Bing, we must talk—I want to come home."

It was now his turn to raise an eyebrow. "Perhaps in my office sometime. Call me." We met, and I offered to do anything he wished to end my exile. "Write this to me in a letter."

Moe Gale, my agent, who by now felt he had undermined my career by steering me into *Aaron Slick*, was relieved. "Bing obviously wants a public apology." Together we worked out a letter that appeared in the *New York Times* and the *Herald Tribune*. I expressed deep regret and promised never to be unfaithful. Mr. Bing accepted me in a letter that appeared on the front page of both papers: "To admit one's mistakes the way you have is a sign of moral courage and decency. I shall be willing to forget the past."

And he told me, "You will open in *Trovatore* on March 11."

"Yes, sir. Whatever you say."

He said, "Welcome home."

> *Bing was a stubborn man, but always honest. His word was his bond, and he rightly expected others to hold to their word. When I mentioned that some artists were making $1,500 a performance more than I, he was incredulous. He ordered an assistant to produce the payroll lists, and immediately raised me to parity with the others. He never quibbled, and we remain friends to this day.*

With my singing career once again on the track, I wanted to solidify my emotional life, build a home and family. Roberta and I were married at my agent's temple, the Park Avenue Synagogue. It was a splendid production, with over 1,000 guests, cameramen, and 2,000 gawking spectators outside. To add a touch of comedy, my brother Gil, the best man, while driving me to the ceremony, was trapped in a Greek parade among the *evzones*, the husky men in short skirts, and we arrived a half hour late.

The marriage continued in that offbeat, disconnected vein. We immediately rejoined the Met on tour in Boston, as scheduled, and Roberta, who had never been away from home, was constantly on the phone to her mother. Soon she took off to make a movie for Fox, titled *Tonight We Sing* and based, by ominous coincidence, on the life of S. Hurok. I continued on the tour.

We were together only three weeks in the next couple of months, and very soon we looked at each other and wondered, What are we doing here? It was an empty, foolish feeling to realize that we actually had only two things in common: We were both singers and both Jewish. Ten weeks after the wedding we filed for separation, and a Mexican divorce followed. All very civilized, but since the baritone is usually the heavy, I was blamed by the scandal sheets and other public gossips for unspecified transgressions against some unknown code. Actually, we had a very successful divorce: Roberta and I have sung onstage together for twenty-five years.

There was a short period when Elsa Maxwell invited me to her parties, mainly because I was a bachelor, wore decent clothes and sang at the drop of a chord. Elsa was the satellite that revolved around the sun of the Duke and Duchess of Windsor, and Jimmy Donohue, the Woolworth heir, was a bright meteor irresistibly drawn to the Duchess.

Jimmy loved opera—I heard him sing entire scores in French, German, and Italian while accompanying himself on the piano—and made large contributions to the Met, arranged lavish dinners and parties for musicians, and adored the Duchess, who called him Bunny. He squired her around when the Duke was busy, and since friends assumed he was a homosexual, it was all very friendly.

Jimmy and I took turns dancing with the former Wallis Simpson at one of Elsa's soirees in a small ballroom at the Waldorf; the Duchess was just as charming as Jimmy and an excellent dancer. The Duke left the party early to work on his memoirs. At about two in the morning, Jimmy said he was hungry. The Duchess invited him, Elsa, and me upstairs to a suite in the Waldorf Towers. "David's asleep by now—I'll do scrambled eggs."

She laid on a bountiful spread with toast, champagne, and coffee. The party rolled on: Jimmy played, I sang, and Elsa was ringmaster while the Duchess glowed with untiring energy.

At 3 A.M. I explained that I had a morning rehearsal. "Oh come now," she said, "you're too young to leave so soon," and brought out more champagne.

At 4 A.M. I got as far as the doorway, where Elsa took

one arm and the Duchess the other, to propel me back to the piano for a Gilbert and Sullivan duet with Jimmy. When the Duchess went into the kitchen, he said, "I know a lot of people think the Duke is homosexual, but he's *not*. He just loves to have people entertain Wallis."

At five, I opened the door and waved good-bye. The Duchess's face was a little drawn now; she said simply, "Please don't leave me now."

Elsa and Jimmy chorused, "We're staying, dear!" as I made a hasty, somewhat befuddled exit.

A few years later, Jimmy slipped into a deep depression, which he alleviated with barbiturates and alcohol, and one day he was discovered dead. Elsa is gone, too, and the Duke passed away in Paris in 1972. The Duchess is now even more alone.

I retreated to the peace of my apartment on 65th Street, surrounded by hundreds of cans of Campbell soups. I had appeared in an ad for them and they generously shipped cases and cases of their best, possibly as a wedding present. I never had to leave the apartment for a midnight snack, but the cans were depressing at dinnertime.

The woman who cleaned the apartment, Gussie Rock, assured me, "Oh, I have a girl for you! I work for her— sweet, beautiful, keeps a neat house—and she's a pianist. Isn't that perfect? She can play for you when you sing!"

It was the old refrain of the Catskills—I shivered. Gussie introduced me to Marion Machno over the telephone, and after we got over our mutual embarrassment, we arranged a dinner date, mainly, I think, to keep Gussie happy. I developed a feverish cold that night. Marion came over to console me with—yes, it was a comedy scene— homemade chicken soup. Marion was, as Gussie specified, sweet, beautiful, neat, and under her care the soup revealed its legendary curative powers. I instantly sensed a soul mate.

We were married shortly after, in a rabbi's study on 86th Street. We hadn't planned a reception because of schedule changes, so our families stood around on the sidewalk wondering, *Now what?* Since some were kosher and Marion's father was vegetarian, we trooped into Steinberg's vegetarian restaurant nearby on Broadway for the wedding dinner. We had a brief honeymoon in Miami, and then joined Richard and Sarah Tucker in Cuba, where he and I sang *The Barber of Seville.* And Roberta sang Rosina.

Destiny is a more acceptable word for accident: It's reassuring to believe that we, or the stars, or Somebody Up There is controlling the most important steps in our lives. Still, my vocal equipment was an accident of heredity; my first marriage was an accident of propinquity at the Met— and would I have met Marion if we had not shared the same cleaning woman?

There are so many possibilities for accidents in the performing arts that no one is immune. Gerald Ford introduced a great soprano at a White House concert, "Here's a lady who sings everything from Strauss operas to Verdi ballots—Miss Beverly Stills!" Ed Sullivan announced Birgit Nilsson as "Bridget Nelson." A concert chairman in Los Angeles brought me on for a medley from *Porgy and Bess* with: "Mr. Merrill will sing songs by George and Ira Gershwin, the finest husband and wife team ever assembled!"

In my youthful exuberance, I used to play Escamillo with the bravura of Errol Flynn. I would spring onto a table in Lillas Pastia's tavern to sing my "Toreador Song." The table rested on wheels, so the stagehand could roll it off swiftly for a scene change; one night on the road he forgot to prop a wedge against the wheels. I sailed off into the wings, in full voice, and without missing a beat, strolled back to finish the song.

Ljuba Welitsch, the red-headed bombshell, threw herself into roles utterly unfettered. At the end of the second act of *Boheme*, I (as Marcello) picked up Ljuba (as Musetta), hugged her, and tossed her into the air in gay abandon, as directed. She wore a flared skirt that whirled up around her head—and no panties. The prompter choked, and Bing raced backstage to scold her, "Don't you ever do that again!" He couldn't understand that Ljuba never bothered to wear underwear.

> *Divas in the era of bloomers and pantaloons had incredible letdowns. Emma Calvé dropped hers at a matinee to the sound of horrified whispers. A dubious box-holder humphed, "Since they look clean, I assume it was intentional."*
>
> *Frances Alda wore pantaloons under a long skirt as Mimi, opposite Caruso. When she bent over to pick up a prop, buttons snapped and the underpants slipped to her ankle; but she hobbled behind a sofa and stepped out of them. Caruso, who loved a laugh almost as much as a high C, bent over as he sang his aria, picked up the pants, bowed to Mimi, and stretched them out on the sofa for the audience to examine.*
>
> *A performance of something called* Cleopatra's Night *in 1920 featured male and female pants. It was one of the Met's accident-prone dress rehearsals with audience, and a slave girl was supposed to stab herself, falling dead at Cleo's feet. The poor soprano fell down a stairway, and her thin chiffon gown unerringly flew up over her head. She stood up, pulled the costume over herself, lay down once more and closed her eyes. Then the tenor, presumably swimming in a pool nearby, stepped out of it, dry as a plaster statue; a white makeup towel, in place of the leopard-skin that had not arrived, was wrapped around his bottom like a diaper and held together with a large safety pin.*

The Kriendler brothers, owners of the 21 Club, were opera buffs: Mack, who had studied with excellent teachers, would drag me up to the second floor of their establishment, to prove to friends that he could belt out an aria as loudly as I could. The youngest, Pete, confided that his wife Jeanette burned with unquenchable passion to sing at the Met. "If you could only get her onstage as a super," Pete said, "I would be grateful to you for the rest of my life." Well, I persuaded the man in charge of extras to interview her.

Months later, I sang Barnaba, a cruel spy of the

Inquisition in *La Gioconda*, a densely populated opera that attracts mobs of 200 and 300 Venetians to its canals—sailors, monks, nobles, ship workers, peasants, and various unclassified women. In one of these scenes, I had to break through the mob and run down a flight of steps to downstage center for a strenuous aria, concentrating all the while on the opening notes of my music.

As I shouldered my way through the crowd, a hand came out and clutched my wrist. I muttered, "Let go! What is this?"

"Don't you remember me?" The voice came from a woman hidden under the heavy brown makeup and black wig of a fishmonger.

I hadn't the foggiest notion. I tried desperately to free my arm: "What do you want? Let go of me, dammit!"

"Bob, I'm Jeanette! I want to thank you—"

I reached my position a beat before the opening note. I adore Jeanette, and that is why I have never put a friend onstage again. I was about to kick her.

I shared a dressing room with a baritone making his Met debut as Alfio, the rough wagon-driver in *Cavalleria Rusticana*. The director insisted he smoke a pipe, to "develop the characterization," on his entrance. Since he did not smoke, the singer had to take lessons from a prop man in lighting and puffing. The night of the show, he inhaled one puff and lost his voice—the prop man had filled it with the cheapest tobacco. That pipe burned the baritone's career in New York.

Rigoletto's costume bedeviled me when I subbed at a matinee in Tulsa for Leonard Warren. His costume was three sizes too large; I could manage the hunchback jester's long jacket, but his cotton-filled hump was far out of proportion and, worse, the strap that held it on my back kept slipping down during the performance. In the last act it rested on my bottom, like a second rump. A reviewer described me as "the most outrageously deformed Rigoletto I have ever seen."

In the last act of the same show, the assassin Sparafucile murders my daughter Gilda instead of the tenor I had paid him to kill. He stuffs the girl in a sack and drags her into an inn. Well, our Sparafucile was a slender five-foot-seven bass who could scarcely lift his feet. As he dragged the girl through the inn door, the bag slipped out of his hand and she cried, "Oh, my head!" Now I was scheduled to drag her off to the river. "Let me out! Get a doctor!" came the muffled plea from inside the sack.

"How can I let you out?" I whispered. "It'll ruin the scene."

"I'm dying!" she groaned.

"Can you wait till the Duke's refrain is finished?"

"I've got a concussion!" she cried.

I opened the sack to let some air in; by the end of the act, she had recovered sufficiently to take her curtain call.

Tosca leaps to her death over a prison parapet, landing safely behind the set on a mattress. Stella Roman, feeling insecure one night, demanded two extra mattresses. She leaped—and the mattresses bounced her back onstage. She had to kill herself all over again.

I never wear a hat onstage. I always carry it, having learned from the contretemps of my colleagues. One tenor, costumed in a red wig of curls under his hat, made his entrance in *Lucia* with a grand gesture: He bowed low, whipping off his hat, but the wig came off with it. He stood there, bald as a bowling ball, wondering why the audience roared.

In *Lucia* again, Tommy Hayward was to make his entrance down a long, winding staircase. The orchestra hit his cue, and I looked up, to see his wide-brimmed cavalier hat floating from the top of the stairs to the stage. It was like a slow-motion movie shot of a tree leaf drifting in gentle circles. We watched, fascinated. Tommy had anticipated his cue and been pulled back into the wings so swiftly by the stage manager that his hat made the entrance.

Somebody devised a spectacular effect for the "Anvil Chorus" in *Trovatore*. Every time the hammers hit the anvils, an electric spark flew up: Both the anvils and hammers were wired to offstage switches. But, of course, the wires crossed or the insulation wore off—each blow gave the men wielding the hammers an electric shock. The choristers vibrated and hopped like puppets; some of them dropped their hammers and ran.

The announcement of an "entirely new production" is often greeted with groans by the performers. New means trouble—the kinks are seldom corrected by curtain time. The Met's new *Barber of Seville* employed a lamplighter who touched the candles in the street lights with a long pole, which signaled an electrician backstage to turn on the "candlelight." The two lamps were at opposite sides of the stage. I was in the wings, on edge as usual, vocalizing to get up steam for "Largo al factotum," when I heard the laughter. As the lamplighter touched the candle at left, the electrician turned on the light at the other lamp, and the lamplighter ran back and forth trying to catch up with the electrician. I had to come out at the height of the laughter to sing. The audience, however, usually sympathizes with the performer in these crises, and it responded with a warming ovation.

Baritone Jess Walters, who has sung in leading houses all over the world, now teaches at the University of Texas. The tale of his debut in Amsterdam is a case history of preposterous mishap and clever improvisation. As the Count des Grieux in *Manon,* Jess had an important scene in which he begged his son, who had joined a seminary, to come home. Somehow, the son never came on for his scene. A chair was part of the setting, so Jeff instantly played to it, as if the son were sitting there; he sang his aria to the chair and even persuaded the nonexistent son to sign a paper before Jess made his exit. The audience applauded his ingenuity, and the management signed him for a long run.

Jeff later arranged an audition in the United States, but had no money to fly there. One of the Dutch baritones said, "That's no trouble," and suddenly developed laryngitis, so Jess filled in for an extra paid performance. The next week another baritone had an upset stomach. In a few weeks, Jeff could pay for his airline tickets.

Animals are unpredictable and great hams. In *Boris Godunov*, Dimitri the Pretender makes a grand entrance on the back of a horse, to address the peasants in an aria. The elegant horse possibly did not think the audience was up to his usual standard, so he turned around and faced the back of the stage; to make his disdain clear, he urinated. Unhappy Dimitri, high in the saddle, was forced to sing his aria to the scenery while the horse swished his beautiful tail. It was a well-rounded performance. The Met now uses attendants in costume to lead the animals on and off, and the men carry small brooms and shovels for emergencies.

American singers pride themselves on performing in five or six languages; most foreign artists sing only in their native language. This doubles or triples their hazards when they sing in English. The Met produced an English-language version of *The Bartered Bride,* for which the young Italian tenor, who could not speak the language at all, promised faithfully to study the score beforehand. He was a little uneasy in rehearsal; on performance night, he panicked. He made his entrance, the conductor gave him the downbeat, he opened his mouth wide—and nothing came out. Another downbeat—still nothing. On the third try, the prompter yelled from his box, "Sing, you jerk!"

And the tenor's first words were "Sing! you jerk!"

The prompters love the music and occasionally sing along. One had such a fine voice he made the sextet from *Lucia* into a septet. On another occasion, I was singing a cadenza in good voice, running up and down the scales, and then . . . I forgot how to get out of it. I interpolated and improvised for several minutes, staring at the prompter with "help!" in my eyes, and he merely nodded. I resolved the cadenza somehow, whereupon the prompter stood up and cried "Bravo!"

Vacation with the family in Italy—what a joyous thought! Fly to Naples, motor up the west coast to Rome (where I would record two albums), then wander up to Milan, stopping to explore the ancient cities. I was a dreamer: Operatic accidents followed me all the way up the boot of Italy.

We would be a company of six—Marion, the children,

age six and seven; a small French poodle, Mimiche; and Linda, a German governess who had worked for us in New York—carrying fourteen pieces of baggage. Among the luggage were two large cartons, two and a half feet square, of toilet paper. It was 1963 and we had been warned that paper was precious, especially in Italy, and even the best hotels supplied a harsh texture. With two children and a dog, I was prepared for anything. Two large cartons were wrapped in heavy brown paper and loaded on the plane as baggage.

At Naples airport, Linda was waiting, but the large station wagon we had ordered was not. The rental agency promised, "Tomorrow." Since we had expected to drive out that same afternoon, we made no hotel reservations. We piled into two taxicabs and cruised around town until we found rooms in a second-class establishment that had an unfortunate resemblance to *Porgy and Bess*'s Catfish Row. The cab drivers then demanded reparations, which totaled tens of thousands of lire.

It soon became clear why opera reached a peak of perfection in Italy—it is everyday life. The simple request for an explanation of the fare became the crashing finale of a Verdi extravaganza. The scene opened with impassioned solos by each driver: one established the theme of honesty; the other, imminent death from starvation. This developed into a quartet when two hotel porters came out. Mimiche, meanwhile, howled a frightened *obbligato*. Gradually, a chorus of street people appeared, creating a counterpoint of American lust and greed as opposed to eternal nobility of the Roman people. The alternating themes built to an uproarious climax, topped by my soaring *"Basta!"* I called on the hotel manager to arbitrate, and we ended the scene by settling for exactly what the cab drivers demanded.

We received two small rooms: The children, governess and dog occupied one, but there was no room for both luggage and the cartons. We opened one covertly on a street behind the hotel, extracted a few rolls, and rewrapped it. These were gifts for friends in Rome, I explained to a porter, and had to be stored carefully in the baggage room.

My foresight was vindicated when we saw the hotel's blotting paper. Little Mimiche, frightened by his new environment, required large quantities.

In the morning, our station wagon arrived: not the large one we had been promised but a small Fiat. We tied the luggage on the roof rack and two cartons sat in the back with me, David and the dog, so they would not get wet in the rain. Linda and Lizanne jammed in the front seat with Marion, our chauffeur. The west coast was lovely, from what I could see between the boxes. During the drive, we left the cartons open for emergencies, and every time the car swerved on the turns of that road, the boxes tipped and the paper fell over me and Mimiche. It was also the hottest summer in the memory of even the oldest gas station attendants, and little of the balmy Tyrrhenian sea air seeped in to me. By the time we reached Rome, I was dehydrated and suffering from various unfocused angers.

Fortunately, the Residence Palace Hotel was ready for us with two bedrooms, a sitting room, and balcony, and we were prepared for the hotel, having rewrapped our cartons with elegant gift paper and marked them HANDLE WITH CARE. When the bellboy dropped one in the lobby, I immediately gathered it up protectively. For the rest of the trip, Marion and I carried the boxes ourselves.

The balcony was most unusual—no railing. Simply a small brick edging about two feet high, the perfect height for children to trip over in the dark. I did not sleep that night, awoke at sunrise, and entered into a duet of despair and betrayal with the hotel manager until he agreed to put up a temporary fence immediately. Two days later, white electric wire was strung around the balcony, supported by wavering mop handles. In those two harrowing nights, I slept little and by day rehearsed *Rigoletto* and the difficult *Falstaff* under a taskmaster second only to Toscanini, Georg Solti, as the thermometer rose to 110 degrees. Our hotel had no air conditioning.

Marion cheered me on with, "It can't get much worse, can it?"

To cool off, we bought a small plastic pool that fitted

neatly on the balcony. Marion, always the pragmatist, asked, "How do we get a hundred and fifty gallons of water up here?"

I cornered the hotel man who mopped the floors and watered the plants between siestas. Again, a seriocomic duet, consisting of a baritone recitative and the porter's uncomprehending shrugs; some paper money was exchanged, and he agreed to supply our water from the roof, where his hose connected. He would aim it into our pool, three floors below. I prayed that no one would stroll out onto any balcony between him and the pool during hosing time, which was every day because the sun lowered the water level three inches in twenty-four hours.

And, of course, we had to take the children sightseeing. As we wandered through the Vatican and St. Peter's, Lizanne asked, "What is the Vatican?"

Simplifying matters, I answered, "This is where God lives." The children, impressed now, peered into the chapels, around the columns and arches and behind the high altar.

David complained, "But God isn't here. Where is He?"

"Oh, David, you're stupid," Lizanne said. "Don't you know nobody works in Italy between one and four?"

We ate lunch in the villa where Mussolini had kept his mistress. When the official in charge learned that I was an opera singer, he opened the private bedrooms, ordinarily closed to tourists, so we could inspect the grandiose fascist-style decor at our leisure. Mimiche, not at all overwhelmed, left an afterthought on the polished floor. We snatched her up and fled; I had no idea she was a political commentator.

After the recording session ended, we had a discussion: Where shall we go now? Our governess suggested Switzerland, which she had found lovely and cool. We held a vote: five to one for Switzerland. Mine was the one. Once more we piled into the station wagon and headed north along the coast for Milan, the cartons cracking merrily onto my head and lap everytime we rounded a curve or stopped short. First stop, Pisa. The heat waves around the famous tower made it seem to be shimmying rather than leaning. As we climbed to the top in the over-100 temperature, Mimiche, evidently maddened by the heat, broke away with her leash and raced to the edge of the parapet. If I hadn't stepped on the strap of the leash, she would have committed suicide off the Tower of Pisa.

We ate a wretched lunch, and reached Milan by evening. Once more we carried the beautifully wrapped cartons through the hotel's marble lobby. After dinner, Lizanne developed raging cramps, and we didn't sleep that night. By morning, her stomach had swelled. The concierge could not locate a doctor: "It is not only summer holiday, it is also Sunday." I heard that Gladys Swarthout and her husband, Frank Chapman, were in Milan. They phoned friends who sent a family physician; Lizanne, he said, had picked up ptomaine, probably in Pisa.

While she rested, I held a vote on the next stop. "Do we go home now from Milan, or do I jump out the window?"

Before we flew home, we had lunch with Gladys and Frank. Out of heartfelt gratitude for their rescue, I asked them to accept a gift: "A carton and a half of American paper."

They were delighted, although Frank hesitated politely. "It's worth its weight in gold."

I insisted. "It's already gift-wrapped."

7

My Friend Ruby

Richard Tucker was with me at my debut, and I was with him at his final exit. The preposterous coincidence of two boys from similar backgrounds making it to the Metropolitan Opera in the same year developed into a thirty-year duet of friendship and admiration; we sang two hundred performances together.

Ruby's presence seemed to fill the entire stage; though he was five feet seven, his forty-two-inch chest made him look as enormous as a defensive linebacker. Whatever he did had that same expansive scale: his laughter, his eating, his willpower, his generosity, his drive. He was a cantor from a small synagogue who became the greatest dramatic tenor of his time in the Italian repertoire, and he remained on top at the Met for three decades.

Rudolf Bing, its general manager, put it exactly: "Caruso, Caruso, that's all you hear. I have an idea we're going to be proud some day to tell people we heard Richard Tucker." That was in 1956, and Ruby had not yet reached his prime.

He had been scouted by a cantor on the Lower East Side when he was an eight-year-old alto, Reuben Ticker, and sang for the services over the years. Although a cantor, he was supporting himself as a $30-a-week salesman of silk linings in the garment district when he proposed to Sarah Perelmuth at an IRT subway station. They married, despite opposition from her family: who needed a singer who couldn't make a living at it? Sarah's brother Jacob was already Jan Peerce, bringing in thousands of dollars from radio programs and Radio City Music Hall. And Jan's eyes focused on an even higher goal—opera.

Ruby, with a little nudge from Sarah, decided to study opera, too. His top note at that time was a high B; few tenors would have the courage to continue studying without a high C. He found his teacher in Paul Althouse, who had sung Wagnerian roles at the Met for many years. Ruby was just as methodical in his learning as he had been in his selling on Seventh Avenue. As Althouse loved to tell it, Tucker came into his studio, took off his hat, sang, put on his hat and went home. He never suffered the disabilities, the soul-destroying terrors of neurotic temperament. He wanted to learn, so he learned; he wanted to sing, so he sang—it was as simple as that.

By the time he was thirty, Ruby had become Richard Tucker and won second prize in a Met Opera Audition of the Air. He had appeared in only one opera, with the Salmaggi company in Brooklyn, when he received a call from Frank St. Ledger, the Met's casting director. He remembered the sweetness and power of the second-prize tenor's voice, and asked him to substitute for an ailing Enzo, the lead role in *La Gioconda*.

Caruso, after years of successes in European opera houses, was shrugged off by the critics in his New York debut for "tiresome Italian vocal mannerisms." Tucker, in his first time at bat, hit a home run. And received a six-figure contract.

Tucker, like Caruso, was not conventionally handsome, but their voices had a sensual throb that enthralled women. They followed Caruso on the street when he was out for a stroll. Tucker, the paragon of the faithful, bourgeois father, willed himself into believing that when he sang a romantic aria, women had orgasms. This is impossible to prove by scientific polling, but I did notice on occasion women in the front rows with lips half open, eyes closed, swaying uneasily to Rudolfo's "Che gelida manina." It was certainly a tribute to the power of positive singing.

Tucker and I formed a concert team in 1969 and toured the country every year. It was almost an "Odd Couple" relationship: We didn't change much, but we learned a great deal from each other. Eventually, people began to confuse our identities. They thought I was Tucker, or that we were related.

"I just saw your brother-in-law in *Carmen*," they'd tell me. "But *you sing better!*"

Another variation: "Why should I know you from someplace? You're Richard Tucker?"

"No, I'm Robert Merrill."

"Funny, you don't look like him."

One summer my wife, Marion, and I were walking down the Via Veneto with Jack O'Brian, the columnist, and his wife. I spotted a couple coming toward us and turned to Jack. "I'll bet a hundred lire they think I'm Richard Tucker."

"That's a sucker bet," Jack said. "You know them."

"I swear I never saw them before."

Jack instantly accepted the bet. The woman strolled up to me and gushed, "Oh, Richard Tucker! You're our favorite tenor!"

It was simple deduction: The tourists' clothes looked
American, something about her beehive hairdo said Long
Island, and since Tucker lived on Long Island, they had to
be his fans.

Richard was somewhat conservative in his choice of
clothes. I broke him down little by little. On tours, we both
enjoyed walking through a town before the performance. I
would look for a haberdashery—I collect shirts; his vice
was just as insidious—he collected stocks. We made a deal:
I'd let him drag me into his broker's office if he'd come into
my haberdashery.

He wore white shirts with short-point collars, a black
suit, black shoes, black coat. I persuaded him to try a spread
collar, with a discreet red and white stripe.

"Oh, hell, I'll look like Rudolph the Reindeer in the
Macy parade."

"Put it on. I'll buy you the shirt."

Later he relaxed into a plaid sport jacket, and from
there the road to ruin was short—he abandoned black suits.
But he never could convert me to the psychedelic highs of
the stock market. I remained an incorrigible nongambler.

When I sang at The Sands in Las Vegas, I had the bad
luck to sit down at the blackjack table next to Lou
Costello, of Abbott and Costello. I laid down $2 on a
card—he bet $1,000. I felt I had to maintain some status
as a fellow performer, so I upped my bets to $50. I left the
table only once, to sing for the second show, and by next
morning I had dropped $1,000.

A cloud of guilt flowed over my face as I confronted
myself in the bathroom mirror: "Your father never had
$1,000 to his name—and who's going to carry those bags
under your eyes?"

From that night on, I invested only $25. If I lost, I
stopped playing.

But Richard relished challenges. The stock market,
with its baffling scenarios, unseen actors and audiences in
the millions, was the biggest, toughest house in the world
to win over. He loved to watch those symbols and numbers

chasing themselves on the electronic tote board: "They're like cues—you got to react fast."

"Come on, Ruby, you agreed we're going for a walk."

"I only need a minute to check ITT."

The storefront brokers' rooms were filled with smoke and senior citizens and stock junkies, who welcomed Tucker as one of their own. They took him for a retired clothing manufacturer. He'd wade right into metaphysical discussions of warrants, trends, puts and calls, ins and outs—and that killed the afternoon. For me it had all the excitement of watching paint dry.

In Detroit I found myself alone at the electronic device that delivers prices and trends of stocks at your request. I idly tapped out "S-E-X," and the machine reported "UP."

When our concert town ran out of haberdashers or brokers, we settled for a movie. We could both save our voices there and, if it was a spectacularly silly picture, even take a snooze.

A cold winter night in Wichita, Kansas—or was it Wichita Falls, Texas? We were stranded at the airport when our connecting flight was delayed five hours, so we went into town for a movie. Three houses were playing Elvis Presley films, which we had already slept through. The fourth presented "Behind the Green Door." Richard looked over the promotion stills outside and winced. "This is a dirty movie. I'll be embarrassed."

I assured him it was the central topic of our concert committee luncheons, and I felt embarrassed at being left out of the conversation.

"Well, I'd hate to be spotted going into this joint," he said.

"Look, anybody who might recognize us wouldn't believe it."

Tucker pulled his hat low over his eyes, turned up his coat collar, and we drifted into the Star Theater: ALL TICKETS $5. A skinny, six-foot boy, his face glowing with pimples, sold the tickets and ushered us to our seats. The gloom was barely relieved by red lights on each wall, and I had an immediate eerie shock of *déjà vu:* The smell of a chorus dancing on a late summer afternoon, and men slumped down in their chairs, newspapers or coats on their laps. It was the same intent audience I had played to in Philadelphia with Zonia Duval.

From the vaguely lit flicker on the screen, I assumed we had come into the middle of Act I. An orgy was convening around a large woman whose flesh overflowed the screen. Tucker nudged me, "Hey, that's Kirsten Flagstad."

Our laughter brought the boy factotum to our side. "Quiet down, you're disturbing the patrons." We nodded and turned our eyes back to Act II. The attractive ingenue was tied to a post, and three girls were stimulating her entire body. Their working conditions were crowded, but they seemed to enjoy their jobs. Now, a black man paraded into the arena, behind a tremendous phallus.

Tucker whispered, "That's unbelievable. It must be a prop."

I agreed. "Looks like one of those long Cuban breads."

His laugh reverberated off the wall, and in a moment I felt a tap on my shoulder. "I'm warnin' you," our censor muttered. "This is a respectable theater."

We sat quietly for Act III. The film was grainy and out of focus here, so the action seemed to be floating under water. From what I could discern, we were approaching the finale—a scene more frantic and hilarious than anything in the history of *opera bouffe.* Sitting astride individual trapeze bars were a peculiar quartet—two tenors, a baritone, and a bass—and our ingenue was catering to all of them simultaneously.

The audience was silent, puzzling out who was doing what to whom and where. Tucker could not restrain his guffaw: "If the trapeze bars break, those guys will turn into sopranos!"

The factotum appeared quickly, shaking a menacing finger. "People paid good money to see these actors, and you're disturbing them. Now you get out, or I'll call the cop."

Tucker slowly pulled himself out of his seat and straightened up to the full majesty of the nobleman he had played so often, Don Alvaro. "This is a rotten show," he declaimed in his rich, open tones, "and the air smells worse." He turned to me. "Let's get the hell out of here!" And we strode up the aisle with a dignity that would have pleased Mr. Bing.

As the usher followed us, I couldn't resist adding: "What's more, that girl is a lousy actress."

Our mutual admiration did not, of course, prevent breaking each other up onstage. After you've played the same role fifty times, you begin to look for any diversion to disturb the routine, to keep your partner on the tips of his boot-toes.

In *Forza del Destino*, I (as Don Carlo) hunt for Don Alvaro, who seduced my sister and caused the death of my father. Unknown to each other, we meet on a battlefield. As Don Alvaro is carried off, wounded, he entrusts a casket of letters to me, to be burned if he dies. Suspicious now, I open the box.

We had a sold-out audience at the old Met. I peered into the box Tucker handed me, expecting to discover a picture of my violated sister. Instead I lifted out a beautifully detailed photo of an orgy, in which the men all wore black socks. I turned upstage to hide my exploding laughter and saw Tucker in the wings, pantomiming "Shame! Shame!"

I repaid him, in a small way, the next time around. In the grand duet before he hands over the box, Don Alvaro calls out my name, Don Carlo, several times. Suddenly, I saw the blank stare that signaled desperation—Tucker could not remember my name! He hummed several notes, and I waited a few moments to heighten his despair. Then I whispered, "It's Moishe. My name is Moishe." Richard's eyes brightened and he sang out gratefully, "Don Moishe!"

In times of crisis, we stood shoulder to shoulder. Our consumptive Violetta on one occasion was Eleanor Steber, who was blessed with a sumptuous voice and a bosom to match. She was costumed in a low-cut, loose-fitting gown for her death scene. Now, a designer can create a costume that defies fire, rips, soiling, even the bulges of the stomach and the seat, but he cannot defy the law of gravity.

In the writhing torment of her final aria, one of Miss Steber's outstanding attributes shook loose from its mooring and gradually slipped out before our apprehensive eyes. Ruby and I instinctively closed ranks downstage in front of her; facing the audience and singing our hearts out, we elbowed her loveliness back into the gown.

Richard had a stainless steel will on matters that were deeply important to him: his voice, his family, his religion.

He gave the best of himself every night; he never held back. "People don't come to see you hit singles and bunts," he'd say. "They want home runs—Babe Ruth, Hank Aaron."

Interviewers often came up with the same question: How would you compare yourself to Caruso? His answer: "Caruso was the first tenor—I'm the first Tucker."

His teacher Althouse died when Tucker was near the summit of his career, still he went searching for another instructor. "I schlepped around to the best ones. I told them I'm not looking to learn anything new, just tell me if I'm okay on the old stuff. If I'm getting sloppy, correct me. And you know something, everybody rejected me! They said, 'You're making a quarter-million a year—what can we teach you?'"

His wife, Sarah, traveled with him more than half the time on the road. If she remained at home, Tucker called her immediately after each performance. The telephone was an extension of his gregariousness. He could not walk past a phone booth in a hotel or airport without calling his booking office, his vocal coach, local friends, his New York broker, the weather bureau. Above all, the family. He phoned each of his three sons several times a day.

We were recording *Forza del Destino* in Rome when he

received a call from New York: His first grandson was about to have his Hebrew circumcision ceremony. Tucker took off in the middle of the session, after being warned he would have to pay the cost of each day lost by his absence. He returned in two days, exhausted but pleased, and the record company deducted several thousand dollars from his royalties.

In *Traviata,* Violetta's death scene requires eight minutes, but to those onstage it seems interminable. I don't think she really dies of tuberculosis—it's old age. Tucker tried to go home as swiftly as possible after a show to his Sarah, his sons, and his supper; he could barely hide his impatience as he waited for his sweetheart's farewell gasp. He'd grumble to me, *sotto voce,* "If this dame doesn't kick the bucket soon, I'll miss the 11:12 to Great Neck."

In every city he visited, Richard searched for a present for Sarah. During the height of the plane hijacking scares, he carried to the Chicago airport a lavishly wrapped anniversary present, a negligee. At that time, the penetrating ray to check parcels had not been developed; packages were opened for inspection. Tucker absolutely refused.

INSPECTOR: *But, sir, I'll rewrap it just as it was.*

TUCKER: *You'll tear it. You'll ruin my present.*

INSPECTOR: *I'm sorry, it's the law.*

TUCKER: *I want to talk to your supervisor.*

(SUPERVISOR appears, ominously suspicious.)

SUPERVISOR: *The package must be opened, to protect all the passengers, including you.*

(TWO POLICEMEN arrive.)

TUCKER: *Do I look like some kind of nut? I have to appear in a concert tonight. I'm Richard Tucker. What do I need to hijack a plane for?*

SUPERVISOR: *I don't know anything about Richard Tucker. The law says—*

TUCKER: *You don't know anything about Tucker, huh?*

(He wraps his arms around the package as if it's a football, shoves it against his stomach and lowers his head, ready to plunge through the security barrier.)

Tucker won.

Ruby lived every day in the warmth of his Orthodox faith. He wrapped the phylactery ribbons on his arm to pray each morning. So powerful was the pull of the telephone that I often found him in his room with a receiver in hand, praying while the party at the other end talked. He hated to waste time.

He wore the ritual *tzitzit*, a prayer shawl that resembles a vest, under his shirt all day. Since he lost about five pounds in perspiration at each performance, he made a complete change of clothing before he left the theater, and he carried an extra prayer vest for this purpose. Non-Jewish friends, if they visited while he dressed, wondered whether the vest was a protection from chills. Or bulletproof.

He would not make the sign of the cross in a performance; he turned upstage so that his hand was hidden. Yet he sang on Friday night, the Hebrew sabbath. "It's not really work, singing—it's my pleasure." During the Hebrew holidays, he served as cantor for services in Chicago.

In 1953, Tucker signed with the English record company EMI to make recordings with Maria Callas at La Scala. When he discovered that the conductor would be Herbert von Karajan, who had been identified with work for the Nazi party, Tucker was aroused.

"I told EMI they had to find themselves a new conductor or a new tenor. They got Tulio Serafin, who was not a hit name like von Karajan. The records didn't sell like a house on fire, and EMI dropped me. That little protest cost me a quarter of a million in royalties."

Some years later, when Tucker made his debut at the Vienna Opera, von Karajan refused to conduct for him. He did pay a visit to Richard's dressing room. "He gave me a stiff 'Welcome to the Staatsoper, *Kammersänger* Tucker,' then he turned around and marched out. He was a gentleman. He had his obligations and I had mine."

On our walking tours, Ruby would occasionally wonder if any of our tribe lived in that town. He developed a simplified census. We strolled through a supermarket, looking for boxes of matzos: One dozen boxes, he calculated, indicated a Jewish community of fifty or less; two different brands of matzos meant a thriving settlement, with a community center and a good delicatessen.

Since it was difficult to eat kosher in small towns, he usually ate Chinese, carefully avoiding the pork dishes in favor of vegetables, fish, chicken. I didn't have the heart to tell him that the Chinese often used bits of pork to flavor these dishes.

When he confronted kosher food, eyeball to matzo ball, he conquered his willpower. He ate. He fought a good, clean, hopeless fight to keep his weight below 180 pounds. As soon as Metrecal appeared on the market, he ran a test. With peculiar results. "It's putting weight on," he groaned.

"How often do you eat it?"

"After every meal."

For breakfast he took only one glass of fruit juice, corn flakes or Wheaties, and coffee. He ate no lunch and, inevitably, after his performance, he was ravenous. He gulped down a bourbon or two, several glasses of fruit juice, three or four slices of bread and butter to keep from collapsing before the appetizers arrived. Then a soup, followed by the biggest steak in town, accompanied by starches on top of starches, a large salad, two desserts, coffee and mints, assorted fruits. He'd go to bed at one A.M. and be up by six, raring to move on to the next city and a new restaurant or friend's house.

I suggested, "Why don't you eat something in the middle of the day? Some crackers."

His eyes filled with reproach. "How can you eat crackers without cream cheese?"

Once a year, the Tuckers hosted a buffet party for at

least a hundred people on their lawn. It was a ten-dessert production, an outpouring of affection for all the people he and his wife held dear: his colleagues at the Met, his booking office, stock brokers, old friends from Brooklyn, new friends he'd met on tour, his makeup man, his dresser, switchboard operators, the owner of his favorite deli.

A new friend was like a gulp of oxygen to Tucker; they quickly became old friends and never forgot each other. Chicago was his town: he'd sung there many years for the Met and the Chicago opera and for holiday services.

> (SCENE: A hotel lobby in Chicago, headquarters for a convention. As soon as we walk out of the elevator, hundreds of middle-aged women swarm around us.)
>
> FIRST WOMAN: . . . *heard you sing, was it fifteen years ago? in Cincinnati.*
>
> TUCKER: *Ah, yes. I had a wonderful dinner at your house. What a delicious honey cake you made.*
>
> SECOND WOMAN: . . . *you recall, we picked you up at the Gainesville airport?*
>
> TUCKER: *Of course. Your husband is in the horse-raising business. He wanted to give me one.*
>
> MERRILL: (Aside, to TUCKER) *Come on, save your voice!*
>
> (TUCKER won't budge. He stands there, lost in recollections.)

In Dallas, Richard saw a young French-horn player bent over in anguished pain. He called a physician friend, who advised an operation for hernia. Since the boy was all alone in Dallas, Tucker bought him a plane ticket for home, so he could be with his parents during the surgery. He'd never met the horn player before.

He spent hours listening to young artists, and he'd recommend them to regional opera companies, even the Met. When he met that performer again, he'd ask happily, "Say, did you get that job I sent you for?" Some of those who benefited considered this sort of question patronizing.

He recommended Placido Domingo to Rudolf Bing as a replacement for himself, despite Bing's judgment that the young man needed polish. This gave Domingo his debut at the Met. Tucker was unable to appear in *Ernani* at La Scala, and again recommended the Spanish-born tenor. Again it was a debut, and Domingo's reception there catapulted him to the eminence he enjoys today.

"He might have thanked me." Tucker shrugged it off.

It is a wretched fact of life in opera: If you don't help a young performer, you're a bastard; if you do, you're resented. I stopped listening to new voices long ago, after I heard a very talented young man sing Escamillo in Toronto. A friend introduced us, and the singer asked me, "What do you think?"

"You did very well. But you're forcing. You ought to work on breathing and projection."

"What's the matter?" the baritone said. "Are *you* worried?"

Tenors are notoriously touchy; their nerve ends are very close to the surface. Now, when you have two tenors feuding . . .

The two most stable tenors I have ever known, solid family men, established, secure in their *macho*, were Tucker and Jan Peerce. But there was an obvious coolness between them. I never could understand why; since I was (and still am) a friend of both families, I was always in the middle.

Since Jan and I live in New Rochelle, he offered to give me a lift to the airport. At the check-in counter, the clerk cheerfully announced, "Mister Tucker of the opera just checked in, so I arranged three seats together."

Jan murmured something about needing privacy, and the clerk placed us together, two rows behind Tucker. I had lunch with Jan, but I didn't want Richard to think I had gone over to the other side, so I asked Jan, "Do you mind if I go up and say hello to him?"

He did not object. Richard grumbled, "What's this bit,

you and Jan . . .?" And I explained the ride to the airport.
Peace.

When we landed, Tucker hurried off—and missed the
sponsors' welcoming committee. The chairman shook
hands with Jan: "Welcome to Cleveland, Mister Tucker."

Peerce's face reddened. "What do you mean? I'm not
Tucker—I'm Jan Peerce!"

Tucker had an unquenchable passion for arriving at
the concert hall a full half hour before the show "to check
on the piano." Whether it was a quest for perfection or
simple nervousness I'll never know. I like to arrive five
minutes early, see if we actually have a piano, and go right
on. I lose a great deal of energy if I hang around backstage,
worrying about the weather or Will I go blank on the
words? or What is the name of this well-wisher I'm thank-
ing?

Inevitably I'd receive a call in my room:

TUCKER: *I'm waiting in the lobby.*

MERRILL: *But the limo won't pick us up till—*

TUCKER: *I called them to pick up twenty minutes early.*

MERRILL: *I'm resting. Please—*

TUCKER: *Don't you care if the piano is placed wrong?*

MERRILL: *For godsakes, it only takes a minute to
check.*

TUCKER: *Will you do me a favor and come down now?*
(At the hall: The piano is exactly right. We wander
around backstage for about fifteen minutes.)

TUCKER: (Discouraged shrug) *What the hell am I doing
here so early?*

I made a bet with Tucker, in my dressing room at the
Met about twenty years ago. A small bet, the kind you never
collect on. He was forty then, and had come offstage
muttering about a soprano who fluffed her cues and ruined

his entrance. "I don't need any more of this crap. I'm quitting when I'm fifty. Take it easy, move to Florida, enjoy life."

I bet him he'd never quit. "You enjoy it right here. With your technique, you can go on forever."

Fifty came, and fifty-five—and he forgot about retiring. He was the master of thirty leading roles and at the peak of his form. A few years ago, he became obsessed with the desire to play Eleazar, the old Jewish goldsmith in Halevy's *La Juive.* It is a melodramatic role that makes heavy demands on a singer, and its music has never been popular. In fact, thirty years had elapsed between its premiere at the Met and the one Caruso sang in 1919. Tucker, who admired and studied all of Caruso's records, felt he could do better. "I'm a cantor, I've spent my life in synagogues. Let's face it, Caruso was never a Jew."

The Met management was not enthusiastic, but Tucker pushed ahead with the project. A concert version in London was well received. A full production in New Orleans brought him enviable reviews, followed by another in Barcelona. Several singers, who can be very objective about other artists' acclaim, assured me that Tucker's ovation in Spain was the most exciting they had heard. He came back for our 1974–1975 concert tour with a great buoyancy and sparkle; I'd never seen him happier. The Met had agreed to produce *La Juive* in 1976 or 1977. And he would wear Caruso's own costume, from the Met's storehouse.

Eleazar had been an obsessive personal challenge for Caruso, too. He was at the height of his powers and popularity; he no longer had to prove anything to anybody. Still, he spent an entire summer studying the score; he modeled a clay head of the old man, to test dozens of noses and beards. He visited Lower East Side synagogues to observe the liturgy and cantorial style, and he hired a Yiddish actor to coach his inflections and gestures. In creating his costume, Caruso used actual Hebrew prayer shawls. He was not at ease on his opening night, November 24, 1919: the wax nose impeded his breathing and the long beard tickled. Nevertheless, the critics acclaimed his Eleazar as the triumph of his career.

The next year, on December 11, singing in *L'Elisir d'Amore* at the Brooklyn Academy, Caruso began to cough blood. He played two more "heavy" shows, *Forza* and *Samson*, then he sang *La Juive* again, with great beauty and power, on Christmas Eve. At the intermission, he almost collapsed from the pain in his side. Artur Bodanzky, the conductor, begged him to cancel, or at least omit some of the music. Caruso insisted he would continue to the end. He finished the performance, and never sang again. The following year, he died.

January 8, 1975, Kalamazoo, Michigan: Tucker and I rehearsed for our concert at the university until one in the afternoon. Our program closed with a medley from *Fiddler on the Roof*, and the last number we sang was "L'Chaim" ("To Life"). We always relished that finale—a lot of bounce, and we'd link arms in a little dance. After rehearsal Tucker went up to his room for a nap.

Half an hour later, the room clerk phoned me: "Mister Tucker's gone to the hospital." I raced there in a taxi with our accompanist, David Benedict, through a torrent of gray rain. What could have hit Richard—food poison? a throat infection? The doctor outside his room said, "He's dead." My legs crumpled, as if a sandbag had dropped on my head. I sat down and wept.

Ruby had not rested in his room. He'd made his usual quota of telephone calls and started to write a letter of recommendation to an Illinois university on behalf of a voice student. The girl found him slumped over a desk, reaching for a pen. Richard's big, generous heart had collapsed. He was sixty.

There was an exasperating hassle for possession of the body. The police insisted that the law required an autopsy, but I knew his wife and family would object, because of his Orthodox faith. I recalled the name of one of his Kalamazoo friends, who, in turn, located a rabbi to explain this religious problem to the police. Reuben Ticker's body was saved for Orthodox burial.

In October of that year, Terence Cardinal Cooke presided at a memorial mass for him, the first such honor ever accorded a Jew in Saint Patrick's Cathedral. The Cardinal had been one of his close friends, and Tucker had sung at many fund-raisings for the Archdiocese hospitals and schools. I didn't know he had also helped raise $6.5 million for Notre Dame.

In December, the Metropolitan Opera conducted an auction to help meet its operating deficit. The costume of Eleazar, which Caruso had worn, was bought for $3,000 by Placido Domingo.

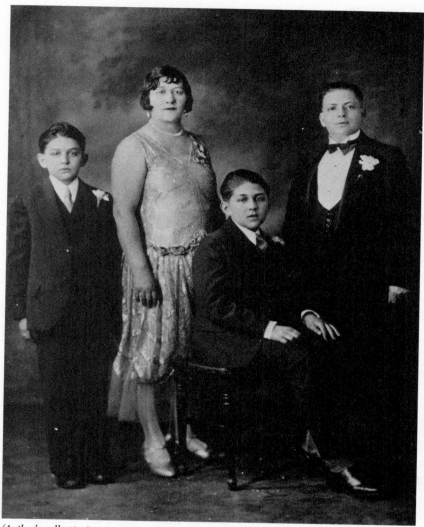

Brother Gil, left, and my parents, on the celebration of
my thirteenth birthday.

(Author's collection)

Danny Kaye and I in woozy after-dinner harmony with
New York's Governor Thomas E. Dewey, who had once
studied opera.

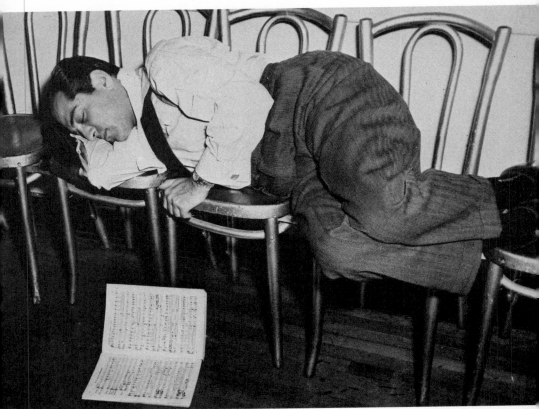

Flaked out after an early call to record a 1950 *Carmen*.   (Author's collection)

Concert partner Richard Tucker.

(Author's collection)

(Author's collection)

Hollywood in the fifties: The girls were a dancing swirl of blond hair, satin gowns, and names that ended in "a"— Lana, Cobina, Sheila . . . .

The Wistful Couple: Duke and Duchess of Windsor.

The Luv-ing Couple: Richard and Liz.

(NBC photo)

Tallulah momentarily subdued—a singalong on the *Big Show* with Margaret Truman before my duet with her.

(Author's collection)

Desi Arnaz and Lucille Ball funning in Las Vegas, about 1954. The other man is Jack Entratter, the resident oracle.

Marion: wife, critic, manager.

Mario Lanza: "I always wanted to be just a boy—to say, to
hell with all the cruel things
in life."

My daughter, Lizanne, toured in *Fiddler* for two seasons as my daughter, Chava.   *(Author's collection)*

As Archie Bunker in a TV operatic spoof of *All in the Family* with Sonny and Cher. Terry Garr, second from right, plays Gloria.

Opening night of Rudolf Bing's first production at the old Met (1950): *Don Carlos* with Jussi Bjoerling, Delia Regal, Fritz Stiedry, conductor. I'm Rodrigo.

Toscanini leads Jan Peerce, Licia Albanese, me, and G. Newman through *Traviata* (1947).

As Rodrigo again for the opening of Bing's farewell season (1971).

Las Vegas: Louie sang "Vesti la Giubba" and
I retaliated with "Honeysuckle Rose." *(Author's collection)*

Ginger Rogers on Bell Telephone's TV hour.

Filming *Aaron Slick*: The city sharper tempts farm girl Dinah Shore with a satchelful of money. Adele Jurgens, left, is my confederate.

(Author's collection)   *(Author's collection)*

On his fourteenth birthday, son David meets Casey Stengel, who assures him, "There's no future in pitchin' like yer father pitched."

(Author's collec

Joan Sutherland in *Travi* celebrating the twenty-fifth niversary of my de

(Author's collection)

Danny Kaye: An aria gets mugged.

Red Skelton: "I know I'm nuts, but if I keep 'em laughing, they'll never put me away." *(Author's collection)*

To Bob my dear friend always Red Skelton

Ezio Pinza, even when re-hearsing, exuded soulful sex appeal.

Lily Pons: "To act with me is very simple. I will move to-ward you—never move toward me."

Lawrence Tibbett really
savored the rich man's life.

Grace Moore, who often sang
Louise, and Gustave Charpen-
tier, who wrote it.

With Leontyne Price: Chalking up our names for posterity on girder for new Met. William Schuman, left, was president of Lincoln Center. *(Author's collection)*

8

The Midget Who Bit
Madame Butterfly

> *... the tragedy of singing: If you write a book, there it is.*
> *Paint, carve, it remains. But sing a song perfectly in your*
> *opera and it vanishes completely after the last quiver.*
> *Radio or records don't repeat it exactly as it was that night*
> *before that audience. It's that sense of being intangible*
> *and evanescent that singers suffer from.*
> —*Frances Alda:* Men, Women and Tenors

The life of the singer is incredibly fragile: It hangs by two thin cords in the throat, approximately the diameter of buttonhole thread. If not used correctly, they stretch and lose their elasticity. They are affected by damp or dry weather, by any change of climate, by air conditioning. Unlike the pianist's and violinist's instruments, they cannot be tuned. Dozens of distempers, bacteria, and neuroses can destroy them.

The nonclassical singer is subject to sudden changes in musical fashions that are as destructive as worn-out cords. Remember those lavish Warner Brothers musicals of the thirties? Dick Powell, who started as a crooner singing through a megaphone at a neighborhood movie house in Pittsburgh, sang in dozens of those films, from *Blessed Event* in 1932 to *Star-Spangled Rhythm*, and suddenly they went out of style. In 1945 Powell went looking for another career; abandoning his wavy hair and dimples, he transformed himself into the laconic, tough private eye in *Murder, My Sweet* and parlayed that character into a string of movie hits, plus successes in radio and television.

> *Powell was a rich man when he and his third wife, June Allyson, heard me at The Sands singing one of his numbers from a thirties musical, "I Only Have Eyes for You." When Jack Entratter introduced us at his table, he looked up glumly and said, "I wish I had the guts to sing again."*
>
> *But he seemed to have a more intense concern overshadowing his vacation here. I saw him several times in the town's clubs, staring in silence at the shows and at June. Still the open-face, all-American girl who might have lived next door to Andy Hardy, she waved "Hiya" to me. But Powell, withdrawn from the hubbub around him, never glanced at me or said another word. There was very little joy for them in this fun capital of the West.*
>
> *Jack, who knew everyone in Vegas, remembered June from the days when she was a dancer in New York's Copa, which he had managed. "They got problems," he said. "They came here to figure out what went wrong with the marriage."*
>
> *Dick's fanatic devotion to his career had led to divorce from his second wife, Joan Blondell; as she put it, "His telephones were jingling all the time."*
>
> *"What happened?" I asked Jack.*
>
> *"All that success, all that dough, and now he can't make*

it with his own wife. They have a son and an adopted
daughter—Dick goes in and out of impotency."
And Dick was faithful. He only had eyes for June.

Operatic fashions change with glacial speed, yet even here careers grow shorter and shorter. Giovanni Martinelli holds the record for longevity at the Met—thirty-two years. 1976 marked my thirty-first year. Dorothy Kirsten retired after thirty, and Caruso's entire career lasted twenty-five years. Ferruccio Tagliavini and a few other tenors performed only ten years at the Met.

Careers are speeded up today. With jet planes providing instant access to theaters all over the world, a first-rank star, adding income from recordings, television, and radio, can earn $500,000 a year. And fade into obscurity, worn-out in just five years.

Tenors and sopranos are particularly prone to disaster. The public pays the great ones up to $7,500 a night, and part of their thrill is similar to the circus artist's balancing of his bicycle and six children on the high wire: Will he make it? If the coloratura or tenor cracks on only *one* note, the critics instantly write that the performer is "slipping." And the end of a career comes swiftly.

Do you wonder that singers are tangled bundles of insecurities that pop out in grotesque hypochrondria, in gullibility and superstitions that would shame a witch doctor?

When I came to the Met, the makeup man was Papa Senz, a delightful Middle European who had created faces for the legends of the 1900s—Caruso, Chaliapin. He told me, "Caruso—you name thee sickness—he had it." Migraine headaches, skin rashes, a morbid fear of infections and falling out of bed; his throat was a never-ending terror because he smoked fifty to sixty powerful Egyptian cigarettes a day. His valet traveled with a custom-fitted trunk that carried atomizers and syringes, salt water, Seidlitz powders, assorted pills and nostrums that the tenor picked up everywhere in his tours. He carried his own supply of linen sheets (because he felt cotton caused his skin rashes) and pillows and a thick mattress, which were arranged around his bed to catch him if he fell out. He never did.

Caruso waged a constant war against his imagined infections. He changed outerclothes and underwear after a walk in the street, then took a bath. The hotel room was quickly sprayed with disinfectant, followed by a French perfume. "While he seet een my chair," Papa said, "he smoked and sprayed the throat and quick took from his vest pocket a little mirror to examine inside thee throat." He also carried two small bottles of salt water in his costume pockets to help clear the throat. He'd gargle onstage if necessary, and turn away from the audience to spit it out. Once he spit over the shoulder of Geraldine Farrar, and she promptly slapped his face.

He had to spit before an aria in *La Gioconda*, and chose the safest spot, a ship that was part of the set. Since then, tenors have been spitting on that ship before that aria—for good luck.

Feodor Chaliapin, a basso on the same Olympian level as Caruso, was afflicted with stage fright all his life. He eased it with vodka. As Papa Senz told it, Chaliapin would sit dozing in his dressing room while Senz worked his magic. Suddenly, he'd open his eyes, and inspect himself in the mirror. "Vot is diss face you giff me?"

"Mefistofele—"

"Not *Boris?* Holy mother! Send for de *Faust* score! I must see de score!"

The Met has a husband and wife package: She is an excellent mezzo-contralto, he is a dependable bass, and if the opera wants her, it has to take her husband. As a result, we get double-strength hypochondria. I always know when he's singing, because he wanders through the halls vocalizing "*Moooooo! Mmmmmooooo!*" My dressing room door is usually open: I'm gregarious. He and his wife always drop in, and they have an ailment for every night of the season and two for matinees: stomach plugged up . . . had bad meat last night . . . the eggs are not fresh in America . . . rusty water . . .

They always stick their tongues out to show they're

white and fuzzy, not healthy pink. "See, in the back, like a flame. Tonsilitis. Laryngitis," he laments. She complains of gasoline odors, noise in the hotel, carbon monoxide, air conditioning, cramps, and backache. But she has always given a first-rate performance. I am evidently their free therapist.

Many European singers are afraid to take baths before the show because they might catch cold. But why two or three days before? I have had to sing a romantic aria with a soprano whose aroma singed my eyebrows. The basso Nicola Moscona had a sense of smell as refined as his pitch. He could walk to the door of the rehearsal room and detect when a certain soprano had arrived. Since we had no air conditioning in the old Met, he refused to enter the room. This unhappy woman suffered from severe internal stresses, too: She would vent a stupefying gas. You could see it coming in the midst of an aria—a wistful look in her eyes, a clenching of her hands. Her partner could shift downstage, but the chorus had to bear the brunt.

At its worst, tension can actually make you lose your voice. I was singing a duet in *Otello* with Jimmy McCracken when his mouth opened wider . . . and wider . . . and no sound came out. He shook his head with an exasperated shrug and walked off the stage. I finished the duet with the prompter, yelling the notes from his cubbyhole at the footlights.

Singers are more credulous than horse players; they'll clutch at any tip that seems to promise escape from the laws of probability. I have dispensed the most outrageous nostrums to my colleagues on the assumption that they couldn't believe such nonsense, but I've had to stop deluding myself.

There is a widespread belief, particularly among tenors, that sex before a performance damages the high notes. This fear seems to weigh most heavily on the minds of the Latins. They abstain for several days. The wife of Mario del Monaco burst into Rudolf Bing's office and accused him of breaking up her marriage because he was using Mario in two and three shows a week.

When I sang *Rigoletto*, a young baritone, Giorgio, would stop into my dressing room to talk over interpretation of the role. It is possibly the most strenuous, the operatic equivalent of the uncut *Hamlet*. And, of course, he came up with the inevitable question. I played along with it:

> ME: (Casual shrug) *Oh, I enjoy it two or three times the morning before—*
>
> GIORGIO: Non posso! Non posso! *I stop three days before.*
>
> ME: (Incredulous) *Why? It develops the inspiration, the emotion.*
>
> GIORGIO: (Appalled) *It no hurt the upper register?*
>
> ME: *No, no. Remember Caruso?*
>
> GIORGIO: Si. *Every place he sing, a woman sue him for making a baby.*
>
> ME: *It even helps the lower notes. Especially one hour before the show.*
>
> GIORGIO: *Incredibile*! (He walks out with the gleam of revelation in his eyes.)

In his next performance, Giorgio had to hang onto the furniture to stand up.

Tommy Hayward listened to everybody's suggestions for improvement. He noticed that Mario del Monaco cupped his ear with his palm, to hear his own sound when he rehearsed. I told Tommy that Mario had worked out a way to hear himself even onstage. "He uses nose putty to push his ear lobe forward—like a radar disk."

When I saw Tommy onstage in *Traviata*, I collapsed against the wall. He'd put so much putty behind both ears that he seemed to be wearing headphones on a space ship. The audience laughed all the way to Venus.

A new bass asked me, as I walked by his room, "What do you gargle with when your throat's tired?"

"Mr. Clean."

Some weeks later he embraced me with thanks. "Mr. Clean is great—once you get over the bubbles!"

The frailty of the voice has supported alchemists and quacks for centuries. Some years ago, my nasal membranes went so dry I had to push my voice with all my energy to reach the last act. I shuttled from doctor to doctor, who prescribed nose sprays that made me even drier. After five years, I was ready to abandon singing. Then Lucine Amara, who had been through the same trauma, suggested simple pure glycerine, applied with a bit of cotton in the nose. A 49-cent bottle of Saint Lucine's elixir saved my career.

Understandably, almost every singer has a talisman, a good luck charm, a fetish to propitiate the gods in advance. Opera people never wish you good luck before a performance. They say, *"Merde"* or *"In bocca el lupo"* (Into the wolf's mouth). The assumption is that the gods will always double-cross you, and so if you expect disaster you can fool them.

Caruso was convinced cigarettes could never harm him as long as he wore a dried anchovy around his neck. Martinelli kissed pictures of his entire family before he went on. In our Newark *Aïda*, he made his entrance and remembered he'd forgotten to kiss one child. He ran off, kissed all the pictures while the orchestra repeated frantically, then entered again.

Lilli Lehmann warned her friends: Never put slippers on a chair or table before the performance. Luisa Tetrazzini pitched a jeweled knife into the floor of her room; if it stuck one out of three times, she knew all would go well. A soprano with whom I sang in San Francisco made her entrance assisted by a kick in the rear from a friendly stagehand.

I checked into a hotel on tour with Jan Peerce. The suite he had reserved on the seventh floor was not available, and he absolutely refused the offer of one on a lower floor. "It's something I've never done," he explained. So he shared mine on the eleventh floor.

I worked with a Spanish tenor in Buenos Aires who had a framed photograph of a distinguished, fatherly-looking gentleman on his dressing table. Before he went on, he spat vehemently at the face: the teacher who told him to abandon singing.

Favorite charms include bracelets or necklaces or stockings or any piece of costume worn in a debut or smash hit. A bass at the Met has worn the same athletic supporter for about twenty years. His wife is constantly patching it. When he retires, I suppose he'll have it bronzed.

Many states require taxi drivers and garbage collectors to be licensed; beauticians in New York state must have 1,000 hours of training. In most cities, even dogs need a license to walk the streets. But anyone who can hammer a piano or hum a scale may become a singing teacher.

My instructor, Mr. Margolis, who also taught Jerome Hines, had his studio next to Carnegie Hall. Occasionally, I'd bring friends up there to hear the incredible sounds billowing out of the open windows of a studio opposite to us in the Hall. That teacher operated on a unique theory: Women could place their voice up front—"put it in the mask" is the trade term—to achieve maximum resonance by singing "meow!" Men could place their voice best by howling "woof! woof!" So the air was filled for hours with barking and meowing, amplified by the passing poodles and schnauzers on 57th Street. With ten in a class at $10 per half hour, this man was coining about $500 a day. And not one cat or dog received a cent royalty.

For his prize pupils, this charlatan would open, at no extra charge, a large thermos jug. "Take a deep breath—that's the wonderful air I brought back from La Scala!"

We achieve some compensation for our insecurities with outbreaks of temperament and rebellion. Some singers blossom out with the arrogance and temper of Fafner the dragon. I must admit I have always considered my self-esteem to be sweetly reasonable, mainly because I've never had to claw and club for what I wanted. And still my wife tells me, "I've heard you do it better."

Ego should not be confused with an empty head.

Frank Corsaro, the director, has said, "If you want a tenor to look as if he's thinking, have him walk down a flight of stairs."

Ferruccio Tagliavini and I left the backstage door of the Met on 40th Street and walked past a newsstand at the corner of Broadway. A Senate committee was hearing testimony on criminal organization from a self-admitted expert and the afternoon newspaper announced in large black type: VALACHI SINGS TODAY.

Ferruccio, perplexed by the important headline, muttered, "Hope he's not another tenor."

The tenor is thinking constantly of the care and feeding of his high Cs. His world revolves around these notes, and very little else exists for him. When I sing with a certain VIP tenor, he is so preoccupied with what's going to happen in his throat that I feel I'm doing a solo recital. We were near the end of a duet in *Andrea Chenier*, with half a page of music to go, when he walked offstage and motioned me to follow. I assumed he was ill and hurried after him while the orchestra continued the duet.

In the wings he lamented in Italian that his suspenders were broken and he was about to drop his trousers. I could find only one button missing, and tried to persuade him the suspenders still had five strong buttons to uphold his modesty. But no—he *knew* he would lose them. I ran to find the seamstress and while she sewed the button, I hurried onto the stage so the audience would not become alarmed. The tenor made it back to center stage in time to hit the final high ones.

I sang this same opera with a tenor, world-famous for his inflamed ego, at the Teatro Colon in Buenos Aires. The national radio had its headquarters in the same building. Sometime during the third act, a quickie revolution broke out; soldiers marched in to take over the radio and some came backstage with submachine guns to secure the opera house, too.

Our tenor walked off after his big aria, to a tremendous chandelier-shaking ovation, and after a few minutes noticed the unmusical types, unshaven and muscular, in dirty camouflage suits and boots, leaning on those heavy guns. "What is this?" he asked me.

"It's a revolution."

He nodded modestly. "It's always a revolution when I sing."

"Di quella pira" in *Trovatore* is a killer aria; so many tenors dread it that they often have it transposed a half tone lower. When the conductor came in to tell Giuseppe de Stefano this was the only orchestration available that night, he said cheerfully, "That's okay, maestro. You conduct any key you like—I sing the high C."

The Met curtain once closed too soon on Kurt Baum's aria. He simply pushed the curtain open with his sword to sing the last note. Later, after some difficulty on a high one, he came into my room dejectedly. "You notice, Bob, when I go for a C there's dust flying all over the stage? For everybody else they spray with water—for me they sweep."

Jussi Bjoerling, a dear, kind friend, was nevertheless a tenor. When we recorded the quartet from *Rigoletto*, Jussi's voice soared over all of us on the first take. The conductor told him to be more subdued for the second take—and we could not hear his voice at all.

"What's the matter?" the conductor asked.

Jussi insisted, "Since I begin the quartet, it's my *solo!*" And the first take was the one that was pressed.

Over the years I have sung that thrilling duet, "Solenne in quest'ora," dozens of times in the third act of *Forza del Destino*. Afterwards the tenor, who appears to be mortally wounded, is carried off on a stretcher. When I sang it with one ovation-happy tenor, the stretcher-bearers were new and eager. They lugged him away while the applause continued. He leaped off, took a couple of bows, lay down again and gestured—"Take me away."

Wives of tenors get into the act, too. The day after one of Mr. Bing's newly mounted productions opened to unanimous dismay, one wife called the wife of the man who had sung the leading role.

Mrs. A: "It was just what I'd expected. Are you satisfied?"

Mrs. B: "Not as much as you are."

Prima donnas insist on their bows, dead or alive, no matter what the dramatic continuity requires. It's a shoddy custom, permitted in the European provincial houses, and many artists can't break the habit, even at the Met. Montserrat Caballé is a singer of highest international rank, and yet . . .

In Act IV of *Trovatore* she sang Leonore's impassioned "Tu vedrai che amore in terra," which of course unleashed a thunderclap of applause. She bowed several times and exited. As I made my entrance and began a recitative detailing some plot secrets, I noticed out of the side of my eye that she was returning for more bows, and since she was not supposed to see me, I retreated to a dark corner of the set. Finally, she had her fill of bravos and walked off. I finished my recitative, she reappeared—gasped, as if she had not seen me a moment ago—and we went into a tumultuous duet which set the scene for the climax. Again applause, again she stepped to the footlights for her bows, and again I was left upstage with anticlimax all over my face.

> In that fondly remembered Golden Age of opera before the First World War, audiences must have been desperately hungry to suspend disbelief in anything their prima donnas deigned to hand out. Nellie Melba on her tours around America played Desdemona so theatrically that women wept after Otello strangled her. If she was sufficiently applauded, Mme. Melba would rise from her deathbed and signal stagehands to wheel on a piano, at which she accompanied herself for an encore—"Home Sweet Home." After this ovation, she stretched out dead again on the bed, and poor Otello had to stagger on with the final five minutes.
>
> Melba was a prima donna assoluta, absolute in the sense of a sixteenth-century monarch. In the second act cafe scene of Bohème, the young Fritzi Scheff sang Musetta and aroused the audience of Covent Garden to "bravos" and "well-dones." Melba, infuriated by this lèse-majesté, stalked off the stage and refused to continue as Mimi. The manager was forced to bring down the

curtain and announce that Miss Scheff had suddenly taken ill, but Mme. Melba, knowing the audience's disappointment, had graciously consented to sing the mad scene from Lucia. *And she did, without changing costume. Whatever the opera might be, Melba wore her own grandiose, all-purpose gown of brocades, silks, and velvets, set off by genuine jewels from her admirers; gold chains and necklaces draped her monumental chest, creating a glitter that preceded her entrance.*

Today, only a few *prima donnas* dare to uphold their grand tradition. But they do their best.

Shortly after I came to the Met I sang my first Lord Ashton in a *Lucia* that starred Lily Pons. I was flattered, and a little thrilled by the prospect of meeting her. She was the Met's glamour girl, who enlivened *Lakme* with a brief, diaphanous costume, a bare stomach, and a jewel in her navel. I rehearsed enthusiastically with our tenor Ferruccio Tagliavini and yet by the time the curtain went up I still had not met Miss Pons. I made my entrance, sang the first scene (in which she does not appear), and when I came offstage, an assistant stage manager took me by the elbow and rushed me to her room. "Miss Pons wants to see you," he said.

(SCENE: Miss Pons' dressing room. The usual grimness of this cell is enlivened by her Chinese silk dressing gown, whose silver brocade, under the makeup lights, makes her entire five-foot figure glow. Her legendary legs are hidden by the gown; her large, soft brown eyes and gamine face are the essence of late-1940s chic. Four Persian cats are curled decoratively at her feet. As I enter, they attack. One claws my wig; another, my leg. The other two ad-lib hostility.)

MISS PONS: (Extending her hand) *A great pleasure.*

ME: (Shaking her hand) *It's my pleasure, too.*

(A quick double-take as I realize I should have kissed her hand. I brush off a cat to cover this gaffe.)

MISS PONS: *You may wonder why I asked you to visit today.*

ME: *Why, yes . . .*

MISS PONS: *To act with me is very simple. You must remember only two things. One: I will move toward you. Two: Never move toward me. This way, you will always know where you are, and I will always know where you are.*

ME: *I understand.*

MISS PONS: *Most important—in Act Two before I faint, you must move the chair instantly so I can fall into it. You understand?*

ME: *I understand.*

MISS PONS: *Very good. Until we meet onstage—*

(A wave of the hand dismisses me. As I turn to exit, I see that one of the cats has relieved itself on my boot.)

Our distant duets came off perfectly. And even when we embraced, I knew I was somewhere in the same city with a great star.

Zinka Milanov, who loved to be admired but was much too honest with herself to be arrogant, occasionally had a relapse. We were chatting at a reception when a young man gushed, "Madame, I love you! I loved your Gioconda, I loved your Desdemona, your Aïda—I just want to kiss the hand of—"

"What's the matter? You didn't like my Leonore?"

On first hearing Montserrat Caballé, Zinka remarked, "She reminds me of the early me."

She even argued with Toscanini on political matters, claiming that Trieste belonged to her homeland, Yugoslavia. He silenced her with "Madame," pointing to her head, "if you had up here what you have here"—pointing to her overhanging bosom—"you would be the greatest soprano of all."

There seems to be a direct correlation between the upper register and high temper. And when tenors and sopranos battle, they approach the storm and fire of *Götter-*

dämmerung. The feud is a grand operatic tradition that has always been with us.

Olive Fremstad and Johanna Gadski, two formidable Wagnerian antagonists of the 1900s, drew genuine blood in *Die Walküre.* The arm of Fremstad, playing Sieglinde, somehow scraped or was pulled (as she charged) across the metal-studded breastplate of Gadski (Brünnhilde). Fremstad remained in character and let the blood flow during the curtain call. At the end of the applause, she rubbed the blood off on Gadski's face.

Geraldine Farrar and Caruso had a realistic battle in the last scene of a 1915 *Carmen.* She twisted and fumed so angrily while he sang that he clutched her wrists to keep her still. She bit his wrist. Caruso, bleeding, furiously shoved her away and she landed on her *derrière.* After the curtain fell, she was up and kicking, pulling Caruso's hair. When the curtain rose for the calls, they stepped forward bloody, but bowed, and when it fell, they renewed the battle.

Grace Moore nailed Jan Kiepura, the notoriously vain Polish tenor, for a lesser offense. She was a warm and gracious beauty, but when she had to defend her position onstage, she became a slugger.

Kiepura had pulled a sly trick in *Bohème.* For the Café Momus scene, the tables were decorated with fruit. Kiepura picked up a lemon, cut it open and sucked on it as she sang. Grace's lips puckered up, in helpless response, and her sound suffered.

"I moved fast," she said. "In the next performance." Kiepura had been directed to move his chair down front, to sit with Grace, as he sang "Che gelida manina." Grace had a friend nail the chair to the floor.

"It ruined his whole aria," she told me. "He kept tugging at it and cursing the stagehands. He just couldn't believe a lady like me would do a thing like that."

In Corsica she sang *Tosca* with a tough old campaigner as Scarpia. In rehearsal, he placed her carefully on the couch for the rape scene as directed, so she would be in position to sing "Vissi d'arte." In performance he threw her to the floor so hard she had no breath to start the aria. Grace struck back in the following performance. At the end of Act II, Tosca kills Scarpia, sets two candles at his head and places a crucifix on his chest.

"I went into town that morning and bought a crucifix that weighed thirty pounds, and I dropped it on his groin. He screamed bloody murder and lay so still I thought I *had* murdered him. But he revived for the curtain call. I wouldn't take a bow until I had my manager on one side and my chauffeur on the other."

Grace was bested only once, to my knowledge—by an extra. Somewhere in the Midwest on a tour, Grace was singing Cio-Cio-San. The city had a strict child labor law which prevented hiring a small boy to play her son, Trouble. Our personnel man saw the Ringling circus near-by and hired a thirty-five-year-old midget with a sweet, unlined face.

In the last act, Madame Butterfly hugs her child for a poignant farewell, sets the boy down and commits suicide. She clasped the midget to her chest—and couldn't set him down. He was nibbling on her bosom. Her aria was going nowhere; If she couldn't put him down, she couldn't kill herself. She glared over his shoulder at the assistant stage manager and moaned, "Get this little bastard off me!"

The midget finally let go and walked to his chair, murmuring, "Thanks for the mammary."

Mary Garden complained that the baritone playing Scarpia opposite her was too short; since she never weighed more than 110 pounds and stood five feet four, he must have been Tom Thumb. He played it anyhow, to Mary's discomfort. As she sang her "Vissi d'arte," reclining on the couch, he pretended to comfort her while he ran his hands over her body, tickling and tweaking. Mary tried to swat him away, then curled into a fetal position to protect herself. Finally, she leaped up and ran to the footlights to end the aria, cracking notes all the way.

A short tenor has a genuine problem maintaining his dignity vis-à-vis the soprano who is taller and heavier.

Enrico di Giuseppe, who has had a fulfilling career at the Met, told me how he grew above his five feet five. He lamented to his teacher, Richard Bonelli, that lack of height would handicap his career. Bonelli gave him ten words that changed his life: "Rico, you will have to sing taller than anyone else."

Frances Alda, who possessed a monumental *poitrine*, is believed to be the first soprano to sing "Vissi d'arte" while reclining. The tremendous sensation she created may have been partly the audience's surprise that her profile was the same lying down as standing up.

It's ridiculous for a baritone to attempt rape on a soprano who weighs forty or fifty pounds more than he does. I've known Toscas who say, "Please don't put me down on the couch—I'll never get up." That's why it was so refreshing when Dorothy Kirsten appeared for a rehearsal. She had been a protégée of Grace Moore and kept herself appropriately svelte.

I asked solicitously, "Shall we try for the couch?"

She looked me square in the eyes and said, "Put me on the floor, baby, and let's go."

Anxieties do not always, of course, inflate a singer's self-esteem. Sometimes the artist simply cannot cope with the demands of everyday life and becomes a pair of glorious vocal cords attached to a Baby Leroy.

Bruno Landi probably had one of the most beautiful lyric tenor voices of his time. You could not resist liking him; he was generous, and as kind and cherubic as a young priest. He performed at the Met for many years, yet he wore a silver tag-holder under his shirt that carried his name, his current address, and his phone number. He was afraid to walk across the street, and would stand on the corner, waiting for someone to guide him. He sang in the United States and England for years, yet he never learned any English beyond the value of dollars and pounds in *lire* and possibly "hello," "good-bye," and "I don't know." He never had to learn "yes" and "no" because he could not make these decisions without his wife.

She was an excellent soprano, and on the week she had to sing in New York, Bruno and I were scheduled to do *Barber of Seville* in Mexico City. Since he could never fly alone, and I knew Italian by courtesy of Verdi and Puccini, she urged me to take the same flight. "Make sure that he gets on the plane, and off the plane, and he's fed." I nodded mechanically as she listed all the calamities he could fall into. I thought she was being overanxious.

Since we could not book two seats together, Bruno sat directly in front of me. As we taxied for takeoff, he brought out two rosaries and began praying; he turned his head several times to make sure I was there, and I saw the perspiration flowing down his face. Once in the air, I wanted to shave. The seats were crowded together, so I helped myself out of my seat by pulling on the back of Bruno's. His seat tilted about an inch, and he screamed, "Help! The plane is crashing!" (My translations are only approximate since his Italian was always *prestissimo*.)

"Bruno, Bruno, it's *me!*" I assured him.

He relaxed a little, but asked me to get two barf bags for the landing. He did not need them. I took him by the hand to the customs station and I handed over my passport. Bruno could not find his. He searched himself, the customs men searched through his luggage for it, and Bruno began to cry. I do not mean moan or lament—he cried like a baby awakened in the middle of the night, his body shuddering with hysterical sobs. The security police arrived now, and Bruno begged them not to put him in prison—he would die there.

I ran back to the plane: The passport was on the floor in front of his seat. I checked him into the hotel and then we had to face the problem of dinner. He had been told of Montezuma's revenge—what was safe to eat? I found the cleanest, brightest restaurant, but nothing was suitable. Salad gave him gas, chicken had small bones that stick in the throat, pork had trichinosis, liver burned his heart. He settled for beef broth.

Next day we took a cab to the theater for rehearsal at 2 P.M. The theater was shut tight. An hour later, the stage door was still closed. Bruno was certain the opera had been canceled or this was not Tuesday. I found a phone to call the impresario, but that took a half hour because the Mexico City system at that time was like talking through a water hose. I was informed the rehearsal would start soon. Time has little meaning for artists in warm countries.

Well, I led Bruno by the hand through the next two days. I found a barber to shave him, and the hotel valet dressed him. We had dinner about four o'clock before the opening, and in the middle of his chicken broth he choked and coughed. He remembered he'd found frogs in his throat that morning and now—he must have a voice teacher, to work himself back into shape.

"I don't speak Spanish," I said. "How the hell can we find one we trust?"

He began blinking, fighting back tears. "I cannot appear in my condition."

The manager of the restaurant went through the phone book with me until I found a teacher who spoke English, at the other end of the city, of course. We took a cab out there, and the teacher promised to put Bruno into a taxi after the session. I went back to the hotel to nap.

I was awakened by a panicky call from Bruno: "The taxi driver can't find the hotel."

"Where are you?"

"How should I know?"

"Can't you see a street sign?"

"If I can't speak Spanish, how can I read Spanish? Call the police!"

"Bruno," I said, "why don't you just put the driver on the phone and let him talk to our Mexican operator?"

He arrived at the hotel half an hour before the 9 o'clock curtain, which was lucky because the actual curtain time would be 10:30. I was making up in the theater when, through the wall, I heard Bruno screaming, and being threatened by yells in Spanish. In the corridor, Bruno was surrounded by the manager and his assistants.

Bruno would not walk onstage until he had his fee check in his hand. That's what his contract called for, and collecting his pay was one fear Bruno had overcome. The official who signed paychecks was not there at night. The curtain was held up another half hour while the assistants scurried around, looking for the man who signed checks. Bruno warned that all this commotion was destroying his voice.

I took Bruno aside. "Will you take cash?

He answered carefully, "From who?"

"The box office." That did it. They counted out the pesos into an envelope, which I sewed into his costume, and the curtain rose. Bruno straightened himself up into a passable cavalier, Count Almaviva, and the show began to roll. My "Largo al factotum" went well, followed by the scenes with Dr. Bartolo and the letter and Rosina, and then I faked the introduction on my guitar for the Count's serenade to Rosina, "Se il mio nome." (The actual guitar music is played by a musician in the wings.) Bruno walked over to me, turned his back to the audience and stuck out his tongue. "Roberto, see? It's all red. *I can't sing!*"

I had to take several deep breaths. The entire company and the whole auditorium were in the hands of an unpredictable child. "Bruno," I whispered through my teeth, "you've *got* to sing."

"Impossible," he mumbled, "impossible to sing."

I strummed the guitar as I strolled around, nudging him into position while he kept sticking out his tongue and mumbling, "Impossible, I'm sick—impossible." And the tears were rolling. The audience enjoyed this heartily because it all seemed to be part of the action: The resourceful Figaro encouraging the hapless Count to sing.

The lunacy of the moment hit me like a wet rag in the face. "I got you this far," I hissed, "and you're not going to ruin this scene. If you don't sing, goddamn you, I'll break this guitar over your head."

I raised it with my left hand, spun him around with the right, the guitarist struck the opening note . . . and Bruno sang the loveliest serenade I have ever heard.

9

The Bangkok Groupie

In the nineteenth century Adelina Patti toured America in a custom-built railroad car, a home away from home: walls and ceilings covered in tapestry, except for the drawing room, where the ceiling featured paintings of the Muses by eminent French artists; all furniture upholstered in silk damask, lamps of rolled gold, a bath of solid silver and, to open the front door, a key of eighteen-karat gold. Lillian Nordica made her way in a car named Brünnhilde, which boasted a music room, three bedrooms, bath, kitchen, and servants' quarters. Nellie Melba's car carried her own collection of paintings, silver candelabra, silk sheets, and several gold alarm clocks—she was always punctual. Everywhere the prima donnas stopped, they were received as royalty, and in fact some were very close to it. The Duc d'Orleans, pretender to the throne of France, was Mme. Melba's lover.

In the 1930s, the owner of a southern railroad would hitch his private car onto the Met's ten-car train at Baltimore. During the week in Georgia, the rail magnate provided lavish dinner parties for the cast in his car. On the way back north, the Met train stopped at his farm in Maryland for a day of relaxation and free play—he sponsored milking contests in his cow barns—and then he served a farewell banquet.

I was born too late. After World War II, the Met toured sixteen productions with 500 people in Pullmans (the scenery and equipment moved on twenty-seven flatcars); and as expenses rose, the number of cars and productions declined. By 1972, we were down to eight shows, transported by truck, while we squeezed into two chartered planes.

The Met played wherever there was a theater and an audience, sometimes in great new culture centers, more often in converted movie palaces, arenas, convention halls, auditoriums that presented ice-skating and roller-derby shows. *Hänsel und Gretel* was presented in a hall from which a circus had just departed, leaving two elephants in the basement to be picked up several days later on the circus's return swing. The elephants were chained to the concrete floor and happily filling up on hay. After the overture started, the building shook like a ship in a storm. Officials checked the elephants and found them quietly munching away. The curtain rose on the first scene and again the floor quivered. Stagehands this time caught the naughty elephants slamming their trunks on the building's huge iron boiler. Two stagehands were delegated to throw hay at the animals to distract them, and the opera carried on. The elephants' reaction may be one of the best critiques of *Hänsel und Gretel* that I've ever heard.

After a few weeks on the road, the Met cars did have a certain fragrant resemblance to a circus menagerie. Many of the artists traveled with their wives, and the European spouses were delighted to cook for their husbands. So many things can go wrong in a six-week tour, with its unfamiliar hotels and restaurants, that home-cooked meals were a welcome reassurance. But the women, and many men, would try to duplicate those fragrant Spanish, Polish, Hungarian, Italian, French specialties on the train. They busily installed Sterno heaters and electric hot plates in the tiny compartments; during rehearsals, the cooks would journey into town to pick up fresh chickens, cheeses, onions, sausages, oregano, garlic, so that a walk through the train corridors was literally staggering. Many cooked after the performance, as the train moved on to another city, and the rocking of the cars, together with the pungent aromas, stimulated some of the company with tender stomachs to various states of nausea.

The train attendants were not a happy crew. I recall the moment, as we entered the dining car in New York, that one steward looked to the other and moaned, "Oh Christ! We got *them* again!" Opera artists, having visited some unheard-of cities, had unique tastes and diets with which they bedeviled the waiters: "I want you to use this Dijon mustard for my dressing." "*Al dente, al dente*, you understand?" "I want Hungarian red pepper, not the sand that comes out of a bag." "Put these greens in with my chicken soup." "Don't you know what broccoli is?"

Tipping was furtive. The Met management did its best, understandably, to hold down expenses, and our per diem, for food and hotels, was modest. During the early fifties, it was about $20 a day for principals, $8 for chorus. The principal performers, as a matter of status, left a generous bounty. But the chorus people and musicians usually sat until their waiter went back to the kitchen before leaving a few coins and making a hasty getaway.

Members of the company paired off to economize on hotel rooms. One of the Met's older staff conductors teamed up with a frugal percussionist to discover, among the magnolias of a Deep South city, an equivalent of the Times Square fleabag. That evening our maestro did not arrive at the theater by eight o'clock, as required, and the assistant stage manager could not call him because the inn had no switchboard.

Eight-fifteen passed, and still no conductor. Another assistant was dispatched to search the main streets. At eight twenty-five the maestro (let's name him Antonio) hobbled in, helped by the percussionist. Antonio, groaning and grimacing in pain, was doubled over like a collapsed puppet. I waved him into my dressing room, and while our tenor poured a triple shot of brandy, Antonio poured out his grand-operatic tale of low farce and incredible chance.

The May day had been hot and dusty. In the hotel room he had taken off his clothes and spectacles (without them he was nearly blind) to slide into a cooling tub. He dried off and turned to the mirrored oak chiffonier for a change of underwear. The drawer was warped by age and dampness—"also the evil eye"—so that he had to struggle to open it. The conductor bent down, lifted out his shorts, and pushed the drawer hard to shut it—right on his other baton.

"Impossible!" I exclaimed.

"*Assolutemente!*" he moaned. "If we try this scene onstage we never reach such perfect timing in one hundred years!"

Trapped by the drawer, Antonio had fainted against the chiffonier. His roommate revived him with a wastebasket of cold water, dressed him, and lifted him into a taxi for the theater. Dressing had not been easy, because the maestro's vitals had swelled to the size of grapefruit, so that he could not straighten up.

And that was the position in which Antonio conducted a tender *Traviata*—leaning against the podium, feet planted wide apart, and cursing softly all the way.

Card games helped the days fade into night and into sunrise again on the train: bridge, pinochle but mainly poker. Musicians generally played among themselves; among singers, the opera caste system prevailed, although occasionally assisting singers sat in with the principals, on the theory that losing to a soloist might help one's career. It never did. I have never been a sharp poker player; I do concentrate but I'm not inscrutable in my bluffing—I couldn't even bluff my own mother. Occasionally I sat in with Salvatore Baccaloni, Pinza, and Tagliavini, who played in Italian with great gusto and whoops of triumph as they slammed down their winning hands. Pinza treated a half-dollar *con amore*: He played to win. His purse, which he set on the table, was a leather pouch with drawstrings, out of the sixteenth century. Baccaloni's game was as confused as his English; he played because it gave him an opportunity to clown around. Tagliavini vocalized with the "Pepsi-Cola hits the spot" jingle when he wasn't chattering about his girls. It was a jolly quartet.

One night, after my performance had gone particularly well, I developed a winning streak, drawing to full houses like a riverboat gambler. The air around the tables changed as swiftly as if we'd crossed a tunnel into Alaska. Except for Baccaloni, who poked into my pockets, pretending to pull out cards with a mad glee. Tagliavini stopped talking, and Pinza, who resembled a burly Sicilian Don, glared at me balefully. After I was $100 ahead, I realized I might not have great luck when I sang with these men; I immediately developed lapses of memory, losing heavily enough to break even, and I bowed gracefully out of the game, for the rest of my career.

The Cincinnati Zoo Opera: I played my first Barber of Seville *for the Met with Pinza as Basilio and Baccaloni as Dr. Bartolo. It was outdoors, and, thankfully, the young prompter was hidden in the bushes; Figaro must be very precise and accurate to pick up the hundreds of cues that volley among the performers. I had studied this opera with the greatest Barber of all, Giuseppe de Luca, but Pinza and Baccaloni held all the cards: It was their language. Just for the hell of it they ad-libbed in rowdy circles around me, and I couldn't recognize any of the cues I had so laboriously worked out with de Luca. I felt my characterization beginning to unravel. The young man in the bushes started to scream wildly—he thought we couldn't hear him—and this received answering roars from the lions in the zoo.*

Baccaloni took pity now, and tossed my lines to me—and lost his own cues. This threw Pinza into uncontrollable laughter, and he fed lines to both of us—all out of sequence. Now Baccaloni broke up, and I stood there sputtering, desperate enough to slug both of them. Baccaloni pulled me out of it, and we ended to great applause. The local critics hailed the "gleeful exuberance" of the production. Fortunately, very few critics understood Italian.

When the train reached our headquarters town, the night games were carefully carried over to the hotel rooms. Giuseppe di Stefano was one of the passionate gamblers. He played all night before a 2 P.M. matinee of *Rigoletto* in Minneapolis. At 1:45, a taxi pulled up to the stage door, and he ran out, unshaven and reeking of tobacco, directly to the stage and into the first scene without makeup. The tenor's role is high and very difficult; he was young, not yet thirty, and sang it without too much extra effort. After a few years of smoking and gambling and other all-night games, he had to force his tones.

Money never troubled him; he ran his fees up to the skies with a little gimmick that he showed me with a guileless, boyish pride. Friends sent him cablegrams from Rome and Milan and Buenos Aires—"Can you come for ten performances at $8,000 each?"—and when he negotiated a fee, he'd pull one of these out of his pocket—"I just have an offer from La Scala."

He made his debut at the Met with me shortly after he arrived in America, a likable, wonderfully gifted, and impossibly handsome young man. Only his English was shaky, so he asked me to stand by at his first press conference. Came the inevitable question:
"What did you do before you sang?"
"I study to be a priest."
"Why did you give that up?"
He looked at me, shrugged and replied, "I lika the girls."
When he sang his last concert with Maria Callas at Carnegie Hall, I went backstage at intermission. He embraced me warmly, but he was tired. Maria had called

*at five in the morning to come cheer her up, he said,
because she was nervous. Now, his throat was itchy and
did I have a cough drop? I gave him one. He sang much
better in the second half. At the end of his bows, he took
the cough drop out of his pocket and held it up so I could
see he hadn't needed it. I suppose the drop had served its
purpose as a charm.*

Mario del Monaco carried a folding rule in his pocket,
to measure the type sizes on our advertising posters. If any
name was larger than his, the tenor refused to go on until
the offending poster was taken down. Or another was put
up, with his name in the largest type.

As di Stefano dressed for a performance in Philadelphia, he noticed that the program billed Franco Corelli in a
coming attraction as "The Greatest Tenor in the World." Di
Stefano balked: "I no sing with this insult."

He shed his costume, dressed and walked out to his
car. Opera officials caught up with him in the parking lot, to
beg him not to disappoint the sold-out house. He suggested
he might be able to recover his voice if all the offensive
programs were destroyed. Management agreed.

Pierre Monteux, of the flaring white mustache and
twinkling eyes—all he needed was a flowing white beard to
play Santa, he loved children so much—conducted on one
tour with great élan, even though he was over eighty. We sat
around the table in the dining car, and several parents
displayed photos of their children. "Maestro, my daughter,
Helen, three and a half."

He examined it, beaming. "Ah, *jolie, très jolie.*"

"Maestro, this is my boy, David, only twelve and he
wants to be an engineer."

"*Vraiment?* And so handsome, too." He opened his
wallet and took out a snapshot cracked at the edges. "My
son, Claude, the flutist, forty-one."

Touring for six weeks with your fellow artists, sleeping
head-to-head and separated by thin compartment or hotel
walls, forces you to see fissures in their lives that you would
rather not see. And, worse, there is often a moment of crisis

in which, much later, you feel you could have done something to prevent the wretched crackup. But then you realize you're not living in an operatic scenario, which can be rearranged or cut.

Another hot, dry day in a southern city: Most of the company was cooling off in the hotel pool. Among them, an up-and-coming tenor and his lover, a ballerina. He was married and their relationship, from what I could see, had been going on for several years.

I walked into the lobby and noticed the tenor's wife at the reception desk: The clerk was handing a key to her. I had met her before and liked her, but I sided with my professional colleague. She obviously had arrived without notice; no doubt she had picked up the key to his room, which was next door to mine. Should I warn him? Could I head her off?

I stepped into the elevator and greeted her. Should I suggest lunch, to get her out of the hotel? But, of course, she would want to have lunch with him. I could offer only a half-hearted "You'll like this town," and entered my room to change for the pool.

A few moments later, she was hammering on my door. When I opened it, she demanded, "Who's the woman? Her underwear's all over the place! Where is he?"

He was probably at the pool with the dancer. "I really don't know," I said. "He's not singing tonight."

She noticed my trunks. "Is he swimming?"

"I don't think so. I haven't seen him all day." She stood there, quivering. I took her elbow gently and asked, although I felt it was too late, "Won't you have lunch? There's a restaurant—"

She ran down the corridor and down the stairway. I turned back into the room, stretched out and tried to take a nap. The climactic scene would be played out at the pool, and I did not need to see it.

The denouement: Divorce, marriage to the ballet girl, and he continues singing for the Met.

I slept a great deal on the road. I was dozing before the evening performance of *Trovatore*, and suddenly I heard, as if in a dream, a woman's screams and thuds, chairs falling. I sat up, put my ear to the wall. It was the room of the tenor with whom I was to sing that night, and from the sound of the woman's cries, he was beating up his wife.

We'd dined together frequently; she was a charming, vibrant woman, he a rather withdrawn esthete, and they had happily displayed snapshots of their children, living in Milan. As the cries continued, I called Charlie Kullman, from his room on the other side of mine. We considered the possibility of calling the hotel manager, or our company manager. We could have, I suppose, rapped on the door and inquired what the hell was going on. But neither of us could face that—how would she look? bloody? And I had to sing with the man.

The wife appeared at the theater that night, calm, lovely as ever in heavy St. Tropez makeup and dark rose sunglasses, as large as auto headlights. And her husband delivered a poetic, impassioned performance, one of his best.

We recorded together in Florence a few years later. Marion was eating lunch alone in the hotel dining room, and the tenor's wife joined her. In the woman-to-woman conversation, she revealed that he beat her often, evidently to relieve his tensions before a performance.

Sponsoring committees in almost every city laid on dinner parties and receptions. Some members of the Metropolitan Opera's board of directors even put in appearances for the better parties, usually in the South. Oh, those buffets in Atlanta!

(SCENE: Party for the principal singers, in a multistory French restaurant in Atlanta. A buffet table, decorated with floral arrangements and large cornucopias of wax fruit. Dishes steaming with shrimp creole, lobster newburg, chicken cacciatore; cold platters of *saumon en croute*, patés, roast beef, Smithfield ham. I turn my back to this and resolutely eat a fresh fruit salad.

TIME: About 11 P.M.)

A WOMAN: *Mr. Merrill, when do you eat before a performance?*

ME: *At four o'clock.*

A WOMAN: *Wouldn't you like to eat now?*

ME: (Indicating the salad) *I am.*

PORTLY BARITONE: (Overloading a plate, to A TENOR) *I'm taking this for my wife.*

A TENOR: (Gulping lobster and shrimp simultaneously) *What I wouldn't give for a good pastrami sandwich.*

(Several SINGERS enter, carrying their leather music portfolios. One opens hers, spreads a plastic bag and inserts fried chicken, ham, beef slices, boiled shrimp, cinnamon rolls.)

MISS PORTFOLIO: (To me) *I'm taking this for my mother.*

DOUBLE-CHIN BASSO: (Hungrily biting into a wax apple) *Chrissakes, that's a dirty trick!*

(A commotion on the floor below. There I find the PORTLY BARITONE sitting on the floor, breathing heavily, his shirt collar open; he clutches a chicken leg in one hand. A DOCTOR examines him with stethoscope.)

DOCTOR: (To HEADWAITER) *Call an ambulance.*

MEMBER OF MET BOARD: (To ANOTHER MEMBER) *You know, we could save substantially on per diem if they would let chorus and musicians eat at these affairs.*

ANOTHER MEMBER: *Is Bing obligated to pay for that ambulance?*

Bing did request, I understand, that sponsors not entertain unless the entire company could be invited; the caste system restrictions had become embarrassing. In his autobiography, Bing revealed that he was unable to charge the Atlanta sponsors any fee close to the actual cost of the productions because the Met's board of directors could not bring themselves to demand more money from such pleasant people.

On tour, I find that fifteen minutes or more of yoga breathing and headstand exercises relax me before a performance, yet standing on my head stirs suspicions of strange sexual practices.

Chicago: Thoroughly soaked after a humid day of travel, I checked into my hotel, enjoyed a shower, and went into a yoga headstand by an open window, nude, of course.

A chambermaid entered the room, stopped and surveyed me. From my upside-down view, I could see her head tilt quizzically. "I'll be finished in ten minutes," I said.

"Oh?" she said. "I thought you was waiting for somebody." She backed out slowly.

Philadelphia: On my head again. I had come to sing that night and appear on the Mike Douglas show the next day. My wife had wandered out to shop, and I was relaxing.

Into my inverted view came a bellboy, carrying two chic suitcases, followed by a very attractive young woman. "My God," she groaned, "what kind of freak is this?" and hurried out.

The next afternoon, Mike's guest sitting beside me was the actress Barbara Parkins. And she told a very amusing story about her first day in Philadelphia: A bellboy took her to a room in which some naked degenerate or nut was standing on his head. "And I thought they pulled up the sidewalks here after four o'clock!" she exclaimed.

Since she hadn't recognized me right end up, I just laughed along.

Playing in unfamiliar theaters, contending with pickup extras and stagehands fresh out of *East Lynne*, created hazards we hadn't even dreamed of in New York.

Madama Butterfly: Butterfly's child, Trouble, is always an affliction. He is supposed to be three years old, but a child that age cannot be left alone onstage. In St. Louis, our personnel manager discovered a beautiful, small five-year-old girl who looked perfect dressed in boy's clothes. Her mother stood by offstage for rehearsal, and the child was a model of Japanese decorum. On the night of the performance, before the soprano embraced her for the last act farewell, the girl peered out into the audience and cried plaintively, "Where's my mommy?" Butterfly picked her up, to soothe her, but the child now screamed louder, "No! No! I want my mommy!" as she beat on the soprano's chest, effectively destroying Puccini's passionate climax.

In a later performance, our stage manager, determined now to play it safe, picked up a suitable life-size doll in a local thrift shop. In Act II, Sharpless asked the child's name and shook his hand vigorously, ending up with the doll's arm in his hand. Hoots of laughter. Our baritone instinctively shoved the arm back into its shoulder socket, but it fell to the floor. More hoots. At length, Butterfly gathered up the child and its arm and continued with the scene. Lamely.

Rigoletto: The American Guild of Musical Artists, to which all principal performers must belong, requires costumes to be cleaned regularly, but the road schedules make this difficult. As the jester Rigoletto, the costume I wore had been previously tenanted by a baritone whose cooling system malfunctioned; the stage manager knew when I was in position for an entrance by merely sniffing. I demanded it be cleaned, so somebody took it to one of those one-hour cleaning shops. It came back reeking of benzene. In Act I the Duke of Mantua's ballroom glittered with candelabra, and inevitably I brushed up against a candle, provoking the benzene into flames. Rigoletto rolled around on the floor to extinguish them; I'm sure some of the audience thought this was a clever, but dangerous, touch by the director.

Aïda: A young baritone, substituting for a fat Amonasro, entered in his simple loincloth, three sizes too large, to sing before the King of Egypt. He took a deep breath to begin his aria—and the loincloth fell to his knees. Amonasro quickly pulled it up in front, and it slipped down in back. He ended well, clutching both front and back, but the uproar from the audience drowned out most of his efforts. It had not occurred to the new singer to wear an athletic supporter.

One of our Aïdas was a surprisingly slender soprano who did not fill out the costume designed for this show. When we reached Cleveland, the production manager decided an Ethiopian princess should be voluptuous and dispatched a prop boy to search through the trunks for a size thirty-eight built-up bra.

On her entrance, Aïda created the curious effect of the burlesque comic who stuffs two basketballs under his shirt. The production manager raced backstage and accosted the prop boy. "You idiot! That's not a thirty-eight!"

The boy was as jittery as a sparrow. "It was dark down there—oh, dear!—I must have given her Falstaff's ass!"

Paris, May 31, 1966: Opening night at the Odéon Theater of the Metropolitan Opera's *The Barber of Seville.*
It began inauspiciously enough.

Since it had been a holiday weekend, the prop men could not find, in all of Paris, the pint of whipped cream I needed as the Barber to lather the basso for his shave. They did uncover some sour cream, which I tried to mix with beaten eggs, but that would not work. I ended up using the custard from Parisian cream puffs.

On opening night, we found, after the first act, that the small locked cabinets in our dressing rooms had been burglarized; I lost an heirloom watch and my wallet, and almost everyone in the company missed something. We asked ourselves, What are we doing here?

Jean-Louis Barrault, the eminent actor-director who staged *Faust* the previous season at the Met, had invited us to play at his theater in Paris. Since the Odéon was a much smaller house, and the Met did not have a government subsidy as the European theaters did, Bing had to scrounge around for $140,000 from private donors to bring two economy-size productions, *The Barber* and *The Marriage of Figaro,* both based on comedies by Beaumarchais. We assumed the French would be pleased with this tribute to their countryman's genius.

We arrived just at the flash point of France's anti-American anger generated by the Vietnam war and the black civil rights riots. (A month after we departed, De Gaulle ordered French forces out of NATO and kicked its headquarters out of Paris, but I don't believe we can blame the Met for this.)

To fit the theater and the budget, Bing sent over only thirty people for the chorus, an orchestra of thirty-eight, and eight ballet dancers. When I recalled Arturo Toscanini's vivid tales of the first Met encounter with the French in 1910, I thought we had done well to bring our own musicians.

> *Four huge productions were mounted,* Otello, Aïda, Falstaff *and* Manon Lescaut, *plus* Cavalleria Rusticana *and* Pagliacci, *with a company of 200, including Caruso, Alda, Scotti, Emmy Destinn. But the French musicians— "Pensioners!" Toscanini exclaimed. "Postoffice bureaucrats! Short work—long lunch! The string section all wood butchers."*
>
> *To wake them up in rehearsal, he lifted his watch out of a pocket and slammed it at the wall. By some miracle it did not break, and the French tried to follow his tempi. Frances Alda, watching from the rear, returned the watch to the Maestro. Some minutes later, he pitched it in fury against the first violinist, and missed. Again the orchestra paid some attention to the baton. Mme. Alda retrieved the watch, now in pieces, and handed them to Toscanini. "Now the beasts scream—time for two-hour lunch!' 'Aspetto!' I say. 'Here is lunch! Eat this, you pigs!' and I throw the watch pieces all over them!"*
>
> *A protest demonstration was led by a chauvinistic singer, who complained the Americans were taking bread and butter out of French mouths. Several reviewers were also unhappy, but their irritation was soothed by the Met press agent's application of large franc notes, and later showings achieved high acclaim.*

What gave us a false sense of security was the knowledge that the Paris Opera, by general agreement of the French public, still ranked among the top three dreariest companies in the world.

On opening night, the city's Beautiful People, among them Maria Callas, were stumbling to their seats a half hour after the lights dimmed. My "Figaro" aria was graciously applauded, but after Roberta Peters sang hers, the booing and hissing began. I thought she delivered it better than I had ever heard her do it before, but this moment seemed to be a prearranged signal. The uproar spread from a group in the rear to the entire theater. I had never heard anything like it, even at Ebbets Field: It was a howling windstorm. Most frightening was the sight of those chicly-gowned women down front, faces distorted, fists clenched, screaming and stamping their feet. And in the midst of all this, cries of "Brava, Callas!"

One man in the house, the composer Henri Sauguet, displayed great personal courage; he stood up and shouted to the audience, "I will never compose another note for you!" Cyril Ritchard, who had staged *Barber*, took off a shoe in the lobby and brandished it after a heckler.

The critics felt "betrayed" by everything—from the opening "Marseillaise," which one said had been led by Thomas Schippers in "goosestep tempo," to the scenery and costumes and even our orchestra, which "lacked finesse." They also scolded the audience. *The Marriage of Figaro* they found a little more endearing. Bing summed it up in his unsparing way to a reporter: "Miss Peters had had a bad night, but the Paris Opera had had a bad century."

The triumph of our visit was the reception given for us by Baron Guy de Rothschild in his Château Ferrières, a wonderland of monarchical splendor, where he laid on champagne and caviar, attended by liveried footmen and illuminated by candlelight sparkling on crystal and mirrors. If only we had played *Figaro* here.

Tokyo, May 29, 1975: Opening night at the Japan Broadcasting Corporation Hall of the Metropolitan Opera's *La Traviata*.

No one came late, no one coughed. The scenery was greeted with "ahs" by the sophisticated audience. I received an ovation when I entered, and I could not understand why; for one of the few moments in my performing life, I simply stood on the stage, stunned. For the final curtain call, the ovation lasted six minutes, a spectacular demonstration when you consider the Japanese tradition of reticence. Hundreds of girls crowded around the stage apron, bearing roses; they were fans, not employees of the sponsor. We did not know the tradition was to bend over the footlights and accept the flowers, so the girls tossed thousands of red blossoms onto the stage.

Hundreds of young people waited at the stage door with stacks of albums to be autographed. At a reception later, an elderly Japanese critic explained my entrance ovation. "We have been listening to your Red Seal records for thirty years—we were glad to see you still alive!"

On my birthday, there was a rap at the door at 7 A.M. In my pajamas, I opened it to meet a very young boy and girl carrying a bouquet of roses and singing "Happy birthday to you!" I have no idea where they learned of the date. The card on the flowers read, "Bless you on June 4 and thank you for May 31" (another *Traviata* performance). I asked if I could give them anything in return.

"No, you already autographed our albums yesterday."

I had flown in with my family before the company because of a concert engagement. We were met at the airport with a giant banner—RCA WELCOMES ROBERT MERRILL TO JAPAN—and baskets of fruit and flowers; the head of RCA Records in Japan vied with the head of London Records—both of whom sell my recordings—to entertain us.

The tour sponsor, Chubu Nippon Broadcasting Corp., paid the total cost of $2.5 million, and tickets for the eighteen performances were sold out at twice the American prices. With this lavish budget, the Met could present *Bohème, Carmen,* and *Traviata* with a company of 325, including John Alexander, Franco Corelli, Marilyn Horne, Luciano Pavarotti, and Joan Sutherland.

There were flowers everywhere backstage at the theater, even potted plants in the rest rooms. The crews worked with pride and efficiency, changing the settings in about half the American time. Joan Sutherland was breathless: "It's too fast—I don't have time to rest."

And at the Kabuki theater, I found another reminder of the Japanese concern for the visitor's peace of mind. A girl hurried after me, up to the fourth landing, to return a ten-cent comb I had dropped.

Early in my travels I discovered that the most refreshing people in town generally convened around the best hotel's swimming pool. In Dallas there was a Junoesque brunette sunning herself each day in a bikini made of two eyelashes; she did not go into the water or read anything. She seemed to be waiting. She introduced herself one afternoon as Miss Cornflower, an American Indian princess. I thought that was a little too much, but anything was possible in Texas.

"Do you know the capital of Thailand?" she asked.

Puzzled by this esoteric interest, I said, "Bangkok?"

And she banged the back of her hand against my groin. I doubled over in pain and fell back into my chair, while she laughed uproariously. I was not only hurt, I was shocked: I couldn't believe a woman would do a crazy thing like that.

"I like opera people," she explained.

As soon as I could straighten up, I beckoned a tenor from the other end of the pool and introduced him.

"Do you know the capital of Thailand?" she asked.

"That's easy—Bangkok."

Bang! He nearly collapsed into the pool. It wasn't much of a joke, but as the comics in the Catskills would say, she sure punched it across. Since I did not want to die young, I excused myself for an early rehearsal.

She came backstage before the performance that night, startlingly impressive under a flower-print cotton. I immediately introduced her to my makeup man, who was only in his twenties but already a Milquetoast.

She asked the question. Bang! His face flushed, he staggered from the room, leaving me to complete the makeup.

"What are you doing after the show?" she asked.

I sat down before I answered. "Going to sleep."

"Me, too," she said. "You have any bourbon around? My mouth feels as dry as a limeburner's wig."

I shook my head regretfully. "Well, don't bust a gut," she said, and ambled out.

After the performance I hurried out of an auditorium

door to avoid Miss Cornflower, and boarded our special train parked at the station. Next stop: Tulsa. I opened the compartment door, and there was our opera groupie, smiling brightly.

"You'll have to get off," I warned.

"Make me."

At that moment, a young buckaroo, a Spanish tenor, walked by on the way to his room. I called him in and introduced him. "Maybe you can answer this lady's question."

He was not sure. "Een Eengleesh?"

"What is the capital of Thailand?" she inquired, obviously interested.

He thought it over for several moments. I had not counted on a language problem, so I whispered into his ear.

"Ah, *si, si!* Bang-krok?"

Bang! As he crumpled, however, he wrapped himself around her waist. When I walked past his dressing room in Tulsa, he could barely lift the stretchers out of his shoes.

Fifteen years passed. I was in Tulsa for a concert, accompanied by Marion. We walked through the auditorium to the dressing room, and across the rows of seats I saw Miss Cornflower, heading in the same direction. Time had stood still for her: Her face was unlined and tanned, and her body was as stimulating as ever. Her exercises evidently worked wonders.

"Hiya!" she called out. "You know the capital of Thailand?"

"Thailand?" I said vaguely. "Maybe my wife here can answer your question."

10

Presidents, Prime Ministers, and the Queen Mother

There is an instinctive comradeship between performers and politicians: Both appear before an audience to sway its emotions for their own purposes. The politico hits certain high notes—"freedom . . . justice . . . peace . . . a Cornish hen in every pot"—to elicit votes, while the singer reaches for the thrilling finale tones to unleash a thunder of applause. In both arenas, it's often best that the audience doesn't understand the language: Many of the love lyrics in opera are as incredibly banal as any political convention platform. This mutual bond may explain why so many actors, singers, and comedians happily campaign in behalf of presidential candidates, who (when elected) enjoy relaxing with performers. We're in very much the same business.

Early fall, 1944: I lounged in a gray-green club chair on the Pennsy train for Washington with Dr. Frank Black, musical director of the NBC Symphony, and Fritz Kreisler, the preeminent violin virtuoso of that era. President Roosevelt was running for a fourth term, and we had been asked to entertain at a dinner in his honor.

I revered Roosevelt: I was twenty-four and he was the only President I was aware of in my lifetime. Before that, I was so preoccupied with my own childhood problems that I had very little interest in a man named Hoover; I was thirteen when he was voted out—mainly, I suspected, because the bank in which my father kept his few dollars went broke. But Roosevelt was our leader in the battle against the Nazis, and all of my family were thrilled that I, the son of a Polish tailor, would sing for him and—they hoped—shake his hand.

Kreisler was in his late sixties, almost six feet tall, and his hands were so tremendous that they made the priceless Guarnerius violin cradled in his lap look like a toy. His fingers did not look delicate or supple; they were more like the powerful claws of my Uncle Sam, the carpenter. But what a raconteur! The four hours of our trip flew by with his genial, witty remembrances of Europe and America at the turn of the century.

He had been a musical prodigy, born in Vienna, who toured the United States around 1889, when he was thirteen. Already about five feet seven, he wore short pants and an Eton collar, and had to conceal his well-developed urges when the young mothers who invited him to their homes insisted on hugging and kissing this sweet boy. "And sometimes those society ladies took advantage of my youth." But there was the afternoon, he recalled, when one of these provocative ladies returned to his hotel and found him enmeshed with her own daughter. It was an exhausting tour.

Kreisler's tales displayed an astonishing range of expertise in medicine (he'd given up the violin for some years to become a doctor), art, engineering, philosophy, chess, languages. Several years before, he had suffered a fractured skull in an accident—"I had a partial loss of memory and spoke only Latin and Greek. My wife knew I was recovering when I switched to French and German."

I had brought the music for "Home on the Range," which I had been told was FDR's favorite, but after we rehearsed it, in the ballroom of the Mayflower Hotel, one of his aides whispered, "Could you do another number?—the President hates that goddamn tune." The ever-ready "Figaro" was substituted.

Bob Hope, our master of ceremonies, introduced me after Kreisler, who received a standing ovation. The President sat in a wheelchair about fifty feet from me. The newsreels had shown him at the Teheran and Cairo conferences, but not in closeups, and I was startled by his physical deterioration: shrunken, eyes sunk deep into hollows, a gray pallor. But ever-smiling. I sang my heart out and was rewarded by another standing ovation. I saw Mr. Roosevelt try to lift himself by his elbows, gently assisted by Vice President Henry Wallace, but he couldn't make it, and settled back into the chair.

After Hope introduced me to him, he shook my hand with a "Bravo!" Then he said, "I understand your parents were born in Europe."

"Yes, Warsaw," I replied, surprised. He had evidently been briefed. "They are both here now."

"Thank goodness for that. Tell them Warsaw will be liberated." Exhausted now, he gestured to his attendant to wheel him away. The President turned his head to me, and with a wan smile and a slight wave of his hand repeated, "Bravo."

Harry Truman heard me sing in the U.S. Senate, in a ceremony commemorating the first anniversary of Roosevelt's death, and invited me to the White House about half a dozen times while he occupied it. He remains in my mind as a man who blended into the background, a face that was part of a large group picture. A vital, shrewd man who could make unpopular decisions, even opposed by his own advisors, he was always modest, always Harry—one of the guys at the party.

When I sang a duet—"Sweethearts"—with his daughter Margaret, José Iturbi accompanied us while Harry turned the pages of the music. The President was a first-rate amateur pianist; he played Chopin and Mozart and could accompany Margaret on any number she chose to sing.

He loved to play Gilbert and Sullivan for his political cronies. On those all-male occasions, Vice President Alben Barkley sang duets with me in his hearty bass. He had a one-piece repertoire, "Wagon Wheels," in which he was determined to sing louder than I. As a former senator from Kentucky, Barkley upheld the bourbon tradition, with a vapor cloud of it haloing his head. In those days, I still smoked an occasional after-dinner cigar, but never close to Barkley.

The President dissolved into a wistful, loving papa every time he looked at Margaret. After I had sung with her, he put his arm around my shoulder and said, "Thank you for being sweet to my baby." It seems so banal in print, but coming from a man who was carrying many of the world's problems on his shoulders, it was very touching.

"He bought me a shiny new baby grand piano when I was eight years old," Margaret told me, "and that meant a sacrifice on a county judge's salary during the Depression. He taught me to play it."

Margaret had her father's warmth and humor, and a graciousness that enveloped everyone around her. She was completely objective about herself. "If my name had been Maggie Wallace, I'd still be a struggling, promising singer," she said. "But being a President's daughter has its disadvantages. It's awfully difficult to say good night to your date at the White House door, when the Secret Service man is shining a flashlight on him."

She was serious about a singing career. Her voice had a lovely, sweet quality, not operatic; she studied with Helen Traubel and made the most of her talent. I suggested operetta or musical comedy, but Margaret wanted to try everything. From concerts she branched out into TV comedy shows, did a song-and-dance with Jimmy Durante and Eddie Jackson, signed a twelve-show contract with NBC, and one summer played a straight stock comedy, *Autumn Crocus.*

By 1953, she was grossing about $100,000 a year. "I'm making more than Dad!" she exclaimed.

I assured her the singer always made more than the accompanist.

She came across beautifully on television, even though the early cameras couldn't pick up her ash-blond hair, her eyes that were sometimes blue-green, sometimes gray-green, and her dimples. We made three appearances together on Tallulah's *The Big Show.* One duet included some director's idea of a "cute" twist: We would whistle a chorus. When we rehearsed it, we stared at each other's puckered faces and broke up. We just couldn't do it without laughing. Tallulah came storming out of the control booth. "Who told this lovely daahling to whistle? God! I'm surrounded by mongolian idiots!"

The whistle became a running gag whenever Margaret and I met. "Bob, let's try it again," she'd say. We would both try hard—and break up again.

Somehow, the ridiculous seemed to be constantly lying in wait for me when I was invited to the Truman White House. Risë Stevens, Kurt Baum, and I were asked to sing for Bess Truman's birthday party; and our accompanist was Dick Marzollo, a young man with hands as powerful as Vladimir Horowitz's. Leaning in the curve of the grand piano, I opened the program with the "Prologue" from *Pagliacci.* The accompanist hit the first four notes—*twaaaaaannggg!* A string snapped, curled up out of the piano and wrapped itself around my wrist. I stood there, trapped, trying to shake the wire loose, but it clung to me like a handcuff. The audience suppressed its laughter as I unwound it, and we finished the "Prologue" with a dull *ping* substituting for the missing note.

The President asked Ed Pauley, his favorite oil millionaire, to fly me to Washington in his private plane for a get-together of old cronies. My accompanist on this occasion was not only accomplished but also captivating, reminiscent of Kay Kendall. The captain of the plane looked like that hot pilot in *Terry and the Pirates,* and after about ten minutes I became part of the comic strip.

PILOT (Motioning me into his seat): *Come on in. Sit here.*

ME: *What for? I'm no pilot.*

PILOT: *Easiest thing in the world. These are your controls . . . just keep your eye on this dial* (strapping me into the seat) *. . . and watch that needle.*

ME: *You must be out of your mind! I can't—*

PILOT: *If it veers to the left, you pull to the right, till it hits twelve o'clock, like this, see? And if it veers left, do the same in reverse . . .*

ME: *But I don't have any insurance for this—*

PILOT: *You'll hear a lot of instructions from ground control in those earphones, but don't let it rattle you. If you have any questions, I'll be sitting back in the cabin.*
(He returns to chat with the pianist. Uneasy but fascinated, I test the controls and they work just as he said they would. After a while I feel like one of the Valkyries, riding above the storm. Though I don't dare take my eyes off the needle. In a few minutes, the ground below lights up like an immense pinball machine.)

ME: (Desperately) *Captain! Is* that *Washington?*
(He takes over. I stagger back to the cabin, with a hot pilot's confident smile on my face.)

ACCOMPANIST: *That was awfully sweet of you, Mr. Merrill . . .*

At the party, I swallowed a few drinks to stabilize my rudder, and I sang something, but I can't remember what.

Outside Denver there is an astounding amphitheater carved high up into the side of Red Rocks mountain.

Shortly after the war in Europe ended, General Eisenhower and his family were among the audience as I sang with the Denver Symphony.

A spring rain began to fall on my head, slowly at first, then in a windy downpour. The audience, accustomed to the vagaries of their weather, unfurled umbrellas or covered their heads with newspapers and pillows. The musicians, especially the string section, ran for cover with their instruments. I finished my number as the water coursed down my face, streaking my makeup and staining my white tuxedo jacket, then I turned to go off. The impresario stopped me, "Oh no! You've got to do something—I can't reschedule—you'll disappoint Eisenhower."

Wiping the water out of my eyes, I noticed that the Eisenhowers were sitting under an umbrella, calmly sipping coffee. Well, if they could stick it out, I certainly could. I called for a community sing: "Take Me Out to the Ball Game," "The Wiffenpoof Song." After a while, the rains passed over, the sun came out, and I was almost dry again.

The General was introduced from the stage. Putting his arm around my shoulder, he hailed my initiative, to my surprise, as "a sample of the spirit that made America great." And he continued in that laudatory vein for several minutes.

A few years later: The General was now President, and I was one of the theater and movie people entertaining at a dinner for him. After the show, we formed a line and he walked by, shaking hands and expressing his thanks. When he reached me, he stopped. "Well, Bob, how nice to see you dry again. We've never forgotten that night in Denver." And he proceeded to tell me, with that irresistibly engaging grin, why he had sat through the rain. "Mamie said, 'If that civilian can stand out there, soaking up the rain, a five-star general can't bug out.'"

A peculiar mental lapse has afflicted me over the years; it's not only frightening, it's downright ridiculous: I occasionally forget the lyrics of "The Star-Spangled Banner." I can't explain it, or overcome it—all I can do is worry about it.

Jack Benny was MC at a rally for President Jack · 157 · Kennedy in Madison Square Garden. Maria Callas and Marilyn Monroe were among the entertainers and I was chosen to open with, of course, "The Star-Spangled Banner."

As we waited in the wings, I told Benny, "Jack, I'm shaky on those lyrics."

"Bob, let me help you. I'll sing the anthem—you go out and make those 18,000 people laugh."

The President sat a few feet away, adding to my tension. I began robustly, reaching "And the rocket's red glare, the bombs bursting in air, gave proof—" I went blank. *Proof of what?* I mumbled and hummed and jiggled the microphone stand, hoping it would sound as if something had gone wrong with the mike.

Kennedy immediately focused on me, and I had the feeling that my knees were wobbling. I dug my nails into my palms, somehow something clicked in my head, and I got over the bombs with "—flag was still there!" I ended on a strong, perspiring note.

We lined up for the customary handshaking, and when Kennedy reached me, he nodded gravely, with the hint of a wink: "Bombing can be rough—I've been through it myself."

On the following day, Mayor Robert Wagner gave a reception for the President on the lawn of Gracie Mansion. I took my two children—Lizanne, five, and David, six—to meet him. Lizanne decided to present one of her dolls to the President as a gift for his daughter, Caroline. She made her own choice from a collection of elaborate and beautiful dolls and carried it in a shoulder bag.

A glowing afternoon on the grass . . . hundreds of New York's social and political leaders pressed around Kennedy . . . television and press cameramen up close as he greeted us . . . and Lizanne, pulling out a shabbily dressed old doll by its feet, handed it to the President of the United States. As he stared at it, bewildered, the doll's dress slipped off—and he was dangling a naked little girl. He broke into semistrangled laughter, and reached for David's hand.

David could only say, "Oh, I know you from television."

On the way home, my daughter explained, "I couldn't give away my *best* doll—that's like my own baby!"

Marion and I were in Vienna when the few years of the Kennedy Camelot collapsed, in a night of fog and confusion. Since I was going there to record *Carmen* with Franco Corelli and Leontyne Price, an agent had suggested, months before, that I could play Escamillo at the Vienna Staatsoper. I refused because I would not have time to rehearse.

On November 22, Marion and I were in our rooms at the Imperial Hotel, enjoying a dinner served by a waiter in white tie and white gloves. After we let ourselves go wild with a Viennese chocolate confection from the dessert cart, the waiter said, "Sir, I must tell you that your President Kennedy has been killed."

I choked. His shaking hand dropped the chocolate on Marion's white dress.

"It may be his father," I said. "He is very sick—"

"No, your President is dead," he insisted, and wheeled the cart out of the room. We turned the hotel's radio to the Armed Forces network: Only one thing was certain—a rifle shot.

The phone rang. Mischa Elman had also heard of the shooting. In a quavering voice, he urged me to come down to the lobby. Marion began to cry. We found Mischa on a sofa, shaking his head incredulously, and as soon as our eyes met, we both began to weep. Dozens of people wandered aimlessly around the lobby, stopping to ask strangers for news: Germans, Japanese, heavy-set men who could only be Poles or Russians, all caught up in that same headshaking disbelief that we encountered for the rest of the night.

Mischa, Marion, and I walked out into the streets to look for a newspaper; there was a soupy fog, and no planes were flying in with foreign papers. We went from stand to stand in that fog, which deepened the feeling of emptiness, nothingness. Eerie figures would suddenly materialize out of the gloom, hunting newspapers, and then disappear. Marion and I couldn't sleep, so we sat up all night, tuned to the Armed Forces radio. The President was dead, but nobody knew why.

In the morning, we dragged ourselves to the recording session. As we passed a newsstand, still seeking a paper in English, a flower-seller asked, "American?"

We nodded. Without a word, she handed us a small bunch of violets.

I recalled the vision of the President, bewildered but gentlemanly, dangling a shabby little naked doll by its legs.

In addition to my lapses in lyrics, I am also adept at forgetting names and spellings. I have on occasion started to introduce Marion and ended lamely, "Of course you've met my wife . . ."

When I brought my recording of *Fiddler* on a visit to the Lyndon Johnsons, Mrs. Johnson asked me to autograph the album for the President. Marion and I were having coffee with her in an anteroom, and as I picked up my pen I had to think a moment: His name was Lyndon, but how was it spelled? I stalled with "I want to think of something particularly appropriate," while Ladybird nodded understandingly. At that moment, a waiter came in to remove the tray, and I whispered frantically to Marion: "*Lyndon?*"

She spelled it instantly.

We also created a slight misunderstanding or, as the newspapers love to label it, "an international incident." The President had requested me to sing for his visitor, Prime Minister Harold Wilson: "You pick your own music." Simple enough.

Marion—who was to be my accompanist—and I chose "The Road to Mandalay," with Kipling's rousing tribute to British adventurers, and "I Got Plenty o' Nuttin'," Gershwin's bit of Americana. And, since I had been performing *Fiddler* on the road, we rounded off the program with "If I Were a Rich Man," and sent the list to Mrs. Johnson's press secretary, Liz Carpenter. She met us at the airport, and on the way to our hotel revealed that the British Embassy, informed of our music, was all in a flap.

"Mandalay"'s imperialistic sentiment was anathema to the Labor government. Since Mr. Wilson had come to Washington to negotiate a loan to bail out his government, "I Got Plenty o' Nuttin'" and "If I Were a Rich Man" sounded like sardonic slaps at Great Britain. Somehow the news of our unhappy choices had leaked to the press before we arrived, so Liz had to smuggle us into the White House through a back entrance to avoid reporters.

Since we had brought no other music, Marion and I rehearsed the three numbers on a White House piano. The rehearsal was filmed for the White House records, I believe; but for some preposterous reason the pictures were relayed via satellite to England.

Nobody, of course, had consulted Mr. Wilson. He and Mr. Johnson, chatting in a room adjacent to our rehearsal, heard me through the wall. After I finished, the door opened, and the President introduced me to his guest.

"I'm sorry about the music," I began.

"Oh, I never cared about that bloody 'Mandalay' anyhow. By all means, sing what you wish."

The more sensational newspapers made a great to-do about those songs, with one cartoon depicting me as a bloated baritone and President Johnson and Harold Wilson singing a dirge over the emaciated body of the British lion.

I was not too troubled: I have always maintained good relations with Great Britain. Why, Sir Winston Churchill honored me with one of his own cigars, although I must admit I had done very little to merit this award.

It was after the war, when Churchill visited our shores, and we were both in Boston at the Ritz-Carlton. I always stayed there during the Met engagement; it had a splendid trandition of service and the elevator men were especially fond of opera, for which I supplied tickets.

On my way down from the tenth floor, the elevator man asked, "Mr. Merrill, would you like to meet Winston Churchill?"

"I certainly would."

"I'm picking him up in a special express elevator, to avoid the autograph hounds. You go back to your floor, push the button in five minutes, and I'll stop for you."

The door opened, and I walked into the elevator, occupied only by Churchill and an aide. The operator closed the door but held the car in place, as he announced: "Sir Winston Churchill, this is Mr. Robert Merrill, star of the Metropolitan Opera—the greatest baritone in the world, and I'd like you to meet him."

After that astounding speech, all I could do was shrink against the wall. Churchill was shorter than I, but his barrel chest gave him great presence, and his heavy, lined face, like a great actor's, demanded attention. I couldn't shift my eyes away.

Sir Winston extended his hand, grunting, "A great opera company. Ah, yes. I always enjoyed opera—wish you would come to Covent Garden!"

The elevator was drifting down slowly now. I murmured, "I've admired your speeches and the way you use your voice—"

Somewhat surprised, he rumbled, "Well—humph! Will you have a cigar, sir?" and pulled a fat one out of an inner pocket.

Just as surprised, I said, "Thank you very much—" The door opened, he nodded farewell, and hurried out to his car.

I walked into our rehearsal displaying the Churchill cigar, and it was laughed off as another Merrill gag. I never smoked it. I wrapped it carefully in cellophane, occasionally showing it to good friends, who would not believe it, either; after a while I put it away in a drawer. In 1965, on the day he died, I opened the drawer to renew my memory of the great man. The cigar had disintegrated.

My relationship with the Queen Mother of Great Britain was a bit more solid: She invited me to guide her on a tour of Brooklyn. On a visit to New York in 1954, she had stopped off at the Canadian Club to dedicate a portrait of her daughter, Queen Elizabeth II, and after I sang the

Canadian, British, and American anthems, we had a cup of tea. The English called her "Mum," but that image of a stolid mother in tweeds did her little justice; she had the extraordinary English complexion—which seems to be nourished by their damp climate—and an easy warmth, and a fluffy, feathered hat that gave her an air of gaiety.

AIDE: *May I present Mr. Robert Merrill of Brooklyn.*

QUEEN MOTHER: *I've heard so much about Brooklyn. Those ballplayers, the Dodgers, why are they called "bums"?*

ME: *That is an expression of affection, Your Majesty.*

QUEEN MOTHER: *Is it a poor, rowdy area, like our East End?*

ME: *Oh, some parts of it are a bit rough. But many people in the arts were born there—Danny Kaye, Richard Tucker . . .*

QUEEN MOTHER: *What an extr'ordinary place!*
(Her surprise may be caused by the fact that the outstanding "English" singers were not born in England. Nellie Melba and John Sutherland came from Australia; Frances Alda, New Zealand; John McCormack, Ireland; and Mary Garden, Scotland.)
(To an aide) *Couldn't we arrange a brief tour of Brooklyn with Mr. Merrill?*

AIDE: *I shall look into it, Ma'am.*

QUEEN MOTHER: *I enjoyed the hot dogs when I visited the Roosevelts in thirty-seven—I trust you have them in Brooklyn?*

ME: *Oh yes. The best hot dogs come from Coney Island.*

QUEEN MOTHER (Delighted): *Possibly we can have a picnic.*

Unfortunately, her schedule could not be rearranged. I'm sure they would have loved the Queen Mother at Nathan's.

Now it can be told: Hubert Humphrey was hooked on peanut butter. After a White House dinner, the Vice President invited us to his private retreat in the Executive Office Building for a nightcap. He hunted through cabinets and the refrigerator to rustle up something to nibble on, and as so often happens with unexpected guests, all he could find were some stale peanuts. This led to his admission that, when he was stuck in his office, he dearly loved a peanut butter sandwich for a quick lunch, and there was no place nearby to which he could send out for one.

Well, I knew of a stall at the Farmers Market in Los Angeles which ground the fresh nuts to order, without fillers or preservatives. Whenever I was in the neighborhood, I dispatched a half-dozen quart jars to Humphrey. And that is how I became Purveyor of Peanut Butter by Appointment to the Vice President.

October, 1968: Marion and I were working in Hubert's campaign for the Presidency, performing at rallies and dinners. His voice was deteriorating from overuse. What could be done? his personal physician asked.

The usual remedy is tea with honey and lemon, but while singing in Buenos Aires, I had discovered some mints that relieved my hoarseness. In addition to collecting shirts, I am a connoisseur of mints, and I was convinced these were the greatest aid to the throat since the invention of the microphone. Marion happened to have a bagful in her purse, so she contributed them to Humphrey. And that is how I also became Purveyor of Mints.

November, 1968: One of Humphrey's aides phoned from Washington. "His voice is going again. Where can I get those special mints?"

"Buenos Aires," I said.

Marion looked into a closet to discover another bag of these magic mites. On the way to Boston, Humphrey's plane stopped at La Guardia airport; I carried the neatly wrapped package into the plane—where it was examined by a Secret Service agent—and Hubert was saved for the final week of campaigning.

My wife and I appeared at rallies in the New York area,

indoors and out, sometimes on street corners; since we were never certain of a piano, Marion accompanied me on a small electronic keyboard, used by rock bands, capable of two and a half octaves. I specialized in "Ol' Man River" and "Sorrento." Occasionally Hubert sang "The Whiffen-poof Song" with me, in his nasal tenor. And once the Secret Service grabbed me after I tossed away a lighted cigar near him.

On the last day of the campaign, we worked eight rallies, and at the end, the three of us embraced, mainly to hold each other up. Hubert, his face limp with weariness and his voice reduced to a hoarse whisper, groaned, "If I only had another week . . ."

He lost by 510,315 votes out of the more than 73 million cast.

On the twenty-fifth anniversary of my debut, the Met staged a gala production of *La Traviata* with the incomparable Joan Sutherland as Violetta. At the end of the third act, Rudolf Bing introduced on stage almost all of the twenty sopranos who had sung Violetta with me: Renata Tebaldi, Renata Scotto, Licia Albanese, and others. It was a lovely and moving moment for me.

After the show, the cast and guests clustered backstage, reminiscing and embracing each other, when Premier Golda Meir stopped in to say hello, with six bodyguards. I was startled by her resemblance to my great-aunt Lesser, a woman of formidable energy and resourcefulness, who had helped our family out of innumerable financial crises.

"Happy twenty-fifth!" Mrs. Meir exclaimed, throwing her arms around me with an aunt's big hug and kiss. Then she added, in Yiddish, "May you have good fortune."

Two years later, I appeared in a festival in Jerusalem celebrating Israel's twenty-fifth anniversary, with Patrice Munsel and Josephine Baker, among others. The setting was the magnificent and ancient Tower of David. I greeted Mrs. Meir with a big hug and kiss and "A happy twenty-fifth to you—may you all have good fortune."

She nodded ruefully, very much like my mother. "It wouldn't hurt . . ."

11
Lovers and Losers: Five against Themselves

In 1945 a record store on Seventh Avenue, around the corner from Carnegie Hall, stocked the old classics. I was listening to a Lawrence Tibbett–Rose Bampton duet from *Simon Boccanegra* when the proprietor pointed me out to a hefty soldier, in Air Force blues. He stuck out his hand. "Hiya, I'm Mario Lanza, and I'm looking for the best teacher." His voice had won a scholarship at the Berkshire Music School, he told me, awarded by Serge Koussevitzky himself. And he had sung in the musical Moss Hart wrote for the Air Force, *Winged Victory*.

I warmed to him quickly: He was a city boy, full of wild energy, from a background something like my own. I took him to Mr. Margolis, who recognized his incredible talent and offered to tutor him, starting with the fundamentals, as he did with everyone he accepted.

Mario was excited, then quickly cooled. "I could lose ten years stumbling around here and not make a living. Who needs all that study? I'm going into movies—what the hell do they know about singing?"

What a gift he had! He could have been at home in any opera house in the world. But he could never discipline himself to study for it, and he spent the rest of his short life with a gnawing self-doubt, quarreling, canceling, gaining weight, losing friends, making excuses.

He zoomed up as the hottest property in Hollywood with *The Great Caruso*, before he was thirty. Despite its musical crudities, it ran for ten weeks at Radio City Music Hall. He made three films for MGM, and even though all of them coined money, the studio released him with a $5 million lawsuit as a farewell present because he refused to show up for work on *The Student Prince*.

This was the first round in his running battle with producers. He rejected direction; his weight yoyoed from 175 to 295 and down again; he indulged his gargantuan appetite for eating and drinking with very little respect for his own talent or that of other singers. Jussi Bjoerling was the only one he admired.

When Mario made *Caruso* his partner in a scene was Blanche Thebom, a highly respected soprano who had sung in the best opera houses. After the scene was shot, she waited with him to hear the replay for sound. In her presence, Lanza ordered a flunky to bar her. "What the hell does she know? Keep the broad out." When Blanche told me this the next day, she was still quivering and ashen.

By 1952, there was speculation that he had lost his voice. He walked out on an engagement in Las Vegas because of a "sore throat." Jack Entratter put it this way:

"His *head* was sore. When a guy gets a sore throat, he goes to a doctor, sprays, takes a nap. This guy was up all night with the vino and the gambling. That's not so bad for a comic like Joe E. Lewis—he can kid it. But Lanza, the Second Caruso, he ought to know better!"

Mario worked off 100 pounds for his next picture, *Serenade*, by starving himself and living on vitamin shots. He worked hard, was never late, and he sang seventeen songs, from pop tunes to arias. It made a lot of money—he told me he had grossed over $5 million in five years—but the music critics still would not recognize him as the legitimate artist he hungered to be. They noted his lack of taste, his posturing and straining.

Mario read the *Serenade* review in *Time* magazine to me, over the phone from California: ". . . looks like a colossal ravioli set on toothpicks, and his face, aflame with rich living, has much the appearance of a gigantic red pepper."

"Isn't that a shitty trick?" he asked.

I had to admit it was vicious.

Now Mario retreated with his family to his villa near Rome. It must have been a magnificent monument; Mussolini had presented it to Marshal Badoglio for his victories over the Ethiopians. I've always regretted I never had the chance to accept his invitation for a visit.

Sometime in 1956, Mario called me from Italy.

MARIO: *Bob, how the hell are you? I'm relaxing here, working out. I got down from two forty to one eighty-five.*

ME: *That's great, Mario. Great. How are the children?*

MARIO: *Fine. Bob, is Bing in town? I want to do* Bohème.

ME: *Mario, I don't think Mr. Bing would let anybody walk out on his stage unless he's seen him on a stage before.*

MARIO: *Hell, he can see me in* Serenade. *I did a sock Rudolfo scene, and my "Di quella pira" is sensational! I even do Otello.*

ME: *They love you in Italy. Why don't you consider a debut there and see how you feel about it? It only takes one—*

MARIO: *So that's my audition, huh? You must be out of your mind. I don't audition for anybody!* (He hangs up.)

Mario made his last movie in Europe, and when death came from a heart attack in 1959, he was only thirty-eight. It was a tragic waste. Mr. Margolis, a better judge than I, seemed confident that Lanza might have become another Caruso.

Some years ago in Las Vegas, Alan Ladd and his wife, Sue Carroll, told me of their shattering experience with this gifted man. He had rented their house while making a film, and after he moved out, they found a disaster area. Alan could not believe it: dried excrement on the floor, carpets ripped, urine stains on the upholstery. When Mario had too much wine, he lost the last bit of discipline he had.

Mario's epitaph was best expressed by himself, with unwitting irony, in a newspaper interview a short time before his death:

"I always wanted to be just Mario Lanza. I always wanted to be just a boy—to say, to hell with all the cruel things in life, and live! because life is a great adventure."

The Bjoerling Quartet, father and three sons, toured Europe and America in 1919 and 1920, singing to joyous acclaim in Swedish costumes for Swedish communities and churches. The sweetest voice was the soprano: jolly, bright-eyed Jussi, age nine. When his father, David, lay on his deathbed, he gathered the boys around him, and admitted he was addicted to the bottle; he made them swear they would never drink hard liquor. This was a wrenching shock, Jussi told me; he had been taught to sing by his father and revered him.

Jussi made his debut at the Royal Opera in Stockholm when he was only nineteen, and in a short while developed into one of the great tenors of all time: "the Swedish Caruso," "vocal velvet." Harold Schonberg of *The New York Times* described his voice as "the greatest lyric instrument since Gigli's . . . without a flaw from top to bottom." And this Swede from the cold north mastered Italian opera with—as Schonberg put it—"more taste than any comparable singer in this writer's experience."

"When I'm really singing well," Jussi said, "the voice

doesn't seem to be in my body at all—it floats in the air about a foot in front of me."

I sang frequently beside this stocky bull of a man with the face of a choirboy; he was buoyant, gracious, and married to one of the most beautiful women in Sweden. Jussi and I played cards, went to movies. He loved Westerns—"Bub, let's see a shoot-'em-up!" I liked him so much it took some years before I would admit to myself that Jussi was an alcoholic.

One evening his wife, Anna-Lisa, a lyric soprano who sang with him occasionally for benefits, phoned me anxiously from the Essex House, their home in New York. "Please come over right away."

Jussi was a little woozy; he'd obviously had a few, and he wanted to go out for a walk. She made it clear that we must not—he would end up in a bar and "that would be disaster." We played cards, watched television, and I spent the night there to divert him. Anna-Lisa would call me at my apartment, when I was courting Marion and baring my soul to her, to inquire if Jussi was with me. And sometimes his wife and I went out to search for him.

She took away his money, but he set up charge accounts around town. The bartender at "21" knew he was not to be served more than one drink, but somehow he inveigled more, and he was so strong I could not budge him. At 3 A.M. I had to call Anna-Lisa, who came over with a fever of 103, to help get him home.

He fooled me a few times on the way to a movie. He would spot a bar with television and switch signals: "We'll watch the fights." One night he ordered an innocent beer; I went to the john, and came back to find him slugging away at the man on the next stool. Jussi had swallowed a few quick ones as soon as I turned my back.

It is possible, as a physician explained to me, that Jussi's problem was an ailment similar to hypoglycemia: abnormally low blood sugar. This condition can be triggered by fears and tensions, and Jussi, always a perfectionist, constantly fretted before a performance. As the sugar level dropped, the irritability and depression intensified while the body demanded more sugar. Alcohol, almost entirely carbohydrates, created an instant surge in the blood, and some relief.

He did try to rescue himself. In Sweden he underwent therapy, taking a medicine that made him abnormally sensitive to alcohol so that one drink caused violent vomiting. It did not have a long-range effect on Jussi, and unfortunately Alcoholics Anonymous was not operating in those years. His wife and I did what we could.

He did not socialize with friends, as so many performers do, and I spent as much time in his suite as at my own apartment. It was heartbreaking to see this world-acclaimed artist sitting in his chair, brooding. Occasionally I started to sing a duet, say, the last act scene from *Bohème*. He joined in reluctantly, slowly, and of course he was marvelous. I tried to assure him, "You see? Your voice is there, you're only worried about the public's response, and they always adore you."

Although he made over forty albums, he evaded the recording studio as if it were his execution chamber. We had agreed to do several albums of duets for RCA, and I spent the night before with him, to guarantee his appearance at 3 P.M. The morning was spent in his suite, listening to the extraordinary Iago-Otello duet which Caruso and Titta Ruffo had recorded. Jussi feared he would not equal the dark coloring of voice that Caruso had achieved, and I was still somewhat awed by my boyhood idol, Ruffo. I tried to boost Jussi's confidence, "You know we can make dozens of takes until it's perfect . . ."

"Wait, wait," he stalled. "Let's hear it once more . . ."

At two-thirty, I literally pulled him by the elbow into a cab. The studio was in Manhattan Center on West 34th Street, formerly the Manhattan Opera House. Jussi would not enter the building: "Bub, let's take a walk." We walked around the block a half dozen times, his tension and irritability increasing with each step.

"It's three o'clock," I announced, hanging onto his arm; reluctantly, with a deep sigh, he walked the last mile to the elevator. Those duets are still best-sellers around the world, and critics have compared them favorably with the Caruso-Ruffo masterpieces.

Jussi and I were invited by Toscanini to perform in a radio version of *Un Ballo in Maschera.* I rehearsed with the Maestro while Jussi sent cables from Sweden that he was on his way. Jussi did not show up.

Shortly after I married Marion, we went to Rome to record *Manon Lescaut;* Jussi arrived with Anna-Lisa and their two children, and Licia Albanese with her stockbroker husband, Joe Gimma. We stayed at the Grand Hotel, turning the work into a festive holiday for all of us. The afternoon before we were to finish recording, Jussi disappeared. Licia and Joe and I immediately searched the Via Veneto and side streets; after a desperate hour we picked up Jussi, looking for a bar. We brought him back to the hotel with the ruse that one of his children had become ill.

The recordings completed, we enjoyed a memorable lunch in the patio of the hotel. Several street musicians strolled in, strumming and singing their usual tunes. Jussi, relaxed and beaming, suggested we join in. Licia sang an aria—I answered with "Sorrento"—Jussi recreated that old vehicle for so many hopeless voices, "O Sole Mio," as if it was his debut at the Met. Out poured all his joy and pain and compassion in a glorious voice that was truly separated from his body, floating in the air about him.

Jussi then went through a period in which he suffered from shortness of breath; whether it was a bronchial ailment or psychosomatic, I do not know. He did not sing for two seasons, and his dejection grew so overpowering that when he came back in 1954, to sing *Bohème* with Cesare Siepi, Licia, and me, he was as jittery as a debutant. We took turns encouraging him backstage, and somewhere in the middle of his first aria, his voice coalesced once more in the Bjoerling miracle of sweetness and passion, charging all of us onstage with an electricity that surged back and forth to create the most voluptuous *Bohème* I have ever sung in. The audience responded with a standing ovation, applauding until midnight.

Jussi was a wonderfully amusing companion, with his

eye for the absurd and wit for the instant summing-up. He had played a boyish Faust—at twenty—to Chaliapin's Mephistopheles. "He always dominate the stage, and not only with great acting—he bribe the man who work the spotlight to keep that light always on him."

In the first scene, after old Faust lamented his despair, Mephistopheles popped up in a flash of light to offer eternal youth. The gigantic Chaliapin wore a tremendous red cape and, with one sweep of his arm, enveloped Jussi. "Bub, I never see the people, never see conductor—I sing the whole act under Chaliapin's cape!"

Jussi sang *Un Ballo* with me in a new production under Herbert Graf. Traditionally, the baritone assassinates the tenor (King of Sweden) with a dagger. Mr. Graf decided to use a pistol then, after some dress rehearsal confusion, changed back to the dagger. But nobody told the prop man. In performance, as I stabbed Jussi, a pistol shot exploded at the same time. Jussi whispered, "Don't worry, Bub! I'll die!" and keeled over, engulfed by the cloud of gunsmoke billowing out from backstage.

Jussi concentrated on singing, not acting. When Peter Brook, the avant-garde English director, restaged *Faust,* he engaged a fencing master to bring more drama into the duel between Jussi (Faust) and me (Valentine). Since the musical cues are complicated, the conventional staging is simply one-two-three, parry and thrust, one-two-three, thrust and parry, etc. The new instructor choreographed the duel. After two hours, Jussi walked into Mr. Bing's office and announced, "I can't sing when I dance. If you want a fancy duel, get Errol Flynn!" He went back to one-two-three.

Jussi was temporarily disabled by a heart attack in 1959, but refused to ease up. On several occasions, when we sang *Faust* at the old Met, an assistant rushed into my room—"The pills, the nitro pills!" I'd dash down the two flights of stairs with the white pellets that relieve heart pain, and as Jussi put two under his tongue I actually saw his heart beating through his costume. It was frightening, and I pleaded with him not to go on.

In March 1960, he was ready to come onstage at Covent

Garden in *Bohème* when he had another seizure. Since some of the royal family were out front, Jussi did not want to disappoint them. He performed, after only a half-hour rest. The final attack took him at his country home in Sweden, in September of the same year. He was only forty-nine.

What a heavenly choir they must have: Caruso, Gigli, Tucker, Bjoerling . . .

A few years after I came to the Met, I was setting up my schedule with the man in charge of rehearsals. He had to phone Lawrence Tibbett. The voice at the other end replied that Mr. Tibbett could not come to the phone. And the schedule-keeper yelled, "Get that drunken bum over here!"

Tibbett had been another of my childhood idols—the great baritone of the Met for twenty years who had sung over seventy roles. I was so frightened by this instability of opera life that I immediately began to buy government bonds and annuities.

Tibbett was the embodiment of the American dream, the hardworking go-getter filled with ideas for improvement and expansion; the future would always be onward and upward. Six-foot-one, weighing over 200 pounds, he had the frank, open face of the good-guy sheriff in a thirties Western. (In fact, his grandfather, uncle, and father had been sheriffs in California, he told me. "My dad was killed in a shoot-out with a bandit named Wild Jim McKinney.") Larry wanted to Americanize opera, sing it in English, popularize it in movies, radio, television. And he was responsible for a considerable string of firsts:

First American without European training to star at the Met.

First American opera singer on commercial radio: the Atwater Kent hour, 1921. In 1945, he was so popular on radio that he followed Frank Sinatra as featured singer on *Your Hit Parade.*

First baritone in films: *Rogue Song* and *New Moon,* with Grace Moore, both in 1930.

He created the baritone roles in two American operas

by Deems Taylor. The operatic version of *The Emperor Jones* was written for him.

He even found time to lead the organization of the first successful union for singers, the American Guild of Musical Artists, and became its first president.

Where did the sheriff's boy go wrong? In the first months of my contract, as I awaited with growing despair an important role for my debut, I stood in the wings almost every day, observing how the stars worked onstage. Tibbett was very friendly and helpful; he explained fundamentals that I didn't know existed. And he talked frankly about his own world.

His mother had operated a large rooming house in Los Angeles after his father's death. He sang in the school glee club and worked out in the gym with Jimmy Doolittle, the future air-war hero. He didn't smoke or drink; he exercised with weights and medicine balls. "A baritone needs to have a diaphragm as tough as a prize fighter's."

He had only six months of study in New York when his coach persuaded him to audition for the Met. He sang the "Prologue" from *Pagliacci* and his voice cracked. He won on the second round with the sardonic "Credo," from *Otello*—the same aria that had won the $125 contract for me. In 1923, Larry's contract paid $60 a week.

He got his first break in the old-style movie way: stepping in for an ailing star. As Ford in *Falstaff*, he literally stopped the show for fifteen minutes in the second act with his raging soliloquy, "E sogno? O realta?" The audience shouted his name until the conductor permitted him a curtain call. He worked hard, seldom went to parties, saved his money and developed into a subtle and moving actor. He had worked with Tyrone Power's father in California in a Shakespearean stock company: "Everything from Puck to Lear, and I was the biggest darn nurse for Juliet that California ever saw."

In 1931, at the bottom of the Depression, when Tibbett was at the top of New York's musical world, he divorced his wife of eleven years and married an American dream girl—the daughter of a wealthy banker. Parties and champagne became a way of life, in a grand East Side apartment and a country estate in Connecticut. Larry invited me to one of the in-town parties: Everyone wore dinner jackets and long gowns, a six-piece band played for dancing, and at about midnight I was startled to hear Tibbett, wobbling with a glass in hand, sing tenor arias. His was an extremely flexible voice, with a surprisingly high top range; still, playing around with tenor high notes does not improve a baritone.

He also appeared often and stayed late at the best parties around town. I heard that, when he spoke of opera, he spoke highly of me. At a lunch with my teacher, Mr. Margolis, he praised me as his likely successor: "And I'm glad he was born and trained in America."

All the while he was losing confidence in his own voice; he canceled performances and missed cues, and I heard of bottles of scotch in his dressing room.

I walked by there once, as he prepared to go on in *Pagliacci*. The door was open, the room clouded with cigarette smoke; made up as the hunchback clown Tonio, Tibbett stared glumly at his face in the mirror as he puffed away on his Lucky Strike.

While I stood in the wings, he came down the stairs reluctantly; his hands shook and I could see him sweating through the clown costume. He had to force himself to walk onstage. Stepping through the curtain, he began the "Pro-logue," holding tightly onto the curtain behind him with both hands. As he reached for the high A-flat, the top note in the "Prologue," he pulled desperately at the curtain, as if to give himself support—and he couldn't make it. It became a loud scream. I was so appalled at the deterioration of this gifted, genial man that I ran out of the theater.

The old Met held Sunday concerts that offered acts and arias from various operas. John Charles Thomas and Tibbett were on the bill and standing backstage as I went out to sing the *Pagliacci* "Prologue." Tibbett waved his arm with the fighter's clenched fist—"Sock it to 'em, Bob!" I was uneasy, singing in their presence, but I made the A-flat. Although both men complimented me as I came off,

Tibbett looked forlorn. He sang for the last time at the Met in 1950.

A few years later, he was arrested in California for drunken driving and paid a large fine. In January 1960, an attractive divorcee was found dead in his apartment; police surmised she had taken an overdose of barbiturates. Tibbett's distorted dream came to an end in July, after he underwent surgery for a head injury. The story that circulated through the Met was even sadder: he had fallen and smashed his head in a drunken stupor.

(1960 was a freakish year of disaster. Not only did Tibbett and Bjoerling pass away, but also John Charles Thomas and Leonard Warren, who collapsed in a heart attack onstage.)

Sex is a never-ending theme with infinite variations in opera. As a preoccupation among performers, it ranks only a half-note below money and good food; and it does not seem to hurt the careers of women, although it certainly helped shorten the vocal lives of several men I knew.

Singing is, after all, a sensual art, by which the voice conveys love, beauty, desire—and these emotions stimulate not only the audience but the singers themselves. The consummation of these passions is aided by two factors peculiar to this profession: endurance and availability. A leading role demands as much energy output as a twenty-mile run, while wearing costumes that weigh thirty to fifty pounds. And opera people usually flock together in the same hotels, where they're not guarded by the phalanxes of flunkies that imprison movie and stage personalities.

Sexuality was always part of the grand tradition of opera, and proudly displayed. Music critics could usually tell when Nellie Melba would be in best voice—her lover, the Duc d'Orleans, was with her.

Lina Cavalieri, a ragged flower girl in Rome, was discovered by an aged marquis who became her Pygmalion, and she developed into the dazzling soprano of French opera and one of the grandest courtesans in Europe. After she ran through a string of Russian princes, she sang with

Caruso at the Met in 1906, was acclaimed by the critics for her "very pretty voice," and married Robert Astor Chanler of the Astor family.

Luisa Tetrazzini, one of the plumpest sopranos of all time, enjoyed a succession of young boys well into her fifties. It was an obsession. When she gave up a season in Europe to run off with a boy, the angry impresario surrounded her ship to England with process servers; she coolly sent her maid aboard, disguised in her diva's clothes, while Luisa, wearing an old peasant's costume, slipped into the steerage hold.

Soprano Frances Alda, who later married Giulio Gatti-Casazza, the general manager of the Met, discovered that four beaux were coming there to hear her, all on the same night. Now, two might be considered an amusing coincidence, but four was too extravagant even for an operatic libretto. Each one told her where he would be sitting; she sang passionately to each of them, and not one ever knew about the other.

Ferruccio Tagliavini wanted me to take a ride in his new Lancia parked at the curb next to the stage door of the old Met. "I wish you to hear that motor," he told me at rehearsals. It was a seven-seat "saloon" model and about as long as a crosstown bus. (In the fifties, Italian tenors upstaged each other with impressive cars. In the seventies, the competition escalated to villas outside Rome.)

But the conductor insisted on running through a duet with me, so I missed a melodramatic scene in front of the car. As it was relayed to me later, by an assistant stage manager, a petite, dark-haired woman, with a vaguely familiar face, stood beside the car, crying. She was obviously pregnant. "Ferruccio! I love you!" she sobbed. "How can you throw me away? I carry your child."

"Impossible!" he said, climbing into the car. "Big mistake."

She was a young Puerto Rican soprano, the stage manager told me, who had made her first appearance at the Met as Rosina in *The Barber of Seville* with me, repeated the role next month—and disappeared. That was all of her career. She had worn a large cross around her neck, and her mother, dressed in black, chaperoned her continually. The girl was so virginal that she stiffened when we had to embrace.

She became hysterical, beating on the car door and screaming that Ferruccio had destroyed her career and would destroy her child. A crowd gathered and one woman shouted, "Call a cop!"

"She's crazy!" Ferruccio yelled, and started the engine. She immediately threw herself in front of the car. Some of the bystanders tried to open the street-side door, to stop the engine. The assistant stage manager saw the possibilities of a juicy scandal for the two morning papers, whose offices were only a few blocks away. With the help of some stagehands, he lifted the young lady from the street and carried her backstage, where a doctor gave her sedation. Ferruccio drove away.

Although he was short and husky, his bell-like lyric tenor, combined with the fair skin and green-blue eyes of his north Italian heritage, seemed to bring young girls clustering around the stage door.

He was married to a soprano who also sang at the Met; but, he said, she was unable to bear children. Perhaps he wanted to reassure himself of his virility.

A few years before that street scene, he had been hit with a paternity suit by a young "music student" who claimed he had signed an agreement to pay $3,000 and $50 a month to support his alleged child, born in New Hampshire. A lower court awarded the money to her, but the case was thrown out on appeal.

"A singer's life," said Ferruccio, "is like a lemon. So long as there is some juice left in it, somebody squeezes."

Ferruccio had never wanted to be a singer anyhow. His father had been overseer of an estate, and the boy was brought up with the children of the house. "I learned the violin there, and I picked up operatic arias from the records by ear, so my father thought I must be a singer. I liked, instead, engineering." He became a licensed electrical engineer.

A musical conservatory in the nearby city of Parma held competitions for entrance. Somehow, his father baited Ferruccio into an audition, even though he was now in his twenties.

> *Parma, the birthplace of Verdi and Toscanini, had a population of about 80,000 and a small opera house, yet it had a large number of discerning, vociferous critics—about 80,000. Ferruccio told me that, as a child, he had heard a soprano named Zepelli break on a high note. The audience hooted and jeered, and as the poor woman stood there helplessly, they began to sing her aria—but perfectly!*
>
> *In* Carmen, *after Micaela reveals her love to Don José, a gypsy lookout fires a rifle, to warn of intruders, and she exits. At Parma, the Micaela was particularly distressing to the audience. When the shot rang through the house and the soprano ran off, a voice in the balcony shouted, "That sonofabitch missed again!"*

"So you understand I was terrified," Ferruccio said. To his total surprise, he was granted a scholarship. He continued to hold onto his engineer's position, until he made his bow as Rudolfo in Florence in 1939. He opened at the Met in 1947 in the same role, in which the critics acclaimed the ease and artistry of his voice; by 1961 the critics noted a significant decline in both these qualities. He returned to Europe and I lost touch with him.

Last year, after my concert in Geneva, a handsome woman and a young girl came backstage. I stared in startled disbelief: The girl was the reincarnation of the one who had stretched out in front of the Lancia. She was Tagliavini's daughter, and the woman was her mother; Ferruccio had used his engineering skills to amass a fortune in the construction business. And the girl was studying voice, determined to carry on the career her mother had abandoned.

Ezio Pinza, after decades in opera, had thousands of admirers, and he did his best to reciprocate their adoration. This by no means shortened his career, but it did lead to a lawsuit.

In March 1935, his wife of fifteen years sued a leading soprano of the Met, Elisabeth Rethberg, claiming alienation of his affection. She charged that it had begun "about April, 1934, and on divers other days and times since then, and before this action at various places in Europe, on the Atlantic Ocean, and in the United States." She demanded $250,000 in damages.

"It was ridiculous," he explained. "Augusta and I were living separate lives for a long time."

Mrs. Pinza threatened to call Lily Pons, Lawrence Tibbett, Martinelli, and others as witnesses, to prove, as her suit alleged, that "the continuous association of my husband and this defendant is a scandal, known to various members of the operatic profession." By May, she dropped the case, and in 1940, Mme. Rethberg's husband divorced her.

Mrs. Pinza might have saved lawyers' fees by imitating the example of another soprano, who stifled much of her husband's philandering by discreetly spreading word that he had contracted a virulent social disease.

Ezio never forgot the poverty of his youth: He'd been an unsuccessful bicycle racer and supported his vocal training by working as a laborer and carpenter. (Carpentry seems to be the French Foreign Legion for young singers.) His success with women must have been based mostly on his virile charms, because his appreciation of a woman was exceeded only by his love for the dollar.

A young soprano lamented to me that Pinza took her to lunch at Maxim's, and when the check came, realized he had forgotten to bring his money. She paid not only the bill but also the cab to Pinza's hotel, where he forgot to reimburse her.

When I followed his act in Las Vegas, he was earning $12,000 a week, yet I would see him walk down the row of slot machines sticking his finger in the payoff slot to see if any silver had been left behind. One of the hotel musicians was with him when he reached a dollar machine. "Do you have a silver dollar?" Pinza asked. The young man dropped one into the machine, and hit the jackpot. Pinza shoveled the several hundred dollars into a pail—and thanked the musician with a dollar. The young man demanded the usual half share, knocking the pail out of Pinza's hand, and there was an undignified scrimmage to pick up the money.

One of the greatest dramatic sopranos of our time was also one of the most uninhibited. As she chatted with several members of the company in the hotel lobby, she ran through a list of her various lovers' high notes and short-comings. After Pinza walked by, she shrugged and held up her pinkie finger.

She offered this tale to indicate the deterioration of good manners in America: She was working with her vocal coach one day when his wife walked into the bedroom to find them in a duet *con brio*. The woman stood there, expressing some objection, and the soprano looked up to say, "Madame, please close the door."

The most spectacular sexual athlete I knew was a tall, darkly handsome Chilean whom I'll rename Claudio. With irresistible dash and the energy of a horse, he enjoyed everything to excess. He had an insatiable appetite; by comparison, Richard Tucker, at his most ravenous, was a babe in a high chair. Claudio had three T-bone steaks at 5 in the afternoon, and after the performance, ordered two more, with dozens of oysters, several wines and desserts.

He possessed a voice of magnificence and power which he abused all his life. He began as a baritone, but his voice soon thinned out, and he turned into a tenor to make his Met debut as Don José. In the fifties, he was singing the most difficult roles, Otello and Tristan, to excellent reviews, while carousing all week, including matinees. He canceled and postponed shows to keep dates with women. By 1959, he could no longer sing a full performance of a Wagnerian opera, and within three years, his tenor voice was destroyed. He ended his career in Europe, singing comedy basso roles.

Claudio, it was generally believed, left a wife and child in Chile and, after coming to the United States, took as his wife an American Indian blessed with money and oil lands. She was not enough for him.

On tour in Cleveland, I received a phone call from Claudio sounding desperately weak: "Please come to my room, three-two-five."

I knew he had canceled a matinee performance because of a sore throat. "Do you want a doctor?"

"I can't talk now. Hurry up."

I ran down the stairway to his room, and after a moment, the door was opened. I walked into a rancid mess of hotel service trays, cups, and saucers scattered about the floor, towels and blankets hanging on chairs and doorknobs. A nicely upholstered blonde stepped from behind the door and introduced herself, "Hello, I'm Sophie." She was complete nude.

"Where's Claudio?" I demanded, suspecting some bizarre blackmail plot.

His deep-throated laugh boomed from the bathroom, and out he bounced, also nude, to lift the girl in his arms. "Isn't she gorgeous? We've been locked in here four days. I know you never believe me, Bob. What do you say, honey? Let's show Bob some tricks."

And he proceeded with great élan to mount Sophie. He not only had a horse's energy and appetite, he had its appendage. I shook my head briskly to clear the steamy vision and walked out the door with a hearty "Bravo! bravo!"

A few years later, when I was in Salzburg, Austria, entertaining American troops, there was a poster advertising Claudio in *Otello*. I stopped by the theater during rehearsal and he was overjoyed to see me. His wife was coming for the opening of *Otello*, and he was terribly troubled. He had so enjoyed himself "with every goddamn broad in the chorus" that he was certain he had caught syphilis. "It's impossible to buy penicillin here—you must please get some from the U.S. Army."

I was able to secure some from the PX, for which he thanked me fervently and invited me to dinner in a house he had rented, outside Salzburg. It was a charming little chalet, and the door was opened by a young, voluptuous blonde, in so few clothes she might as well have been nude. "My name is Berthe," she announced, and led me to the studio where Claudio was working with his coach.

He closed the door to inform me: "I'll be busy here for another hour. I've told Berthe all about you. Why don't you just go into the bedroom and have her for an appetizer?"

I settled for a quiet drink with Berthe while she made dinner. She announced proudly that she sang in the chorus.

12

When TV was Young and Gray

Richard Burton was back on Broadway in *Equus* early in 1976. Chain-smoking nervously backstage, he asked, "How was it? I was concentrating to project to you, luv."

I assured him his voice was robust as usual, filling the theater.

"Another bloody eight weeks . . ." he muttered wearily.

Richard has been concerned about his magnificent Churchillian vocal instrument ever since we met on the *Queen Mary*. Marion and I were returning from Italy; he and his first wife, Sybil, were going to Hollywood for his

American film debut in *My Cousin Rachel*, with Olivia de Havilland. I mentioned some of the pitfalls I had not avoided in *Aaron Slick*. "Oh, of course it's garbage," Burton said. "But I intend to make barrels of money. For Boot [Sybil] and for my numerous family. But I assure you, if I'm doing garbage, I'll be the best garbage in it."

Sybil, delicate and prematurely gray, said little, nodding occasionally with a gentle smile.

Late next afternoon, Richard found me vocalizing on the afterdeck. "Let's have a drink," he said, and guided me to the second-class bar—"I can't abide the snobby one"— and that was where our wives found us four hours later. Few men in the world can talk with the wit and magnetism and range of Burton. He'd known only Welsh until he was ten years old, and he'd abandoned an Oxford scholarship after one year to join the RAF. Since we met when he was about twenty-eight, he must have spent the intervening years reading every book of poetry and history in the English language.

I did not see him early in the day; I assumed he took naps to refresh himself for the late-night talk sessions. One noon he escorted me to the ship's boiler room, where his Welsh countrymen sang on their lunchtime. Burton joined in the intricate choral work, and as he sang, his seething energy relaxed into a benign smile. He asked me to sing with them.

"I don't know the language."

"But, luv, you do have a soul."

I fitted into the harmony, and several of the men nodded encouragingly. Richard never told them I was a professional.

While the musical *Camelot* glittered in New York, Richard held open house in his dressing room at the Majestic, where the main piece of furniture was a large refrigerator, fully stocked with liquids. "Burton's Bar," he called it, "cheapest in town." Everyone dropped in, from the English actor-knight currently in New York to stage-hands to barmen off the English ships. It was a continuous vaudeville, songs and patter and witty chatter, with Burton as MC. He is a mercilessly accurate mimic, particularly of his fellow actors. What an act Burton and Kaye would make!

In Rome for another recording session, I ran into Burton's valet, who told me Richard was at the Grand and would want to see me. I promised I would call and hurried off to the studio. When I walked in, Richard was already there—he wanted to hear *Pagliacci*. At the end of the session, he insisted, "Tell Marion to meet us at my hotel— we'll have a drink with Elizabeth. Bring the tenor." So Jimmy McCracken and I, in our old slacks and work shirts, and Burton, who now commanded $1 million a picture but still dressed like one of the crew, gathered around Marion and Elizabeth at the bar.

Elizabeth, dressed for dinner, informed Richard he was an hour late. She is only five feet two but hers was a towering rage, worthy of Cleopatra. They went at each other in one of those homey, name-calling rumbles that kept them together for years. Jimmy whispered, "I'm getting out before the cops come," and slipped away.

After a while Liz and Richard silently acknowledged a truce. I suggested a restaurant operated by Mama Angelina, who made the best pasta in Rome. We got a back-room table but there was another uproar—of autograph hunters— while Mama excitedly cooked up her specialties. Now Elizabeth announced she must lose some weight for her next picture—she couldn't eat a thing.

Richard exploded. "After all that goddamn rowdydow about my being late for dinner, you'd better eat!" Hostilities broke out once more, while Mama's tears welled up. Marion and I wanted to eat—the Burtons stalked out and entered a cab. It pulled away, stopped, and backed up. Richard poked his head out the window. "Bob, could you lend me . . . I don't have a *lira*."

Rome, one year later: The telephone awakened me in the hotel room. "Bob, it's Richard. Come down for a drink."

It was seven-thirty in the morning. "Richard, I have a recording . . ."

Marion murmured, "What's that?"

"Burton."

She rolled away, pulling the cover over her head.

"I'll meet you in the bar," he announced, and hung up.

I pulled my trousers and a shirt over my pajamas and stumbled down to the bar. He had been up all night, but the almost savage energy within him boiled out over our Bloody Marys. He declaimed Dylan Thomas, and went back to his own years of terrible poverty as the thirteenth child of a coal miner, when the family had been forced to borrow money to bury their mother. "Well, I've taken care of all of them—they have houses and cars—but my pictures are such slush, and I haven't done anything first-rate since *Hamlet*. And everybody expects me to take over from Olivier when he goes. . . . Bob, how do you stay so bloody sober?"

"Liquor never did anything for me."

He sat there nodding with a wry smile as if he were an amused observer of his own secrets while he talked. Marion found us at the bar. "Bob, it's ten-thirty. You'll have to get your head together for the session." She ordered coffee.

"Quite right," Richard said. "Carry on." And he walked out into the gray morning, singing a Welsh dirge.

He is one of the few genuinely independent persons in this world, with wealth, sensitivity, intelligence—and the guts to do whatever he pleases. He gave up drinking a short time ago, by a sheer act of will—cold turkey—and now he sips only an occasional glass of wine. He still retains his low threshold of boredom.

At one of the parties in his New York hotel he grumbled, "Bob, let's get some air." We strolled into a corridor and discovered two of the hotel's attractive cigarette girls. Richard introduced me, then requested a bit of music. I sang a chorus of "My Blue Heaven" à la Crosby. He responded with some lines from "Gunga Din."

The girls, a little baffled, applauded. Richard thanked them for being such a beautiful audience, and we walked back to his party.

The Merrills rattled Burton only once. He invited us over to his New York hotel suite, just after he had paid about $1.25 million for the famous Cartier diamond as a present to Elizabeth. Admission to their floor was as difficult as entry to Fort Knox.

Richard greeted us, and when Elizabeth came in, said, "Show Marion the swag, luv."

Marion does things thoroughly—she once practiced piano for eight solid hours—and that is why she is my business manager. Some years back, when we decided to invest in diamonds as a financial hedge, she found a friendly dealer and studied the intricacies of gem structure. For this she bought a loupe, the small magnifying glass used by jewelers to examine stones.

Elizabeth jauntily tossed the ring across the room to Marion, who fielded it neatly. The diamond was an inch and a half long and an inch thick, shaped like a miniature pear. Marion lifted the jeweler's loupe out of her handbag. "May I?" she asked, and held the glass to her eye.

It was the first time I'd ever caught Burton at loss for a word. "What in hell is this?"

"Perfect," Marion announced. "Absolutely flawless."

The astonished Burtons took turns looking through the loupe, and Richard announced, "Before you leave tonight, you will both be searched."

Nelson Eddy was forty and one of the brightest stars in the movie heaven, as the stalwart sweetheart of Jeanette MacDonald, when he eloped with Ann Franklin, former wife of Sidney Franklin, movie producer and ex-matador. That was in 1939. Since 85 percent of his fan mail came from women, MGM was concerned that they might cool off now that their blond hero was married; but his career sailed onward and upward, into radio and concerts. He and his wife were seldom photographed in public together. About ten years later, I learned why.

I came out to the NBC studios in Hollywood for a radio show, and met Nelson in one of the corridors. He immediately made me a guest on his show. According to the script, the announcer would say, "And now, ladies and gentlemen, the voice of Nelson Eddy—" Offstage, he'd sing "Rose-Marie," and then make his grand entrance.

This night, Nelson turned to me with a big grin and said, "*You* sing it." I sang "Rose-Marie, I love you—," and I don't suppose anybody noticed the difference, until the announcer continued, "Here he is, ladies and gentlemen, Nelson Eddy!"—and Nelson pushed me out on the stage for a startled bow.

The real Nelson Eddy never came through on the screen. As the brave Royal Northwest Mounted policeman in *Rose-Marie*, he looked as if he'd rather kiss the horse than Jeanette. Yet he was a beguiling, impetuous man of many talents. A gifted sculptor, a collector of ceramic T'ang horses, he knew thirty-two operatic roles and could sing in seven languages. He had worked hard for years to perform in Wagner, and actually did sing in *Aïda* in San Francisco. His was a good, serviceable voice, but without operatic timbre or the top notes. Louis B. Mayer's secretary heard him at a concert and recommended him to her boss; after his first two films made Eddy look foolish, Mayer literally coerced him into becoming a star.

As Nelson explained, "I hired a drama coach to teach me how to act. His advice was one word: Don't. Just be yourself. Then Mayer had an opening in *Naughty Marietta* with Jeanette, where I would sing 'Ah, Sweet Mystery of Life.' And I said, 'Hell no, that's the theme music for Forest Lawn Cemetery!'

"Mayer said, 'If you don't take this part, you'll never make another picture in Hollywood. What's more, you'll be so broke you'll never even get into that cemetery!'"

After the radio show, he took me to his colonial mansion in Brentwood for dinner and introduced me to his wife. The romantic throb in the hearts of millions of women had married a charming and cultivated lady who looked about twenty-five years older. She could have been typecast as his mother.

Our tours crossed in the fifties and sixties. I was in Boston, carrying a bundle of starched-front tuxedo shirts under my arm and looking for an instant laundry. "Laundry?" Eddy roared. "Who the hell needs a laundry? Shake some white talcum over it and the audience'll never know the difference."

It worked nicely. He was not broke, and neither was I.
Show business is illusion, anyhow, and its practioners
delight in these little tricks.

> *When I played Philadelphia with Pinky Lee, one of the*
> *dancers showed me how to press a tie without an iron:*
> *Sprinkle some water on it with your fingertips, then run the*
> *back side of the tie carefully over a bare electric bulb in*
> *the dressing room. The wrinkles steam right out.*
>
> *In the Catskills, I needed a white waiter's jacket for a*
> *comedy bit; the one available must have been used to*
> *wash the dinning room floor. Simple, said the stage*
> *manager. He took it to the scenery shop and painted the*
> *entire jacket whiter than white. It was as crisp as if it had*
> *just been pressed.*

Nelson told me he'd made $5 million in his sixteen
films, when taxes were only fleabites; in the forties, he
commanded $10,000 a concert and $5,000 a week in radio.
He didn't need money or work when he went on the
nightclub circuit in 1960 as a partner for Gale Sherwood, a
beautiful and talented soprano. He had told me he was in
love with her, but she would not marry him—he was about
twenty-five years older than she. He toured with Gale and
never divorced his wife.

To lay out a tour of clubs, you often break a long trip
with stopovers that are not up to your usual standard. I saw
him when I appeared in St. Louis; he and Miss Sherwood
were playing in a downtown hotel. The nightclub was
dowdy, the air was stale, and the customers noisy. Nelson
was in his sixties, massive and jowly, with the face of a
Wagnerian warrior he'd always wanted to play. He introduced me from the audience and sang "Rose-Marie" as a
souvenir of our long-ago radio show.

"God, how I hate that song!" he said with a sigh in his
dressing room. "I personify a wonderful, nostalgic era for
so many people—all they want from me is 'Short'nin'
Bread' and 'Ah, Sweet Mystery of Life.' I'm trapped in their
thirties!"

He must have been profoundly in love, to choose this
heartbreaking way to round out his career.

A friend, who saw his last show in 1967, told me Nelson suffered a seizure while performing, something artists always fear. At the Sans Souci Hotel in Miami Beach, he stopped suddenly in the midst of a number. Bewildered, he told the audience, "I can't seem to get the words out," and asked his accompanist to play "Dardanella," a song out of the twenties—"I ought to know *those* words." But the pianist and Miss Sherwood had to help him back to his dressing room; he died in the hospital. His wife survived him.

"I was a kid when I got this show—twenty-eight!" Sid Caesar groaned. "I don't think it was impossible to do a different ninety-minute show every week. Now I know."

Sid was as jittery, bewildered, compulsive and morose as any *shnook* he ever portrayed on his *Show of Shows*. He worked from life. For the two years I sang in that bedlam, he lived in constant terror that he would wake up and discover he was a successful comedian. He worked on his sketches eight days a week, lurching around the rehearsal hall like a Bowery drifter, groaning, sweating, buttoning his jacket up, then down again, as if ready to flee. He smiled only when the skit demanded it.

After a day of turmoil, his eyebrows, lips, and jowls limp as a basset hound's, he slumped into a nearby steak house. I ordered a small beef filet; he had a tumblerful of scotch, glanced at the menu and ordered doubles on everything. As an eater, he was in the championship class with the Chilean tenor, but it never ran to fat. Sid, a powerful six-footer, lifted weights.

From age eight on, Sid hoped to be a serious musician, a saxophone soloist. He performed in the high school jazz band, studied at the Juilliard School of Music at night, played hot tenor sax for Charlie Spivack and others. He was in a Borscht Belt band when a *toomler* suggested he could escape rehearsal merely by helping out in comedy bits. Sid drifted into comedy.

He invited me for dinner, to hear him play sax concertos by Ibert and Debussy, in his out-of-character Park Avenue apartment: eight rooms, governess and cook, two children, a delightful blond wife, Florence, and a collection of modern French paintings. After hors d'oeuvres and a few drinks, Sid wandered out of the room; soon I heard the sound of a saxophone through the walls. "He's practicing," Florence explained. After an hour, she asked me to be patient: "Sid loses track of time." After another hour, she asked me to please understand, and I went home. Without dinner.

Carl Reiner performed with Sid in the comedy bits, but what he *really* wanted to do, he confided, was sing tenor. During breaks in rehearsals I helped him vocalize with some of Mr. Margolis's exercises, but Carl fortunately never mastered singing; he became a highly paid actor and writer.

Mel Brooks was the frantic young gofer with the show. He spent most of the day spraying one-line gags around the hall and getting in Max Liebman's way. Max, as producer, fired him twice, and Sid, as star, hired him back three times. He could pick up a few wild lines out of Mel's barrage. (Although Sid had four writers, he contributed about 35 percent of what went out on the air.) Mel is now spraying gags into big hits, *Blazing Saddles* and *Young Frankenstein.*

Sid's father ran the St. Clair Lunch, near the railroad station in Yonkers, New York. Sid picked up bits of Italian and Russian from the day laborers who ate there, to become an uncanny mimic of accents. He and I concocted raving arguments in gibberish French and Viennese, riding up and down the studio elevators; we started as the doors closed, and the fearful passengers shrank back against the walls, shielding themselves with pocketbooks and umbrellas. Then we threatened to drop a *"bomba."* This byplay gave Liebman the idea of doing foreign movie satires with Sid and Imogene Coca. But never with me.

I asked Sid once why we didn't do one of those elevator scenes on the air. "Oh, no," he answered. "You're a serious singer."

"But you're a serious saxophone player."

He looked at me as if we had just met. "Who told you that?"

Television in the fifties could be spectacularly foolish. I was catapulted into the middle of the great Paar-Sullivan feud, and an omniscient shoemaker proved on *The $64,000 Challenge* that he knew more about opera than I did. It was all *Sturm und Drang* at the time, but television and I survived.

Jack Paar drove me home one night from the airport after we appeared at a dinner for President Eisenhower, and mentioned that the NBC *Tonight* show was up for grabs. "I'm in front. Christ, I hope it works for me—I've been knocking around radio and TV for twenty years now, and something always fizzles out. It's a minimum budget, but . . ." I immediately volunteered to appear with him.

What drew me to Jack was our mutual stuttering: he had cured himself as a boy by filling his mouth with buttons and reading out loud, while I never conquered mine until I was about thirty, by singing. Jack had come out of Canton, Ohio, and bounced around as disk jocky, stand-up comic in the army, and a bit player in five forgettable films, one with Marilyn Monroe; he had been a replacement for Arthur Godfrey and Jack Benny, and flopped on two network TV shows and one on radio.

Jack's first *Tonight* shows were a hassle. The budget permitted him to pay only union minimum, about $220 an appearance. I was singing on Ed Sullivan's *Toast of the Town* for $3,000. Ed sizzled under the collar when he discovered that Jack was attracting his talent for minimum wages and issued an edict: No one who appeared for Paar could ever work for Sullivan. So Ed exiled me for five years. It became very important to thousands of people that I be reinstated. Sacks of mail were delivered at the Met, from absolute strangers, supporting me. Agents and friends supplicated Sullivan. At length, I had a chat with Ed in his apartment at the Delmonico. I explained I had only done my bit to help a friend in distress, adding that I had sung on Sullivan's own second show for bare minimum, too. He relented, and I was rehabilitated.

Opera performers on these early radio and TV shows jangled sensitive nerves at the Metropolitan Opera. Both

Edward Johnson and Rudolf Bing believed these appearances were undignified and subverted the Met's image. And yet, when I mentioned on TV the cities where the Met touring company would play, people who had never seen opera would walk up to the box office and inquire for tickets to the "Bob Merrill show." After some time, the publicity department of the Met asked me if I could arrange TV spots for their other singers.

Paar, a normally bright and droll man, had no time for opera. It became a running gag on the show; after a year I persuaded him to accept two tickets. Since he was celebrating an anniversary, I arranged an informal champagne reception in the Green Room of the old Met. Jack never showed up. He sent, instead, Mrs. Miller, the elderly little groupie who sat in his studio audience every night to exchange laughs with him. And there I was, with all that champagne and Mrs. Miller. Jack explained, "I just chickened out."

Hugh Downs, who cued the opening of the show with " . . . and now, here's Jack!", was an accomplished musician who, for some years, asked me to listen to a symphony he had composed. I'm afraid he chickened out, too; I never heard it.

Jack was accused by detractors of being hostile, arrogant, moody; well, he had to shift moods quickly to keep the show moving. "We don't rehearse this show," he once said. "We just defend ourselves." When one of his guests was uncommunicative or dull, Jack could be very distant. On some nights, I had the distinct feeling he'd rather be home with his family. A very moral man, he enjoyed provoking his guests into spilling sexual innuendos that titillated his audience.

He provoked me into a hot food competition. After the show, he enjoyed spicy foods at La Fonda del Sol, a South American restaurant near NBC. When I wouldn't eat them, he called me a sissy. I'd had enough of hot chilis in Texas, where I lost my voice; but Jack was such a compelling man that I tried some chimi churri sauce with tacos that he labeled "yummy." My tongue came out for air—and I lost my voice again.

The show grossed $10 million for NBC in 1958, and by 1962, when Johnny Carson took it over, Jack was a man of means; he invested in radio and television stations and is retired now, simply relaxing at his home in Connecticut.

The confusion that made me slide into *Aaron Slick* was much like the one that lured me into *The $64,000 Challenge:* I was expanding my horizons and creating interest in opera. Television is a great humanizer; seen close-up on the screen, a performer whom the viewer has only heard about becomes a guest in the house, a pal, even a loved one. It took me two shows to become aware of how the quiz game was tilted, but by that time, I was hooked. Strangers greeted me on the street by my first name, cab drivers called to me through open windows—I was a national celebrity.

My opponent, the Italian shoemaker who came into the studio with his shop grime still under his fingernails, was an adorable little man; he loved opera and played the mandolin with intense amateurism. When the producers asked me to sing "Sorrento" accompanied by him, a flood of love and warmth seemed to flow over the country, coast-to-coast. On my tours, bellboys rushed to pick up my bags, and stewardesses embraced me: "Gee, that was sweet of you to sing with the shoemaker."

The challenge operated in a sly way to let the producers make a winner of whomever they wished. One of the assistants would come into my dressing room (and the shoemaker's—they were separate rooms) before air time and ask a series of questions on opera. Since the quizzes were simple at first, I answered all correctly. Next week, I missed one in the dressing room—and it was not asked on the air.

But I hung on, assuming, in a self-serving daze, that I would in the long haul know more than the shoemaker. But this classic confrontation—the little amateur versus the elitist professional—had an intense hold on the national imagination. The shoemaker *had* to win: We were acting out a deeply-felt myth, and millions of viewers would have felt chagrined, personally defeated, if I had been the victor. The question that cut me down was something as preposterous as, "What did Verdi brush his teeth with?" If I had answered correctly, I might have been mobbed.

Johnny Carson, master of the wicked ad-lib, has an instinctive feeling for comedic situations. He can turn almost any disaster into a laugh.

My number on his *Tonight* show was the everlasting "Sorrento," accompanied by the band's guitarist to create a Neapolitan atmosphere; unfortunately, he was a nervous pop guitarist who started on the wrong note and lost the tempo. Johnny leaped into the breach. Slipping under the camera, he rolled up the legs of my trousers, and suddenly I was transformed into a small boy, wading in the Bay of Naples. The visual incongruity created an audience uproar, giving the guitarist time to recover, Johnny stopped the music, I rolled down my trousers, and "Sorrento" was sunny again.

Johnny, who hosted my twentieth anniversary at the Met party, began honing his comedy sense as a child magician and ventriloquist in Nebraska. He served as a writer for Red Skelton and, like Red, is an inventive improviser. We performed at a dinner of a doctors' convention in the Waldorf-Astoria on Johnny's birthday. A lovely model wheeled in a surprise cake from the doctors—four feet high, topped by a small figure of Carson that looked more like Dracula with acid indigestion. Johnny cut into the cake with a serving knife, and after one inch of pastry, hit wood. It hadn't occurred to anyone that he would actually slice the cake. He rose to the occasion with wild invention, spouting gags, sawing away at the wood, circling in a duel with the tiny figure on top, offering to operate free on anyone with his knife, and finally he began to swallow the knife. It was five minutes of inspired lunacy.

One of the most endearing stand-up comedians of our day, Max Asnas, made his living as proprietor of the Stage

Delicatessen on Seventh Avenue. He delivered his pungent aphorisms with his sandwiches, from behind the counter and at your table, sauced by a thick Russian accent that cannot be duplicated to this day. Short and rotund, with the gait of a duck, he was a natural philosopher—someone dubbed him the Corned-Beef Confucius—and his devastating losses at the racetracks only sharpened his understanding of life's absurdities.

Max considered opera a snare and a delusion. After I talked him into sampling *Bohème*, I asked if he enjoyed it. He heaved the mournful sigh of a prisoner who has known Siberia. "Next time I want to hear foreigners, I'll go to Grossinger's."

To entertain an out-of-town guest, he sat through two acts of *Traviata*. His critique: "I'd rather sleep in my own bed."

His friend, a self-styled opera buff, then sang the aria "Di provenza" with a Yiddish sob, and asked me, "How come you don't sing the lover, a good-looking fellow like you?"

"I can't. I'm the baritone."

"Don't worry," Max said, "you're still young."

A year later, I was in *Traviata* again and offered Max two tickets. "What's the use?" he said. "I already know the story."

Max had been headwaiter at another Broadway landmark, the tiny Gaiety Delicatessen, when I was delivering shoes for my uncle's Paradise Bootery nearby. In those days, you could buy half a sandwich. After Max opened the Stage, between 53rd and 54th Streets, he moved into the apartment house above the store for convenience: He never closed up until four A.M.

Inevitably, the deli, with only eighty seats, became the late-late show club. Fred Allen and his writers, Milton Berle, Sid Caesar, Jack Leonard popped in for the spicy pastramis and left with comedy material. Playwright Elmer Rice was a habitué, as well as Harry Warner of the movie brothers. But Max never lost his uncommon touch.

One of his friends was honored by a dinner at the four-star Chambord restaurant; Max reluctantly climbed into his blue suit and ate carefully among the alien dishes—one of which was pheasant under glass. A Park Avenue dowager, sitting across the table, made conversation: "I'm so sorry I have never visited your famous restaurant, Mr. Asnas. What do *you* serve under glass?"

"What I serve under glass? A saucer."

I brought my children, Lizanne and David, to the Stage when they were toddlers. Max, almost beaming, waited on them himself. My boy ordered a peanut butter and grape jelly sandwich, and Lizanne wanted only potato chips with Pepsi. Max turned to me: "Where did you bring these kids up—in a garage?"

On my way to the Met in a cab, I discovered I had left my money at home. Since I was within striking distance of the Stage, I stopped the taxi and ran in. Max spotted me in the mob standing four-deep at the counter.

"Robert Merrill!" he shouted above the din. "You should be rehearsing now."

I murmured, "Max, I've got a cab outside. Can you lend me five dollars?"

There were immediate grumbles from the standees: "*This* is an opera singer? He don't have five bucks to his name!"

Max, who was a notoriously soft touch for panhandlers, opened the register and tossed a ten at me. As I turned to go, he called out, "Wait. I already made three sandwiches!"—and handed me the bag.

New York cab drivers are sit-down comedians. About a third of them seem to be actors between engagements, and another third, who are not comics or thespians, must be frustrated singers.

As I climbed into a Checker, with two suits in boxes from my tailor, the unshaven driver immediately sized up the boxes. "What line garments you make?"

"Oh, the one hundred, hundred-and-fifty range."

"Listen, I need a suit, my son is getting married. Could you give me a suit wholesale?"

"I think so." By this time we had reached the Met door,

and as I twisted out, he recognized me. Without blinking, he said, "Okay, I'll take two tickets to the Met."

Another night I was late for an evening performance and urged the driver, a woman—from the Bronx, I judged, by her accent—to hurry, please. "They've probably started the overture by now."

"You wouldn't miss much," she replied. "It's only the music."

The would-be singers usually tell me what kept them from a professional career: no money to study, too many children, couldn't stand the climate. One driver, a middle-aged man, demonstrated with "O paradiso." He wasn't bad at all.

Two hours later, when I came out of rehearsal, he was waiting for me at the stage door. He refused to accept payment—he wanted to audition another aria. I found him waiting for me at the opera or my apartment in following days, and I told him I would not get into the cab unless he accepted my fare.

He was in his forties and felt unfulfilled. I tried to persuade him it was almost impossible to start a singing career at that age: "Study it for your own enjoyment." No, he was determined. "I'd like to take a real crack at it."

Walking through the opera house one afternoon, I heard voices coming from the general auditions that were held once or twice a month. I came into the rear of the auditorium, just in time to catch the last few bars of the cab driver's "O paradiso." I retreated immediately.

Mr. Bing informed me later that he had arranged the audition, which is usually done through agents or recognized voice teachers, after the cabbie had picked him up at the stage door and told him he was my protégé. I denied all credit for this, but the driver managed to wangle a job with the chorus. He left opera a few years later to take home more pay driving the taxi.

On my way to NBC, in a cab driven by a clean-shaven, wavy-haired fellow in blue aviator's glasses, obviously a young leading man, I was overwhelmed by his stinking cigar.

It was, in fact, the vilest cigar since the one Aristotle Onassis gave me at a party in El Morocco. We were celebrating my recent debut at Covent Garden. I recall that Alan King was leading a community sing—"Take Me Out to the Ball Game," etc.—and Maria Callas, who was with Onassis, could not sing along because she didn't know this American genre. Onassis, puffing away on his wretched cigar, kept poking Maria with his elbow, "Sing, Maria—sing for your supper!" while she muttered, "But I don't know the words . . . !"

I asked my cabbie, "Please put out that smelly cigar." He grumbled, then slowly snuffed it out. After we drew up to the NBC stage entrance, he recognized me. "Big shot!" he grunted. "If *I* was on the networks, I'd smoke a Havana."

The Brooklyn Dodgers of the fifties were all show biz—buffoons, trick dancers, magicians—led by one of the country's greatest comics, Casey Stengel. About the only straight man in the company was Gil Hodges, who played hard and played square, kept the curfew, drank only coffee, and was sustained by his intense faith in the power of his bat and the Catholic religion.

He was flying to Chicago on a Friday night when the stewardess brought a plate of sliced steak. The gentle giant told the girl, with a rueful smile, that he would have to pass it up. "I'm a little too close to headquarters."

His wife Joan had an almost equal commitment to the music of opera; she'd studied voice and knew almost every note of the major librettos. But Gil, son of a miner from Indiana, was tuned mainly to the sound of hickory slamming cowhide. He was the first man in history to hit four home runs and a single in one game. He moved to Los Angeles with the Dodgers, but the Mets brought him back to New York after those lovable stumblebums had lost 101 games in one season. Gil wiped the clown makeup off their faces, shut them out of saloons, and, while most of the city prayed, guided them to their first pennant.

Nineteen sixty-nine was the year of the spectacular—

men walked on the moon that summer—and Marion and I sat in Joan's box for every Mets game, praying they could walk off with the World Series. After they took the first game, Joan insisted we were good luck charms, and we had to duplicate exactly in the following days what we had done in the first game. I wore a bow tie and ate a bag of peanuts each seventh inning; Marion wore the same dress for the five games.

The city arranged a tremendous victory celebration at Battery Park, for which Mayor John Lindsay asked me to sing "Take Me Out to the Ball Game."

As I stood on that platform in the park—with 100,000 faces staring up at me and the TV camera focused—I blanked out on the lyrics. Putting my arms around the MC, Ralph Kiner, and Pearl Bailey, I urged the crowd, "Let's *all* join in singing 'Take Me Out to the Ball Game'" and whispered to Ralph, "Do you know the words?"

He nodded. "Okay," I said, "you start." I synchronized my lips to his words until they came back to me.

Soon, another crisis. I was booked for a luncheon uptown, and I didn't see one taxi in the bedlam at the Battery. Could one of the Mayor's assistants give me a lift uptown? He could indeed—right in the back seat of the limousine carrying Joan and Gil for the triumphal ticker-tape parade up Broadway.

It was an incredibly exciting and frightening hour: people hanging out of buildings; Wall Streeters, hard-hat construction men, and stenographers breaking through the police lines, with tears in their eyes, to shake Gil's and Joan's hands; and, over all, a heavy snowstorm of confetti, torn papers, emptied wastebaskets. The *Guinness Book of World Records* claims that the greatest New York welcome in history was given astronaut John Glenn in 1962, when the city's Department of Sanitation picked up 3,474 tons of paper. Impossible. The sanitation experts calculating the Mets' reception must have gone snow-blind. I could barely see the front end of our car.

In the midst of all this roaring exultation, Joan, her

head projecting above an igloo of paper, turned to me and asked, "In the second act of *Trovatore*, what is that melody you sing with the nuns?"

At that tumultuous instant, I couldn't recall it. Joan hummed away on several false starts, when suddenly, she cried, "I've got it! Da-da-da-da!" And we triumphantly sang the finale of Act II as we paraded uptown in the paper snow while thousands cheered.

Now Joan managed to drag Gil to the opera with the argument that since I was a Met fan, we ought to support each other. I sang *Rigoletto* and afterwards they visited my dressing room, Gil looking a little uneasy and towering above the others in the background. To relax the situation, I asked, "Well, how did I do?"

"Not bad," Gil said slowly. "You hit in three out of four acts."

Joan was a zealous fan of Franco Corelli, but after Gil died in 1972, running the household and four children made it difficult for her to attend the Met. Each of our dressing rooms has a telephone and a speaker that delivers the music from the stage; Joan asked if I could phone her, when Franco was singing a thrilling aria, and relay the music. Since I was not singing in that act, I stood on a bench, holding the telephone receiver next to the speaker.

Franco's wife walked in. "What the devil is that?" she cried.

"This woman in Brooklyn, she just can't keep away from your husband's voice."

The circumstances and time escape me, but I remember Casey Stengel's nasal drawl admitting, "I always enjoy a good funeral, as long as I'm not, ya know, the main attraction." I think he would have liked the splendid memorial service devoted to him at St. Patrick's Cathedral in November, 1975. He certainly would have added up the attendance: three or four hundred of his former players, fans, altar boys, league presidents, Terence Cardinal Cooke, and a few umpires.

I sang "The Lord's Prayer" from high up in the choir

loft, and the astonishing reverberations made me sound like the Mormon Tabernacle chorus. Afterward, I promised Cardinal Cooke he had himself a new choirboy. He accepted, and assured me the music I had sung "will be around for a while."

> *I am constantly surprised by the secular humor of church princes. Francis Cardinal Spellman, sitting next to me on the dais of a philanthropic affair, invited me to dinner at his residence, for which he would cook his specialty—spaghetti and meat sauce. "Buitoni has been trying to steal it for years," he whispered.*
>
> *In the lounge at Kennedy airport, awaiting a flight to London, I was introduced to the Archbishop of Canterbury. He discussed opera with an aficionado's perception and after the flight was called, added, "We'll continue our chat in the plane." My wife and I settled ourselves in the first-class seats—the Archbishop and his party walked through to tourist class. The primate of the Church of England turned to me and grinned. "I'm afraid God cannot afford an expense account."*

In his eulogy to Casey, M. Donald Grant, board chairman of the Mets, said: "He's Up There, managing a great team." And Baseball Commissioner Bowie Kuhn, quoting from the Book of Wisdom, remarked: "The just are in the hands of God, and no torment shall touch them."

I think the Old Perfessor, if he hadn't been the main attraction, would have volunteered a few "cherce woids to unsolemize the occasion."

13

Conductors to the End of the Line

It has been estimated that [Toscanini] knew by heart every note of every instrument of about 250 symphonic works, and the words and music of about 100 operas.
—*George R. Marek:* Toscanini

"Toscanini wants you."

The spine-tingling command was relayed to me a short while after my debut at the Met. The Maestro planned to conduct *La Traviata* on radio with his NBC Symphony and, having heard me sing "Di provenza" on my show, *Serenade to America*, told Samuel Chotzinoff, "That's the voice I want." I was hired sight unseen.

I immediately dissolved into a warm sweat, suffering all the depression of a condemned man. Arturo Toscanini, now seventy-nine years young, was still the wonder and terror of the music world. Tales of his ferocious demands for perfection swept through NBC regularly like whirlwinds. He was all-powerful and he knew everything: he had conducted the world premieres of *Pagliacci* and *La Bohème*, and it was all in his head—he never needed the score. When he made his first appearance at the Met, rehearsing *Götterdämmerung*, he corrected a cellist on one note. The musician insisted he had always played what the score required—A-natural. Toscanini called for the master score, which proved him correct. The orchestra applauded, and that was the last time anyone dared dispute him.

The night before I was to meet the demon Maestro for the first rehearsal, I could not sleep. I was living at home then, and my father and mother sat up with me, drinking tea around the kitchen table, as they argued to convince me—and themselves—that I should not be afraid of the Great Man. "He *likes* you," my father assured me. "He already gave you the audition."

"What is there not to like?" my mother added.

My insecurities could not be calmed by anything so rational as that. On the long subway ride to NBC, I sang "Di provenza" over and over to myself. I knew the words all right, but that was small comfort.

(SCENE: Studio 8-H at NBC.)

(I enter the huge hall briskly, expecting to see the principal singers assembled. It is empty, except for the grand piano and the Maestro, drumming his fingers on the polished top. He wears a fitted black jacket buttoned to his neck Nehru-style. He is a tiny man and slender, but his face is luminous—a halo of electric energy seems to surround it. And his eyes—they bore into me for several minutes as he inspects me, peering closely because he is almost blind. My courage oozes away.)

TOSCANINI: (Incredulously) *You are the Germont I hear on radio?*

ME: (Lapsing into my stutter) *Y-yes, M-m-maestro . . .*

TOSCANINI: (Inhaling deeply) *How can it be? You look fifteen years old!*

ME: *Oh, no! I'm al-al-ready t-t-twenty-sev-seven.*

TOSCANINI: (After a long pause) Vero? *But Germont is the father. He has suffer-ed, his heart it is smash-ed.* (Hopefully) *You have a son?*

ME: *I'm not ma-ma-married!*

TOSCANINI: Povero ragazzo. *(Two more minutes of silence, as he shakes his head in despair. I stand there, destroyed. Am I dismissed? A long sigh, and he beckons me to the piano. He plays the first notes of Germont's entrance. I sing. The Maestro plays from the score; but he was trained as a cellist, not a pianist, and troubled by his failing eyesight, he hits wrong notes. After we finish, he closes the score reverently, slowly. His lips purse into a gentle smile.)*Allóra! *My boy—I will* make *you a father!*

Together with Licia Albanese, my first Violetta, and Jan Peerce, we rehearsed for ten days. Toscanini lived up to his advance notices. He was terrifying in his rages against incompetence and almost childishly delighted when he achieved the supreme quality he sought. The musicians and singers were raised to heights they had never believed they possessed. For this, they loved him.

> As we became more relaxed with each other, he confided to me: "I always try for 125 percent perfect—if I get 80 percent, I am a happy man."

While he lashed us to reach that superhuman 125 percent, he was also, I'm sure, whipping himself because he could not convey the sound he heard in his head. Rehearsal was his way of exorcising the demons of mediocrity, and this required constant vigilance. He stood on his feet for the entire two or three hours, beseeching us with his body and arms, singing along with the music in his sharp-edged voice. At the end of each session, he was soaked in perspiration. The animal energy of the man at seventy-nine was beyond measure; he needed only four or five hours sleep, so he kept music at his bedside for study and review.

He could be savagely cruel to those who did not measure up, and he never forgave. He had resigned from the Met in 1915, after an artistic dispute with Gatti-Casazza, and no one around him dared mention the Metropolitan Opera; to him, it was always "that place, " pronounced with a sharp hiss. There was a legend at NBC that Toscanini had been required, by company policy, to submit to a heart examination. When told it was in perfect condition, he snorted, "Why not? It has never been used."

He phoned once to inform me that I would not be needed at a rehearsal, and chatted amiably. "What is your next performance in *that place?*"

"*Trovatore*, Maestro."

"Ah. Who is singing?"

"Zinka Milanov—"

He hummed in vague approval. "And the tenor?"

I pronounced his name. Silence. Then a flood of curses—*"Vergogna!* [shame] . . . *bestia! . . . assassino!"* The maledictions coagulated into an incomprehensible scream, and he hung up.

He spared no one, least of all himself. As I walked by his small office after a rehearsal I heard, through the partly open door, the Maestro's curses. I dared to peep through the opening. He was seated at the piano, running through a passage, while a metronome clicked away, and he was calling himself *"idiot!" . . . "pig!"* The metronome had proved him wrong in a tempo he rehearsed that day.

When he pointed his long, bony finger at offenders in the orchestra, thunder rumbled from the tip of that finger:

"I should kill you, *imbecille!* Because you are killing me!"

One day he drew himself up to his full five-feet-one-inch height and roared with wild glee: "I cannot find anybody who knows to play the violin. *Not one man here!* When I retire, I open a bordello. You know what that is? or are you all *castrati?* I will attract the most beautiful women in the world for my bordello—it will be the La Scala of passion! But I will lock the door against *every one of you!*"

His phenomenal memory doomed his "enemies" to eternal damnation. I happened to be in his office—I don't recall why—when he interviewed a conductor as a summer replacement for the NBC Symphony. Emil Cooper had conducted all over the world, including a long term at the Met. He enumerated some of his credits: "Kiev, 1900 . . . Drury Lane, 1914, for Diaghilev's ballet . . . an all-Wagner program at Salzburg in 1920. I heard that you were in the audience. . . ."

Toscanini, twirling his mustache as he concentrated, leaped up. "Yes! Yes! You destroy-ed the concert! Faker! Get out!"

He coached me for Germont patiently and tirelessly. Leo Spitalny, who had persuaded me to sing "Di provenza" on our radio show, attended several rehearsals; he was privileged because he was NBC's music contractor. As Toscanini and I worked on this aria, I looked over to see Leo, the score in his lap, waving his finger to signal me, "Don't leeston to heem—do eet like *I* told you!" I shivered and turned away. If Toscanini had caught him, he would have thrust his baton through Leo's heart—and dismissed me as co-conspirator.

After I finished my solo, the Maestro hopped off his podium and wrapped his arms around me—I was so relieved I went limp against his frail body. "I make you a father, dear boy," he said softly. When I saw how harshly he treated others, I did feel he had adopted me. In the Act II duet with Violetta, I had a problem with a syncopated beat. Toscanini gave me the correct timing by tapping his baton on my head. And whenever I sang Germont after that, I felt the supernatural hand of Toscanini on me.

As the company filed out of his office to present *Traviata* on the air, I was astonished to see the Maestro leap up onto his sofa, then down again, up and down again. Chotzinoff explained, "He practices that all the time, so he can look graceful when he jumps on the podium." Toscanini was subject to the normal small vanities after all. The tailcoat he wore for radio performances had been adjusted over and over, I was told, so that his back, which only the studio audience could see, was also perfection.

Our *Traviata* was universally acclaimed; the tapes of the broadcast, however, revealed a few imperfections. The Maestro refused to release the album of the show unless the flawed passages could be rerecorded. A date was set, shortly before he was to leave for summer vacation in Italy, and it was exactly at the high point of my hay fever season. I appealed to Chotzinoff: "I might ruin it with my nasal tone."

Toscanini understood: He also suffered from hay fever. He promised to repair the faults, but his schedule never permitted the time. The original tapes were pirated, and sold in Europe for $50 and more. Toscanini exploded when told of this: "Why should only the rich hear Verdi? Do their ears have more sense than other people? Never!" He allowed the release of the album, blemishes and all, including the Maestro humming and singing along.

He was eighty-nine when he decided it was time to conduct *Un Ballo in Maschera*, and again he asked for me. To coach me on the role, he recommended Dick Marzzolo, the same man who had snapped the piano string at Bess Truman's birthday party. Dick worked with me for about a week, and all the while I questioned his tempi. "Don't rush me," Dick said. "I've worked with the Maestro for years, I know exactly what he wants."

Toscanini asked for a run-through of my role in the NBC studio; although the broadcast would come from Carnegie Hall, he wanted to hear how it would sound in the control room. Marzzolo and I got past the first eight bars when we heard Toscanini's livid curses on the studio loudspeaker. "Who gave you those tempi? Who? Who? Idiot! Miserable pig!"

We froze. For five minutes we sat in utter despair while Toscanini stared at us through the booth's glass in silence. I knew it was a strategy he used, to let his message sink in while you waited, in terror, for the verdict. He then quietly ordered us to begin again. But Marzzolo's fingers had stiffened into rigor mortis, he missed notes. At length, Chotzinoff said, "That's enough," and Toscanini walked away without another word. He gave me the tempi later.

Having decided that Jussi Bjoerling would not arrive, as he had promised, the Maestro assembled the cast—Jan Peerce, Jussi's replacement; our soprano, Herva Nelli, and the others—for three days of hectic rehearsal in his large Victorian home, Villa Pauline, in Riverdale, just north of Manhattan. His son Walter had filled the house with elaborate recording, control and replay equipment, but the Maestro was hardly interested.

The truth was, he seldom listened to other conductors' work. Chotzinoff persuaded him to hear a young genius, who was touted for creating a marvelous new interpretation of a Beethoven symphony by making elaborate cuts in it. Toscanini listened attentively and Chotzi requested his judgment. The Maestro replied, "The move-ments I heard—*bah!* But the cuts, they sound-ed very good."

For relaxation between rehearsal hours, trays of coffee were served while the old man reminisced. Although he could have been only ten or twelve at the time, he recalled how Verdi conducted *Ballo;* and just as vividly, he remembered the soprano who played Oscar, the page boy, in knee breeches. "Ah! What beautiful legs she had."

Toscanini had a wide-ranging amorous eye. His genius and energy created a magnetic field that pulled women to his side. In his first years at the Met, there was a torrid affair with Geraldine Farrar; others followed, increasing in frequency with age. I sang with a soprano, about forty, who admitted she had fallen under Toscanini's spell while studying a role with him at his home. His black limousine would pick her up in New York City and deposit her at Villa Pauline around midnight. She entered the house through the darkened servants' entrance, and left the same way. The limousine then returned to her apartment in the city as the dawn rose over the East River. This liaison continued for over a year, when the Maestro was in his middle seventies "and still a hellova lover," she said. The soprano was not the first nor the last to come to his home in

*Riverdale or his villa in Italy. His wife, Carla, was deeply
wounded, but never abandoned him.*

His other amusements were rather simple. He displayed a surprising taste for musical comedies of the 1900s,
and enjoyed playing over and over the little tinkling waltz,
"Beautiful Lady," from the show *The Pink Lady.* Friends
gave him, or he bought, corny little tricks from a Times
Square magic store. He once served sherry late in the
afternoon; as we raised the glasses, the wine dripped
through tiny holes in the stems onto our chests. In another
intermission, he told one of the women to sing a passage
"like this"—and squeaked a rubber mouse in her ear. Then,
shaking it by the tail as if it were alive, dropped it into her
lap. Screams from the woman—howls of glee from the
Maestro.

Children responded to him as an equal. He and I
stepped out of an elevator at NBC into a mob of children,
milling around as they waited to audition for the Horn and
Hardart kiddies' radio show. He paused. A smile came over
his stern face as he bowed to them and shook hands.
Bending down on his knees to the small ones, he carried on
an animated conversation; he kissed them and laughed
with them and tossed them into the air. After about fifteen
minutes an assistant came out to look for him: he was late
for rehearsal. He waved good-bye to the children and
marched to the studio. With each step, his face grew more
austere as he concentrated on the music of the day. When
he picked up the baton, he was once more Toscanini, the
deputy of Verdi on earth.

Ballo was broadcast on two consecutive Sundays in
January 1954, and came up to his superlative standard.
During rehearsal, he heard me hold a note I had become
fond of, an E-flat, and he shook his head emphatically. "No,
no. Stop!" After the performance, he told me, with a wink,
"I see you take a big breath—you want again to hold that
E-flat, eh, *caro*?—so I wait for you. Beautiful!"

I thanked him. "Not me," he exclaimed. "Verdi! Ho,
Mayrill, whatta music!"

When I introduced him to Marion later, he congratulated me. "Whatta lucky man, Mayrill!," and patted her fanny. She immediately telephoned her parents in Detroit to inform them of this supreme honor.

A few months later, he conducted his last concert for NBC, and that was his final public appearance. I was blessed to have sung in the opera with which he ended his extraordinary career.

After Toscanini, it is difficult to take many conductors seriously. Oscar Shumsky, concertmaster of the NBC Symphony, told me—after he untangled a world-renowned baton-twirler from his knotted "interpretation"—"I'm thinking of quitting music to become a conductor."

The forties radio show *Music America Loves Best*, for which I was MC, originated on Sundays from Boston Symphony Hall and employed the Boston Pops Orchestra under Arthur Fiedler. The Pops is the Boston Symphony minus about twenty men. We rehearsed from noon to 1:30; the full symphony, under the haughty Serge Koussevitzky, played its regular matinee concert from 2:30 to 4:30; after an hour's rest, the Pops men reassembled to play the Victor show.

I frequently came in early, before Mr. Fiedler, and picked up the baton to rehearse one of my vocal numbers. The aria "Eri tu" went beautifully—after all, how could the experienced Boston orchestra not sound splendid?—when a studio flunky ran in with a message: "Mr. Koussevitzky wants to know who is the guest conductor. He shows promise."

This was high praise indeed. The pince-nezed leader called Toscanini "an Italian peasant," and Toscanini scoffed at "that Russian boor."

Jan Peerce, Risë Stevens and I were hired to record excerpts from *Samson and Delilah*, conducted by the glamorous Leopold Stokowski. He received us for the first rehearsal at his East Side apartment in a silk lounging robe that gave appropriate exposure to his bare legs. (Known as

"Fingers" Stokowski for the expressive digits he used instead of a baton, he was just as proud of his legs, Risë told me.) His wife at the time was Gloria Vanderbilt, and while we rehearsed, their two little boys in cowboy suits dashed in and out of his studio, shooting cap pistols and yelling "Stick 'em up!"

This did not disturb us as much as the realization, when we ran through the score, that he seemed to be learning the music as we went along, making it ten times more difficult: since he used only his fingers, we never knew where his beat was—in his left thumb? the right forefinger? the back of the hand?

I sat in on a rehearsal of *Turandot* that he was conducting for the Met. It was a shambles because nobody in the cast could find the beat. Birgit Nilsson, an experienced Princess Turandot, threatened to walk out. He ordered the horn players to repeat one passage over and over, to make it *pianissimo*. A member of the section told me that they put their horns to their lips but only one man played.

Leopold nodded. "Just a little softer, and it'll be perfect."

> Toots Shor, eminent saloon-keeper, and his pal, Rags Ragland, the thinking man's comedian, were persuaded to attend a concert at Carnegie Hall for the first time in their lives. Toots had only one small criticism: "How do you like that bum Stokowski?—he took more bows than Carl Hubbell after a no-hitter!"
>
> Arrogance is as essential to a conductor's equipment as the ability to stand on a narrow podium without falling off. Artur Bodanzky, who conducted at the Met for fourteen seasons until he retired in 1928, actually composed music for the recitatives in Fidelio, to improve on Beethoven.

A conductor, whom I may as well call Papriki, displayed in his pursuit of women the same finesse that made him a creative interpreter of Wagner. In Vienna, he rewarded a new amour with a full-length white lynx coat. I believe he had an arrangement with a wholesale furrier, because he gave the same prize to a second woman, and a third. All three appeared at the same reception, eyed each other, and made it clear to Papriki what he could do with his conductor's stick.

Years ago, a concert manager told me, he pursued Beverly Sills around the grand piano in rehearsal. His timing was off; as he rested one hand on her waist and the other on the piano, she dropped the open lid on his knuckles.

Another city, another soprano. In Frankfurt, a husband, unaware that Papriki had been making overtures to his wife, asked the conductor to escort her around town while he was away on business. The conductor immediately took her to dinner, and home to her hotel. Then, she said, the evening turned into a Feydeau farce.

(SCENE: Outside the soprano's room)

PAPRIKI: (Reaching for the door handle) *At last, my dear, we are alone.*

SOPRANO: *You've been very kind. Thank you—* (As he opens the door, she slips in quickly and locks him out)

PAPRIKI: *But my dear, you don't understand. Papriki is here to love you.*

SOPRANO: *I'm utterly exhausted.*

PAPRIKI: *You have not even kissed Papriki good night.*
(She opens the door a foot, but the conductor pushes the door open and enters the room. She has left her purse open on the floor. As he reaches for her, he puts his foot into the bag and the catch clings around his ankle. He hobbles after her, one foot in the bag, and finally traps her against the wall.)

PAPRIKI: *Oh, what a lovely breast is this!*
(He reaches into her gown, and a falsie comes out in his hand.)
What an outrage! You have deceived *Papriki!*
(Angered, he stumbles out of the room, pulling the handbag off his ankle as he goes.)

Fritz Stiedry, who had a notable career in Europe, suffered from a curious deficiency as a conductor. He directed Bing's first production, *Don Carlo*, in 1950, with a formidable cast: Cesare Siepi, Bjoerling, Jerome Hines, myself. We crowded around him while he conducted piano rehearsals sitting down.

He stopped me several times. "The score wants *forte* here. Why can't I hear you?"

I sang louder and louder, and still he insisted I was too soft. One of the men tipped me off: "He's deaf in the right ear." So I moved to his left side; now I was too loud. We worked until six o'clock, and then he invited me to his house. "Come for dinner. You have problems we must work out."

I was admitted to the apartment by a maid, who seated me in a side room. The smell of sauerbraten permeated the room, making me salivate; I had not eaten since noon. I waited and waited. Was it possible the maid had not announced me? Or he could not hear the maid? Promptly at 8:30 Stiedry came out of the dining room, wiping the gravy from his lips, and ordered me into the studio. "All right— let's go to work." We rehearsed until 10, and he didn't even offer me a cracker.

His deafness became more obvious. He could not hear entrances on stage or singing on his right, until Bing had to end his services. Stiedry felt this was unjustified, and never spoke to him again.

> Seven P.M.: *A desperate phone call from Erich Leinsdorf. "You must come down to my room immediately!"*
> *I dashed to the hotel elevator. He was conducting me in a production that night for the San Francisco Opera. Was he bowing out? Was the production postponed?*
> *Dressed in white tie and tails, he handed me a small jar of black makeup, and sat on a chair. "Bob, please cover that little bald spot in the back, so the lights don't hit it."*

Artur Rubinstein is synonymous with piano virtuoso, but like the Wagnerian heldentenor who dreams of playing

Pagliacci, Artur always wanted to conduct an orchestra. He performed frequently with the Israeli Symphony, so on a recent appearance he told Zubin Mehta, their musical adviser, of his aspiration. Mehta agreed. "Play whatever you want. The orchestra is yours tomorrow."

Choosing a Brahms symphony, the virtuoso spent the night studying the score. He arrived promptly at rehearsal in the regulation black turtleneck; Mehta and the orchestra's managers sat in the rear of the hall. Rubinstein hopped onto the podium smartly, and the orchestra tensed for the opening beat. He stood there thoughtfully for a moment, and then turned around. "Maestro!" he called to Mehta. "How do I start?"

Each conductor, scenery designer, costumer, choreographer, and director superimposes his own personality on the original score, one layer over the other. Each director's version is necessarily different from that of all other directors; otherwise he could hardly hope to receive the critical accolades: "new daring" . . . "new insights" . . . "a new sensation has arrived!" Unfortunately, in opera there is no time or money for one of those rehearsals George M. Cohan used to call on the plays he wrote: "Tomorrow at ten, we'll meet to take out the improvements."

We had a new director, "daring" but not yet "sensational," for a production of *Pagliacci* at the old Met. Leonard Warren was Tonio and I was cast as Silvio, the lover of young Nedda.

Our Nedda, however, was a woman of a certain weight, about forty pounds more than mine. For our passionate duet, the director thoughtfully placed her in a chair and instructed me, "Get on your knees and put your head in her lap."

I demurred *sotto voce*, "But she doesn't have a lap."

"Well, snuggle as close as you can."

The only place my face could go was into her crotch. This evoked unsuppressed giggles from others in the cast. "It looks bad," I told the director.

But he was determined to be creative. "These are Italian peasants, they're passionate people."

I went back to my prenatal position and we started the duet. On a lovely phrase, my voice wobbled.

"What's the trouble?" the director yelled.

"I think I'm getting an echo."

My best director was the immortal Giuseppe de Luca, the most sparkling and exuberant Figaro I have ever seen. De Luca had sung it at the Met since 1915, and in his farewell twenty-five years later, at the age of sixty-four, his vitality and consummate skill shamed men half his age playing that role. With his round pudding face and halo of white hair, he looked like Snow White's Happy. His eyes were still merry at seventy when I approached him to coach me in Figaro; I had warily arranged to try out the role in Montreal before my appearance with the Met.

When I was very young I had seen de Luca as the Barber, and recalled that I could not take my eyes off him. The secret he divulged in sixteen lessons was simply this:

"The eyes are the window of the soul, and Figaro's soul is gold and silver. In his eyes we see always what he is thinking: How much money is in the Count's purse? What is the height of the balcony? Where is my escape? All in the eyes. They move always. If you close your eyes for one second, you lose the audience."

I have a wide-open bias in favor of the people who carry the weight of everybody else's creativity on their backs and still make it all come together onstage: the singers.

I am an unabashed fan of Leontyne Price. She not only has a splendid lyric *spinto* soprano and an emotional range that glides smoothly from a sensual Aida to a devout Carmelite nun—she also has a joyous sense of humor. Very few divas have that gift and I don't know why.

She toured in *Porgy and Bess* for two years, all the way to Russia, and for two more years she sang in NBC-TV operas, from *Tosca* to *The Magic Flute*, before she actually stepped on an operatic stage in San Francisco, as Aïda. It was a thrifty production, which never helps relieve a debutante's tensions. When I entered as her father, the captive King of Ethiopia, my army consisted of five schoolboys painted black. She ran to greet me, obviously uptight, so I ad-libbed, "No wonder I lost the war—look at my army!"

She stifled her laugh, but it helped loosen her up, and the show became her personal triumph. Several years passed, in leading roles in Vienna, Salzburg, Covent Garden, La Scala (where a critic lauded her as the Aïda Verdi would have loved), before she came on the Met stage as Aïda. Again I was her father, and made up blacker than she. As Leontyne bowed to the bravos and open-hearted applause, I squeezed her hand. "Well, we finally made it!"

"Yeh, daddy. Now let's see you go out and get us a taxi."

In an English version of *The Magic Flute*, the tenor picked up her hand and said, "I will kiss your lily-white hand."

She whispered, "Baby, you ain't gonna find it here."

She lives in Greenwich Village and is a devotee of yoga exercise; beyond that, she says, "A good sex life is the best thing for a woman's voice."

Jan Peerce, my neighbor in Westchester, and I often sang in *Lucia di Lammermoor*. He played Edgardo, passionately in love with Lucia, and I was her brother, who forced her to marry another man. Before the famous sextet, Jan pulled out his sword one night and whispered angrily, "*Shmuck!* Why are you doing this to me?"

Jan took a long time to reach the Met from the Lower East Side. He learned the violin as a kid ("we were too broke to have a piano") and worked his way up to a sideman with Meyer Davis's dance bands. His wife, Alice, nudged him into singing; afterwards *his* sister, Sarah, nudged Richard Tucker into opera. When the Met accepted Jan, he was thirty-seven.

One thing Jan is very serious about is eating kosher. When we toured, he insisted on dragging me to a kosher restaurant or, failing that, to a family that kept a kosher house. Unfortunately, this soul food gives me heartburn. In New Orleans, I tried to drag him to Antoine's or Brennan's. But no, some friends were sending over a homemade dinner, "and you can share it with me." The dinner was one gigantic *challah* bread, about four feet long. Jan sent out for a bottle of milk, and we sat in his hotel room, dunking *challah*. I could have been dipping lobster into butter at Antoine's.

Next stop: Dallas. The opera played in a huge indoor athletic arena, like Madison Square Garden, with dozens of dressing rooms; wrestlers, booked for the following night, wandered in and out. Jan kept his door shut to concentrate on his role. In my room, next to his, I found some white chalk, and printed on his door: MEN'S ROOM.

A constant parade of wrestlers and hangers-on banged and rattled Jan's door, unzipping as they entered, and Jan had a terrible time persuading these giants to leave. Then he saw the chalk sign and stormed into my room. "You sonofabitch! You'll never get another kosher meal from me!"

A New York critic noted that Rosalind Elias, the alluring mezzo who often plays boy's roles such as Cherubino, "possesses certain physical endowments that make the task of impersonating a boy a little more than arduous."

Within these certain endowments, there is a lovable kook struggling to come out. One clue is the fact that she has tattooed her social security number on her abdomen; for another, she wears a diamond ring on her toes.

"Why not?" she says. "I'm Lebanese, and that's an old-country custom." As for the tattooed number, "If anything happens to me, and there's no other identification, I hope this inch of me will be saved so I can be buried with the family."

Rosalind was the thirteenth child in the family, and born on Friday the thirteenth, making it inevitable that she would be deeply committed to astrology. She is also an unrestrained belly dancer at weekend parties in her country house, and anybody who can read Rosalind's social security number, right below the navel, wins a special prize.

I know that skeptics have labeled the tattooing a piece of press agent's nonsense. Well, I attended one of those weekends, and the number is 023-22-9834.

Constance Hope, when she was an executive of Red Seal records, gave a party which Lenny Bernstein attended, as well as Blanche Thebom and the fabled Rosa Ponselle, with the strong, swarthy Roman face and the shyness of a wild bird. In my teens I had been fascinated by the few recordings of this most voluptuous dramatic soprano voice of the twenties; she had retired two decades before the party, so meeting her gave me a shock, as if she had risen from the dead.

Bernstein noodled around the piano as she sat in silence, shaking her head to requests for a song. Suddenly, the sumptuous, dark voice floated over the room, and together we sang the second act duet from *Aïda*. It was a memory to be cherished.

When I played *Fiddler* in Baltimore, I recalled that she lived nearby. She was now seventy-two, I was told, and had recently been hospitalized, but I wanted very much to say hello. Her maid answered the phone doubtfully, and then—Rosa was on the phone, apologizing in a wavering, still vibrant voice, for not seeing *Fiddler* because of her illness and urging me to bring Marion for a visit.

We drove out immediately, hoping we had not made a mistake; it's disillusioning to exhume legends, better to remember them at their prime. Miss Ponselle had enjoyed—or, rather, suffered, because of her neurotic insecurities—an unusual career. After she and her sister, Carmela, had sung in vaudeville, Rosa in 1918 made her debut at the Met in *La Forza del Destino* with the first team: Caruso and de Luca. James Gibbons Huneker, a critic who, like George Bernard Shaw, is still read for the durability of his judgment, praised her voice as "vocal gold, dark, rich, and ductile." Carmela also sang at the Met for a total of five years, then retired to teach.

Rosa sang there for twenty years, each one clouded by her own fears. Almost all performers are frightened before they go on; she lived in terror. Like Jussi Bjoerling, she walked around the block many times, firing up her courage to enter the theater. She was obsessed by the need for fresh air: The windows in her dressing room and the doors backstage had to be opened wide two hours before her performance, even in winter. She exasperated other members of the cast who feared the chill would give them colds; de Luca told me he warned her of a lawsuit if he caught cold on one of her singing days. Her tensions often made her so ill she had to cancel. In 1935, she sang Carmen, a difficult role for anyone except a mezzo, and her reviews were devastatingly cruel. A short while later, at forty, she left the Met and never sang in public again. Her marriage to a prominent Baltimore politician ended in scandal and divorce. The timorous Miss Ponselle withdrew further into herself, although she found some balm as artistic director of the Baltimore Opera Company.

We drove up to the villa, built on three levels, and at the very top, which was rimmed by a balustrade, she waved to us. "Merrill!" she called, and sang out "Ritorna vincitor!" ("Return victorious"), an aria from *Aïda*.

Marion wiped away some tears as we walked to the top level, which surrounded a swimming pool. Rosa Ponselle was wan and tired but the old warmth had not deserted her. Sandwiches and drinks had been set out, and she reminisced. She even burst into some arias *a cappella:* The glorious, lush quality was still there, although she could not sustain a full opera. We were entranced. Several times, we stood up to leave, to save her energy, but she would have none of that. Her only regret, she said, was that she had not recorded more of her music. "I really hoped to do it with you, after that party, but"—and she shrugged—"I was always so afraid. You know, I had to fight myself to come out on that stage. And I always hoped, when I walked around the theater, that I would become sick, or have an accident, so I could cancel."

She presented me with two autographed albums of all the music she had recorded, together with a picture of herself and Caruso in costume for *Forza*. Rosa Ponselle is now about eighty, the end of the line of the Golden Age.

Few performers can retire gracefully, before their special talent has worn thin and their public appearances are sad echoes of the glory they achieved in their prime. Garbo quit while she was on top; so did Jimmy Cagney and Cary Grant. Leo Slezak, the giant Czech tenor who rivaled Caruso, stopped when he was sixty, after he had received the greatest ovation of his career. That night, he realized he might never sing so thrillingly again; he and his wife had a nostalgic cry in his dressing room, and the next morning he announced his retirement. And he stayed retired. Nellie Melba had recurring farewell appearances, squeaking and cracking notes until she was seventy. Helen Traubel and Lauritz Melchior took to caricaturing themselves on radio and television when their voices were gone.

The massive Melchior, after reaching the heights in more Wagnerian roles than any heroic tenor in history, sang his last *Lohengrin* swan song at the Met in 1949. He then developed a comedy routine à la Henny Youngman and his violin: Melchior would sing, say, "La Martinata," and as he approached an unreachable note, he'd stop to tell a funny story, "When I was very young . . ."

Elsa Maxwell booked him and me for a lavish $75,000 New Year's Eve party in the ballroom of a Newark hotel, hosted by one of the Hess family, who owned a department store. On these concert occasions, Melchior appeared in white tie and tails, his chest emblazoned with medals conferred by many countries, including France, Sweden, Bulgaria, and Germany—and Vassar College, which honored him with a gold medal for service to American art. The entrance to his suite in the Ansonia Hotel displayed a placard with scroll letters: *Singer to the Royal Court of Denmark.*

As Elsa and I entered the hotel in Newark, I noticed a novelty shop selling fake medals as ornamental jewelry— the French Légion d'Honneur and others. Since Melchior liked a joke as much as I did, I stocked up on a chestful of brass medallions, and Elsa pinned them on, from my shoulder to my belt, giggling all the way.

Melchior, the six-foot-three "Great Dane," towered over the party guests who clustered around him, inspecting his honors, when I walked over to shake his hand. As I rattled my medals, the group broke into a hubbub of laughter and comment: Were Melchior's medals genuine? or were we both faking? He drew back, stunned, and his jovial Foxy Grandpa face seemed to droop in dismay; he refused my hand and turned away, barely hiding a tremble in his lower lip.

My joke collapsed like a punctured bagpipe. His medals were the concrete evidence of decades of noble achievement; they propped him up now that he was no longer champ, and I had unwittingly mocked his entire life. I hurried out of the lobby and tossed my medals into a vase of flowers. Later I tried to apologize. He walked away from me.

Vienna, 1963: I received a phone call in my hotel room. A low, resonant voice said, "This is Emanuel List. Can I see you downstairs for coffee?" I hurried down to meet the man I had admired since my teens, when he sang in the first Wagner opera I ever saw.

List had retired to his native Vienna in 1952, after fourteen years as leading bass at the Met, specializing in Wagnerian roles. Both his presence and his voice were magnificent, almost on a level with Chaliapin's. List had come to America in 1914 and toured for some years in vaudeville and minstrel shows. He became an American citizen, but attained his eminence in Europe and South America before he reached the Met.

List was in his seventies now, and his face and body

had shrunk so that he looked older. He wore the conventional Viennese double-breasted black suit, well pressed, with the white, stiff-collar shirt and black tie; still an aura of seediness hung over him. He recounted wistful tales of his tours around America, and his recitals and successes in Vienna before his retirement. Coffee stretched into lunch, when Marion joined us, and after a while he admitted he was penniless and needed help. He had no pension and, he said softly, "I have not eaten for two days."

We were shocked; the specter of the great artist reduced to begging for a handout is one that haunts most performers. And yet, since he had been an American citizen, I thought he should be receiving Social Security payments. I excused myself, to see what I could do for him. I phoned a friend familiar with Viennese music circles, who told me that List did have a small stipend from the Austrian government as well as American Social Security; he lived thriftily in a one-room flat, and was hardly in the bleak situation he had described. My friend said that the singer had fallen into the habit of asking for loans from acquaintances and visiting artists.

I then gave List all I had in my wallet, for which he thanked me with dignity. Two days later, he was waiting for me again in the lobby. I didn't want to explore the truth of his story any further—I just could not face him. I turned quickly and walked out of the lobby, but I had the feeling that he saw me.

My dear friend Eileen Farrell is one of the most relaxed, uninhibited sopranos on the stage today. Raised in a vaudeville family, The Singing O'Farrells, she managed somehow to flunk a Major Bowes amateur audition. She arrived in opera by way of radio and recordings. Baking pies and watching boxing on television are her great joys; married to a former New York City policeman, Eileen doesn't take guff from anybody. (When the overbearing George Szell needled her in rehearsals for Beethoven's *Ninth Symphony*—"Softer! Softer! You're too loud!"—she yelled back, "If you want a pop singer, why the hell didn't you hire Dinah Shore?")

Now, a bosom is one of woman's crowning glories, but onstage it can be a man's pain in the neck. In *Forza* Eileen played my sister, lamenting as I lay dying, at one of the old Met's paid dress rehearsals. She sang her heartbreaking aria bending over me, and smothering me with her magnificent *poitrine*. I whispered, "Got a cookie with the milk?" She swallowed a few notes in that round.

At the evening performance, she came back swinging with her treasure chest. I could barely breathe during her aria. As I mumbled, "Okay, that's enough," her upstage hand stuffed a gooey cookie into my mouth.

14

Fiddler on the Road

Ezio Pinza, near the end of his operatic career, entered a new level of singing life by creating the role of the French planter in *South Pacific*. Grace Moore had come to opera from Broadway musical comedies. So I was intrigued by the possibilities when Frank Loesser played the score of *Guys and Dolls* at my apartment, and promised he would expand the singing in the role of Sky Masterson if I took it. (It was played by Marlon Brando in the film version.) But I had achieved my lifetime drive to sing at the Met only five years before, and since this was Loesser's first Broadway score, I felt it was too chancy.

Richard Rodgers talked to me about a musical version of the book *Anna and the King of Siam*. He thought my dark complexion would be useful, and planned to write semioperatic numbers for me. It didn't work out.

When I saw Zero Mostel in *Fiddler on the Roof*, I knew I had to do it; after all, my Polish parents were very close to Tevye's Russian villagers, and Mostel was much more of a comedian than a singer. Since 1970, I have played Tevye over 200 times during the summer months, in every form of theater—indoors, outdoors and in-the-round. As in all tours, I expect the unexpected: outrageous accidents and incredible people pop up; the constant movement from place to place can be unsettling and a grand adventure at the same time. *Fiddler* is a uniquely intimate musical with strong characterization. I was the first Tevye to play it outdoors, and I didn't know whether it could reach out to audiences of ten or fifteen thousand, spread over an acre or two. Theater-in-the-round also adds to the hazards: It demands an entirely different acting technique from conventional stages. But nothing can stop *Fiddler*.

In one of the round theaters, as I implored God to give me a replacement for my horse, which had lost its shoe, a small, spotted dog walked up onto the stage. I had to add, "Oh, God, please try again."

Musical comedy does not employ a prompter, as in opera; still, the actor, as he repeats the same dialogue night after night, becomes weary, bored—and blanks out. One night, I could not remember an essential plot point that I had to convey to my daughters. When you're in trouble onstage, you become busy—you move around, improvising business, hemming and humming to fill in the appalling silence. Finally, I beseeched the girls for a clue: "Dear children, your father has worked all day, his head is tired—surely you can *guess* what he has in mind to tell you?" And daughter Chava gave me the cue.

She was played by my own daughter, Lizanne, who toured for two seasons during her summer recesses from high school. My son, David, came along as my personal dresser and baggage handler. In Atlanta, the man who perched on the roof with the fiddler was delayed one night. I walked onstage, looking up to address God, and was startled to see David fiddling on the roof. He gave me a slight nod, "Go ahead, Pop."

There is a poignant moment in *Fiddler* when I say good-bye to the daughter who is joining her young man in Siberia; I carry the suitcase, with all her belongings, to the railroad station. After begging God to keep her safe and warmly dressed, I walked offstage, still absent-mindedly toting her bag.

My understudy, who also played Lazar Wolf, the butcher, was a very ambitious young man. He'd frequently shake his head as he eyed me. "Bob, you look tired. Are you working too hard?" In one town, where we had been warned not to drink the water, he told me, "Your voice sounds harsh. Maybe your throat is dry?" and graciously handed me a glass of water. I am not paranoiac, but . . .

The indoor theaters were air-conditioned. Since I, like most actors, perspire heavily under the lights, I tried to keep warm when I came offstage. I'd find the thermostat adjusted to make the dressing room cold enough to store furs. And that was not all. One of the most dangerous foods a singer can eat before performance is nuts. The jagged bits stick in your throat and irritate the vocal cords. Several times I found bags of peanuts in my room, and when my understudy brought a gift of fruit, cashew nuts were included.

In my scene with Lazar Wolf, we used a table and two chairs, whose positions were clearly marked on the floor. My understudy never failed me on a conventional stage with proscenium and back wall: His chair was moved upstage, behind me, so that when I spoke to him I'd have to turn my face away from the audience. If I moved my chair beside him, he moved farther back. Grace Moore would have nailed his chair—and his shoes—to the floor.

Since the audience sits around the actors of theather-in-the-round, I had to circle and turn constantly in order to face all the customers. I found myself acting with my back. Opera is, by comparison, a series of postures. You take your position, pretend to look at your partner in the scene (the technical term is "cheating"), and sing out to the audience. In round theater you speak and sing face-to-face. After the summer, when I'd come back to the Met, I found myself actually looking at the soprano, who was so surprised she became uneasy. It required two or three performances to bring me back to the opera's more static technique.

Outdoor concerts may add atmosphere and relaxation to the enjoyment of music; they also multiply the opportunities for disaster, especially since I have, for many years, suffered from hay fever. I was about to sing in a New York park when some clown in the wings, as a joke, began sneezing up a storm. The simple power of suggestion affected me—I came onstage sneezing.

The Met last year presented a concert version of *Traviata* in Van Cortlandt Park in the Bronx. A large flying insect zeroed in on my head as I began "Di provenza." I shook my head, and it landed on my nose. A moment later, it was sitting on the microphone, watching me with its abnormally large eyes, like a supercilious critic in sunglasses.

> *A prolonged stare from an audience while I sing disturbs my concentration. That's why I prefer a dark auditorium with lights in my eye. I grow ill at ease when I see people in the front rows peering at me through binoculars. What are they looking for—my tonsils? Some music students actually use opera glasses to look down a singer's throat, hoping to see how he shapes his tones.*
>
> *I was strolling around a town in the Midwest just before a concert, relaxing, peering into shop windows. I stopped in front of a large market where the fish were piled high, one above the other. The rows of eyes reminded me I was overdue at the concert.*

The park bug listened until the end of my aria, and when I joined the soprano for a duet, it flew to the back of her neck. In the midst of an embrace, I slapped the soprano's back and killed that bug. She then slapped my face.

For Outstanding Outdoor Fiasco, I would nominate a Hollywood Bowl performance of *Carmen* about fifteen years ago. The stage and bowl are so huge that someone had the notion of placing the orchestra and singing chorus onstage *behind* the soloists. To make sure everyone could be heard as we moved about, sound engineers equipped us with tiny microphones, complete with antennae. They were actually miniature radio stations, transmitting our voices to a central amplifier system. The mikes were sewn into the men's costumes, and nestled in the cleavage of the women's bosoms.

It worked beautifully in rehearsal; the engineer could control the volume of each voice. "But what if something goes wrong?" I asked.

"It can't," the expert said. "For a backup, we have three mikes on stands downstage, with red lights. If the red light goes on, you can sing into those mikes."

It was a hot night, but pleasant under the stars. The first act was beautiful. The Bowl has a background of mountains, so in Act II I made my entrance as Escamillo from up high, as if I were coming down from the hills into the gypsy smugglers' hangout. Halfway through my "Toreador Song," I saw the red light flash on at the mikes downstage. My sound had gone off. I promptly strolled out of the scene to the mike and sang into it.

But no sound came out of it. After a moment, it blasted on, rattling the rocks in the nearby hills and breaking a few eardrums. I walked back into the scene with our Carmen, Jean Madeira, who now sounded as if she was singing under water. The distraught tenor, producing no sound with his mike, put his head on Miss Madeira's bosom, to sing into her mike.

At the end of that act, I grabbed the engineer's lapels with both hands. Furious, I cried, "How could it go wrong?"

"We can't understand it," he said sorrowfully. "We were getting police calls on your mike!"

Carmen's perspiration had seeped into her mike, so that she sounded like Donald Duck. The only one on the stage who could hear perfectly was the conductor, Andre Kostelanetz; since his back was turned to the singers, he had been wired with earphones—and he received the police calls loud and clear.

A review was headlined: "'CARMEN' ELECTRO-CUTED."

Moving from city to city every two or three days is disorienting; the usual pattern of my life dissolves, the abnormal becomes normal, and sometimes I don't know where I am—or why.

I recall a dinner conversation with friends in San Francisco, where we discussed the questions of life after death and is there a Heaven? I returned to my suite atop the Mark Hopkins Hotel and fell asleep, dreaming that I had indeed gone to Heaven. I awoke early and stumbled around a room that resembled my own, but surrounded by clouds; after I stubbed my toe on a chair, I wondered, If I'm dead, would I still feel pain? It was an eerie moment, suspended between life and death, until I felt the cold breeze from the open windows. San Francisco's famous fog had invaded my room.

In Dallas, I arrived at the theater center at 7:30 for an 8 o'clock recital. The stage door guardian ushered my accompanist and me into a dressing room; we sat there uncomfortably until 7:50, but nobody from the sponsoring committee welcomed us. I asked the doorman, "Isn't there a sponsor or a committee?"

"Oh, we got plenty of sponsors. It's a big show—ten acts."

"Ten acts? Hell—Am I in the wrong theater?"

"This is the convention hall, mister. Yours is around the corner." The audience was still waiting, but a little restless, when I arrived—out of breath.

My appearance in *Carmen* at Buenos Aires was delayed by a revolution in Montevideo, Uruguay, when the airport was taken over. I reached the Teatro Colon two and a half hours late, as the orchestra struck up my "Toreador Song," and I walked onto the stage in my blue blazer with gray houndstooth slacks. Nobody except the conductor, George Pretre, thought this entrance was abnormal, since shows there usually start two and a half hours late.

Marion and I arrived at the Sans Souci nightclub in Havana, under the Batista regime, to find that the Castro revolutionaries had set off a bomb backstage and blown the arm off a chorus girl. I still had the show-must-go-on compulsion, so I rehearsed my forty-minute act. The club was one of those plush 1930-ish Busby Berkeley movie settings, in pink and white, about the size of a soccer field, operated as a lure for a gambling casino.

The first show, at nine, came off without incident. Then the lights went out—the Castroites had struck again. Instantly, the croupiers threw themselves onto the tables, to cover the money with their bodies. The elegantly dressed crowd, screaming in terror in the dark, fought their way to the exit doors. Marion and I hid in a corner, under a fake palm tree, like two shivering kids. Half an hour later, the lights flickered on, and the gambling continued as if nothing had happened.

We stayed at the Nacional Hotel, a forty-five-minute drive from the club, and set out early each evening because at seven, the revolutionaries set off a bomb somewhere in Havana. One missed us on the road by about three minutes. On the third night, General Batista's brother, also a general, came to see our show, and everybody was expecting a terrorist attack. I peeped through the curtain: The brother in uniform, his cronies, and lavishly gowned women sat around a long table, about ten feet from the stage, surrounded by a squad of machine gunners.

Marion begged me, "Let's go home!" I began to wonder why the show had to go on. The manager explained that if it did not, Batista would make him suffer. Well, the twenty-five chorus girls wiggled through their number. I was given an elaborate introduction, walked down a spectacular semicircular staircase and sang my opening, "Granada." I cut off the applause with, "And now, ladies and gentlemen, for my encore—the 'Toreador Song!'" At the finish, I ran to the dressing room, grabbed my clothes, leaped into a taxi with Marion to the hotel, got our bags and raced to the airport.

After thirty years of travel, there is always the surprise I have never dreamed of, waiting for me at the next town.

The Barber of Seville has given me trouble ever since I sang it with Pinza and Baccaloni at the Cincinnati Zoo. The first act is filled with booby traps; so many cues volley back and forth that a single misstep can destroy the scene. I was the guest Barber in a western city where I had only one rehearsal with the tenor and orchestra. I warned the prompter, a young transplanted Viennese in jeans, to watch my cues carefully. "Don't hesitate to sing them out, so I can hear them."

The opening went well, and as we came to the precarious passages, I noticed the prompter's eyes enlarge, as if in surprise; then he swayed and his eyelids drooped. My God, I thought, the man's falling asleep or fainting—will he conk out before my cues? He steadied himself against the side of his little box, as my cues slipped by. I botched the entire sequence with the tenor and soprano.

The curtain came down mercifully. I sprinted backstage, asking, "Why didn't you cue me? Are you sick?"

His eyes were still not focused. He mumbled, "No, you see I had a girl in the box with me . . ."

"What was she doing in there? Dammit, I blew the whole scene!"

"So did she . . ."

By the time I clean off my makeup and leave the hall, it is 11:30 or midnight; I am tired and hungry, and even in larger cities, restaurants usually do not serve that late. So I find myself thinking all day of my supper after the concert, planning expeditions to restaurants, devising strategies for where, and with whom, to eat.

Over the years, local sponsors and members of concert committees were kind enough to invite me, with my accom-

panist, for a reception, and we were served finger sandwiches or cookies and punch. After a few such letdowns, I
would bluntly tell whoever met us on arrival, "We're
usually very hungry."

The answer was, "Oh, of course—we've taken care of
that." We'd be escorted to a large home and eased in
through a back door to the kitchen, because about 100
guests were having their punch and cookies in the other
rooms. A cook would prepare delicious steak for us and as
the aroma filtered throughout the house, heads would poke
into the kitchen: "What are you eating?" . . . "May I have
your autograph?"

Or, the hosts would hide the liquor. They'd beckon me
into another room, most often the children's bedroom,
where they stashed the bottle of Chivas Regal. Why waste
good whiskey on a hundred people? And, of course, when I
was introduced to the other guests, a sober guy would ask,
"Where'd you get the drink, buddy?"

A memorable reception: As I speared the first shrimp of
my appetizer in the dining room, the doors to the living
room were opened, and there, behind a concert grand
piano, stood eight baritones—to audition for me. I paid for
that dinner: Each of the eight was slightly worse than the
other.

My agency now sends a letter with the contract, explaining that because of early rising and plane schedules, I
prefer not to attend receptions. As a result, when the
performance ends, the accompanist and I wander around,
looking for an all-night diner or truck stop. Our forays
arouse questions and suspicion because we are still in
white tie and tails. The chef-waiter-dishwasher behind the
counter wants to know, "Where the hell have you been?"

The stock answer: "We were best men at a wedding."

There's very little variety in a truck-stop menu, but I
often found that the man behind the counter did not care if
we made our own food. We'd take off our tails and ties to
compose a Caesar's salad with cold cuts, or we'd create
elaborate omelets out of the same ingredients, minus the

lettuce, oil, and vinegar. One night I discovered Aunt Jemima's pancake mix—and we whipped up crepes suzettes. One of the truckmen happened to have a nip of brandy with him, so we even flamed the dish, to much applause. I began to look for accompanists who could cook.

And my agency would receive hurt letters from sponsors who had been told of the two men in tails eating at a greasy-spoon diner after rejecting the city's hospitality. I was not invited back again.

We couldn't even find a diner in a farming town in Nebraska. The only lights were in a woebegone wooden shack with a dusty window sign:

CHINESE COOKING
TO TAKE HOME

It was closed. I rapped on the window and a wizened Chinese gentleman appeared, waving me away as if I had come to burn the place. We both pantomimed starvation before he reluctantly opened the door. He surveyed our costume, perplexed. "You from Noo Yuck?"

"Yes, we eat anything."

"You eat good Chinese?"

"Oh, yes." And I told him about lemon chicken we'd enjoyed, and bass with black bean sauce. "You wait," he said. "I fix something."

We settled ourselves around a yellow Formica table, sipping canned tomato juice. My colleague lifted his eyes to me and glumly shook his head. In half an hour, the chef served a sumptuous six-dish banquet, opening with fish-egg soup. He lived alone and was so delighted, after years of preparing chop suey for the local trade, that he brought out a bottle of rice wine and sat with us to savor the delicacies. He then got up to make "special dessert," but we begged off. I offered to send tickets for the next concert; he asked instead for a photo with an autograph to hang on the wall. "I like pictures."

And, sure enough, my agency received another irritated

letter, reporting that Mr. Merrill's autographed photo had been seen on the wall of an inferior Chinese chop suey parlor, praising the food. I never sang there again, either.

On arrival at the airport, I am usually met by at least one member of the local committee, who drives me to the hotel. I don't want to seem ungrateful, but the questions, with very few exceptions, are ones that recur with numbing regularity: "What city did you come from?" "How do you like our town?" "What is your favorite opera?" (Or composer.) "Would you mind listening to the tenor in our choir?"

I lean back, close my eyes and relax, while my accompanist answers the questions. The next inevitable query is, "Does Mr. Merrill always sleep before a concert?"

Pleasantries are pleasantries anywhere in the world. I sat next to the wife of the German ambassador at a reception in Tel Aviv, after I sang in *Aïda*. "Are you a musician?" she asked.

I nodded. "Some people think I am."

"Do you play a piano, or string instrument?"

"Not exactly," I replied, eating busily to avoid embarrassing her.

She smiled with determination. "Ah, then you are in the orchestra?"

The English ambassador, sitting on her other side, explained diplomatically, "Mr. Merrill sang the baritone role, Amonasro."

"Oh, of course." And turning to me, she probed again. "Then who is your favorite opera composer?"

"Cole Porter."

"Oh!" she exclaimed. "He is mine also!"

The reception committee is probably no less bored than the artist being honored. One of the smaller cities in the Southwest was headquarters for a huge international construction company, whose personnel had been recruited from sophisticated engineering and architectural centers all over America. And their wives, evidently suffocated by the monotony of their lives here, made a gourmet production of the post-concert dinner. After a few liqueurs, one woman went into a bedroom and came out holding her bra, to be autographed. I obliged her. Other wives brought out panties and slips. And then the husbands tossed their keys into a grab bag on the floor. My talented accompanist, Charlie, who had lived a secluded life with his aunt, gasped, "I say, what are those keys?"

"F," I said, and took him home quickly, for fear he would report this to his aunt. I did not want to lose Charlie: He was sober, always on time and an excellent cook.

Our next stop was Tulsa, where an old friend introduced me to a lunch guest, an expensive party girl who, he said, would do anything for a laugh. I suggested to her that Charlie had not had many laughs lately; possibly she could relieve his tedium by posing as a newspaper reporter, seeking more information for a story about us. She was delighted: "Yeh! I hear piano players are great with their fingers!"

I phoned Charlie's room to explain that a reporter wanted to speak to him, preferably now. "Okay, Bob," he said, "if you think it'll promote the concert."

He called me back several hours later. "I don't know how to tell you this, Bob, but you've introduced me to the warmest, most wonderful girl in the world! She started asking me personal questions . . . she was tired, put her head on my lap . . . and I guess I . . . I . . . seduced her. Gee, I hope it doesn't ruin your interview—I'd cut my throat!—but I'm in love with her!"

He played magnificently at the concert that night—I had never seen him more at ease. Unfortunately, the girl had to cover a story in Texas the very next day. Charlie was disconsolate for weeks.

Some years before I married, I received letters addressed from a post office box number in Chicago and signed Geraldine. She sent gifts, such as gloves—they were my exact size—and mufflers, so I wouldn't be cold on my tours. Occasionally, I found flowers in my hotel room, before I arrived for a concert in the Midwest. They were always carnations or miniature roses, with a note wishing me the best of luck for the recital—"And I'll be there."

Notes arrived backstage, sentimental but not mawkish: "I so enjoyed seeing you again. Your voice makes me so happy, I know you must be the kindest gentleman in the entire world of opera." These and the letters were written on blue vellum in a clear, exuberant hand. I formed the picture of a woman in her late thirties, cultivated, probably a schoolteacher, unhappily married or living alone.

I wrote to the post office address to thank her for the gifts, and urged her to write to me, when she learned of a concert near her home, so that I would be able to take her to dinner in appreciation.

She did telephone several times, to say hello, in a bright, well-modulated voice. Each time I suggested meeting for lunch or a drink, she had a different excuse: a bad cold, or she could not leave her mother. This friendship continued for about six years. One day she phoned to my hotel.

ME: *Where are you?*

GERALDINE: *In the lobby, Mr. Merrill.*
(It was always Mr. Merrill.)

ME: *Can you come up and have a drink?*

GERALDINE: *I'd love to, really. But I can't . . .* (I can hear the emotional tension)

ME: *Then I'll come down to meet you. We can have dinner in the hotel dining room.*

GERALDINE: (Almost a sob) *I can't. I'm leaving now.*

ME: *I insist. I want to meet you.*

GERALDINE: (After a long silence, reluctantly) *I'll try.*

(After the years of puzzlement—who is she? why is she afraid to meet me?—I wait restlessly for the obligatory scene. Footsteps in the hall. I hurry to open the door. A woman enters, wearing a flowered hat out of the twenties, heavily rouged, with a fixed smile of desperation on her wrinkled face. She is about three and a half feet tall. I can't mask my shock and sadness.)

GERALDINE: *I do hope you don't think I'm being bold . . .*

ME: *Not at all. Won't you sit down!* (She sits, and breaks into tears.)

GERALDINE: *I shouldn't have . . . I'm sorry . . . I was foolish. But I love your voice . . .*

ME: *Thank you very much, I—*
(I can't help myself; my eyes mist up. After a few moments, she rises from the chair, dabbing at her eyes with a lacy handkerchief.)

GERALDINE: *I'm glad we met. My mind's at rest now. Good-bye, Mr. Merrill.*

ME: *Come on, Geraldine. We're going downstairs to dinner.* (I take her arm.)

Marion and I arrived in Rome, Georgia, an hour earlier than we expected, in our chauffeured limousine from Atlanta. Marion, my accompanist, inspected the piano and lighting at the hall, and we decided to have some Sanka to relax before the recital. Now, Rome is a city of over 30,000 that attracts a surprisingly large audience of 1,600 to its yearly concert. Still, nothing was open on the main street at 7 P.M. except a small lunch counter.

Our Cadillac pulled up to the shop, the uniformed driver opened the car door, Marion and I stepped out. Every face inside was gazing at us through the window. I suppose we did look exotic: Marion in long white gown and fur jacket, I in white tie and tails. Our chauffeur opened the door of the hamburger joint, and we entered.

We sat at a crumb-spotted Formica table. There was a dead silence while the customers, mostly young boys and girls and a family with two tots, examined us. The stares were friendly but puzzled and surprised, as if we had landed from another planet. The boy behind the counter, sporting a scraggly mustache, said, "No table service, folks. Can I help ya, please?"

He had no Sanka or tea. I ordered hot chocolate and toast and a Coke for Marion, and she carried the order to the table. As we drank from the plastic cups in the stillness, I noticed a small boy, about eight or nine, standing at the counter near the register, sipping a Dr. Pepper. He was studying us, tilting his head first to one side, then the other; his stare combined awe with bravado—who the hell cares?

After half an hour, we paid the sixty-cent check. The little boy could no longer restrain his questions. "Where y'all from? Whatcha doin' in town?"

"I'm singing at the concert hall."

He nodded solemnly, and we walked out. Behind the glass of the door, his eyes followed us as we drove off. We were from another world, and he saw he would never be part of it. Exactly what I would have felt at eight if a limousine had disgorged a couple in formal dress at my neighborhood candy store in Brooklyn. I could only wish that whatever the boy in Georgia wanted to do with his life, he might be blessed with a loving family that scolded and drove him to make the best of what he had.

How much could it hurt?